THE ARCHAEOLOGY OF MIDAS
AND THE PHRYGIANS

THE ARCHAEOLOGY OF MIDAS

AND THE PHRYGIANS

RECENT WORK AT GORDION

Edited by
Lisa Kealhofer

University of Pennsylvania Museum of Archaeology and Anthropology

Philadelphia

Library of Congress Cataloging-in-Publication Data

The archaeology of Midas and the Phrygians : recent work at Gordion / edited by Lisa
Kealhofer.-- 1st ed.
p. cm.
Includes bibliographical references and index.
ISBN 1-931707-76-6 (alk. paper)
1. Gordion (Extinct city) 2. Phrygia. 3. Turkey--Antiquities. I. Kealhofer, Lisa.
DS156.G6A73 2005
939'.26--dc22
2005004394

ACKNOWLEDGMENTS

The Editor would like to thank both Santa Clara University for subsidizing the inclusion of the color illustrations and an anonymous donor for production support.

Chapter 8: The research from which this chapter is drawn has been carried out with financial support of Bucknell University, the National Endowment for the Humanities, the American Philosophical Society, the Council of American Overseas Research Centers, the Loeb Library Foundation, the Margo Tytus Visiting Scholars Program of the Classics Department at the University of Cincinnati, and the Parker Visiting Scholars Program at Brown University. Phoebe Schweitzer produced illustrations based on drawings done in the field by the author.

Chapter 11: The Gordion Regional Survey was funded by the National Science Foundation (Award Number 9903149) (1999–2002), the American Research Institute in Turkey (1996), the College of William and Mary, and the University Museum. Ben Marsh patiently compiled the GIS maps for this chapter, and Peter Grave commented on several versions.

Chapter 12: B. Burke, J. Chang, E. Denel, and M. Dixon processed the Dümrek survey ceramics, and PIXE-PIGE analysis was funded by grant #99/115 from the Australian Institute of Nuclear Science and Engineering.

Chapter 14: The research from which this chapter is drawn has been carried out with funds from the National Endowment for Humanities (1995), American Research Institute in Turkey (1996, 1997), and American Philosophical Society (1998). Partial funding was provided by research funds from the University Museum (2000–2004). Jason D. Block assisted the author in landuse and sheepfold surveys in 1998–2000.

Chapter 15: Thanks to G. Kenneth Sams for his vision and long-term support of conservation at Gordion and to the directors and staff of the Museum of Anatolian Civilizations in Ankara for their unending interest, cooperation, and help. The team members of the Gordion Objects Conservation program are always willing to provide help and advice. Special thanks go to Ibrahim Bolat and the rest of the staff of the Gordion Museum, who have steadfastly tended to the monthly environmental and structural monitors in the tomb. Sometimes it does take a village.

CONTENTS

1

RECENT WORK AT GORDION

LISA KEALHOFER

Gordion is one of the few sites in the Middle East, outside of the Levant and Egypt, with ongoing archaeological excavations and research since 1950 (Fig. 1-1). Research at Gordion has always been highly innovative: for example, in the 1950s Gordion provided some of the first radiocarbon samples to the new radiocarbon lab at the University of Pennsylvania Museum, and early magnetometer studies were conducted by Elizabeth Ralph, the director of the Museum Applied Science Center, on the Citadel Mound. More recently, multidisciplinary environmental, analytic, and chronometric projects have advanced new methods.

With a long history of research and excavation, Gordion provides an exceptional opportunity to study specific historical and archaeological questions. For example, studies of both new and previously excavated material are providing insights into the exchange systems of the 1st millennium BC and early centuries AD. Despite its inland location (Chapter 4 this volume), Gordion was closely linked to Eastern Mediterranean trade networks. New evidence also reveals shifting trade alliances and exchange with groups to the east (Chapter 8 this volume).

Gordion is also one of the key sites in central Anatolia that offer a long occupation sequence from the Early Bronze Age to the early 1st millennium AD (Voigt 1997). With a selection of widely dispersed sites like Gordion, Boğazköy, Alişar, and Sardis, we are beginning to understand the nature of early civilizations during the Late Bronze and Iron Ages. How did Gordion interact with the Hittite Empire? How did the Phrygians and Midas create and consolidate a new state in central Anatolia? What was its economic basis? How did it fit into the regional economic and political structures of the day? These are questions that the research presented here is beginning to answer.

From a methodological point of view, Gordion also has brought together researchers who bridge several archaeological and material science disciplines. Interest in the site was originally stimulated by historical accounts, such as those of Herodotus and later Greek and Roman authors, but since about 1985 a broader set of questions about the Phrygians and their landscape has developed. Alongside archaeological research, Gordion has also become an important center for innovations in site and monument conservation (Chapters 15–17 this volume).

For all of these reasons, and others, research at Gordion is significant not only to those with specific interests in ancient Anatolia, but also to a wider range of people interested in more general processes of cultural interaction, state

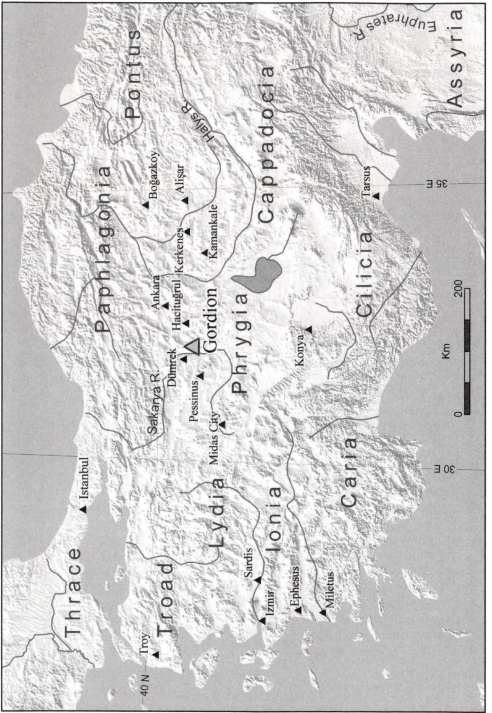

Figure 1-1 Turkey, showing the location of Gordion and other major sites mentioned.

development and collapse, as well as the practicalities of how people protect sites and artifacts for future generations.

This book aims to present an accessible summary of much of the recent research on Gordion and the Phrygians. While the University of Pennsylvania Museum Monographs on Gordion provide a scholarly venue for individual, detailed studies, no summaries of the current research at the site are available. This book seeks to fill that void. Compiling all current research at Gordion is beyond the scope of this project, but the chapters provide a substantial sample of the range of ongoing research projects for the University of Pennsylvania Museum's Gordion Project.

The wide range of research at Gordion is grouped here into four sections: site history and excavations, artifact analyses, regional survey, and site and artifact conservation.

PART I EXCAVATIONS, HISTORY, AND DATING AT GORDION

The current Director of the Gordion Project, G. Kenneth Sams, discusses the history of excavations at Gordion from work by the Körte brothers at the turn of the 20th century to the beginning of the current excavations in 1988. The vast quantity of material excavated by Rodney Young, from 1950 to 1974, continues to stimulate research on a variety of fronts, from architectural conservation (see Chapters 16 and 17 this volume) to re-assessments of excavation contexts and dating (e.g., Chapter 4 this volume).

Mary Voigt, the current Director of Excavations and Survey, presents the goals and some of the achievements of excavations since 1988 (Chapter 3). Recent excavations have explored a very different set of goals, as non-elite areas of the site have been investigated to provide a more representative view of life at ancient Gordion. Evidence related to craft activities (including metal production), mortuary patterns, and cultural/demographic changes are part of the more detailed and textured understanding contributed by recent work. Recent excavations have also refined the stratigraphic sequence at the site, which has resulted in significant changes in its chronology.

Keith DeVries, the Project Director from 1974 to 1988, has most recently been working on understanding the context and sequence of Greek ceramic imports to Gordion. Because these ceramics are extremely well dated (often to within a decade), they provide an excellent way to date archaeological deposits that have few other artifacts that can provide an absolute date. DeVries' critical reassessment of several key deposits (Chapter 4) has contributed to the recent re-dating of the Destruction Level at Gordion (the boundary between the Early and Middle Phrygian periods). Incorporating both new radiocarbon dates and dendrochronology, this re-dating has wide implications for the timing of the development of the Phrygian state (earlier than previously thought) as well as the dating of the monumental mortuary tumuli surrounding the site of Gordion (DeVries et al. 2003).

While Rodney Young focused primarily on understanding the Early Phrygian levels at Gordion, other periods are also present at the site. Andrew Goldman has been working on the Roman period (Chapter 5). Located at the eastern boundary of the Roman Empire in the early centuries AD, Gordion provides an illuminating view of Roman frontier dynamics. While historical records document the broad pattern of Roman road building projects and military expansion during the Flavian period, Gordion provides concrete evidence for how these programs affected those living on the frontier in central Anatolia.

PART II INTERPRETING THE FINDS FROM GORDION

Part II explores a variety of material and artifact studies from excavations by Rodney Young and more recently by Mary Voigt. Integrating present and past excavation data is one of the ongoing challenges of a long-term excavation like Gordion. Having contemporary material from a wide range of archaeological contexts, makes much more sophisticated interpretations about site development, destruction, and reuse possible (see Glendinning, Chapter 7, for example).

Brendan Burke (Chapter 6) investigates the economy during the Early Phrygian period. The catastrophic fire that destroyed the core Citadel area preserved for archaeologists an unusual, nearly intact view of the Citadel at the moment of destruction (late 9th century BC). Within what appears to be a series of specialized buildings there is extensive evidence for large-scale production of textiles (possibly including carpets) and food. Burke suggests that elite-controlled textile production served a key role in the Phrygian economy.

In Chapter 7, Matthew Glendinning describes the elaborate architectural terracottas found in Middle and Late Phrygian contexts at Gordion. By examining the entire corpus of roof and decorative tiles and comparing them with other sites in both Greece and Anatolia, Glendinning shows strong links between coastal sites like Sardis (Lydia) and Gordion during the late 7th and 6th centuries BC. The richly decorated roof structures created by the tiles also reveal the cosmopolitan and affluent nature of late Middle Phrygian society.

The glass objects found at Gordion, like the artifacts associated with textiles and architectural decoration, reveal a very complex mix of external exchange, emulation, and local traditions. In Chapter 8, Janet Jones discusses the glass artifacts found at Gordion, one of the earliest large collections of luxury glassware in the Middle East. She focuses on the technological traditions revealed in these glass objects and the implications these have for understanding Gordion's trade and political connections in the 1st millennium BC. The earliest glass vessels make use of a core-forming technique developed in northern Mesopotamia, while subsequent vessels are clearly Greek made or influenced by Greek designs (but likely made for export to Persian consumers). A later group shows the shift back to eastern interaction and influences as Persian hegemony becomes more important in the mid-6th century BC.

Excavations in the 1990s of the Lower Town (between the Citadel Mound and Küçük Höyük) uncovered one of the most unusual deposits at Gordion: a structured surface distribution of domestic trash, food remains, and human skeletal material. In Chapter 9 Page Selinsky summarizes her analyses of this human skeletal material, focusing in particular on the health status of the individuals and their manner of death. The deposit appears to be a Later Hellenistic or Galatian (3rd century BC) human sacrifice, similar to those known from Europe, providing convincing evidence of Celtic ritual practice. The Galatian occupation lasted more than a century and has provided a rich inventory of material culture. Young's excavations documented "abandoned" houses with their contents mostly intact, which he dated to the 2nd century BC. We now know that there were two distinct events leading to the abandonment of household contents. The *in situ* artifact spatial patterning makes it possible to look at gender roles and gendered spaces within houses, a topic that is currently of considerable interest to both classical archaeologists and anthropologists.

One of the most informative and ubiquitous remains at many archaeological sites is the pottery. Since 1990, Robert Henrickson (Chapter 10) has been studying potting traditions at Gordion from the Late Bronze Age through the Phrygian period. Based on the technological styles of production revealed in ceramics, Henrickson finds that Phrygian potters were very conservative, making use of a limited number of clay sources and maintaining production techniques for nearly 1,000 years, despite exchange of ideas and goods with Greeks and others.

Part 2 provides a richly textured view of Phrygian society. The elite interchange with both the Greeks and later Achaemenid groups, alongside the creation of a uniquely central Anatolian cultural style, highlights the immense size and complexity of the 1st millennium BC interaction sphere. Rapid complex shifts in economic and political alliances are reflected in the Gordion materials. Yet with this interaction we get a glimpse of the more conservative non-elite traditions that governed everyday life for most Phrygians. Future work on the non-elite portions of Phrygian society will illuminate how the Phrygians organized and ruled their state.

PART III GORDION IN ITS CONTEXT

Initial results from the Gordion Regional Survey comprise Part III. With the resumption of excavations in 1988, Mary Voigt also instigated the first systematic survey of archaeological sites around Gordion (beyond the readily visible tumuli). Regional archaeological survey documents the demographic and geographic distribution of towns and villages over time, enhancing our understanding of the economic and political structure of Phrygian (and other) society(s).

In Chapter 11, I present a summary of the Gordion Regional Survey (GRS), initiated with a pilot study in 1996 and continuing 1998–2002. GRS undertook a systematic surface survey of 400 km² around the site of Gordion as well as an in-depth study of the land use history. The goal of the survey was to explore the relationship between agricultural (economic) expansion and political change. While one might expect that large-scale political entities dictated extensive and intensive agricultural expansion, comparisons of Hittite, Phrygian, and later Roman land use suggest that the relationship between political and economic change was much more complex.

One of the keys both to identifying and dating sites in the landscape is the surface distribution of ceramics. In Chapter 12, Peter Grave, Lisa Kealhofer, and Ben Marsh examine the ceramic distribution at Dümrek, a unique Phrygian sanctuary site ca. 40 km northwest of Gordion. Dümrek had long been known by archaeologists, who linked the site to the Phrygians by the form of sculptures (e.g., the rounded, stepped boulders) also found at Midas City, to the southeast. At Midas City, rock outcrops bore sculpted images of the Phrygian goddess Matar or Kybele set within the doorway of gabled buildings, as well as a Phrygian inscription including the name Mita or (in English) Midas.

Using elemental characterization techniques to link ceramics at Dümrek to ceramics from specific periods at Gordion and other sites, the main periods of ritual activity at Dümrek are defined. The use of unusual places like Dümrek began in the Early Iron Age/YHSS 7, when Phrygians first arrived at Gordion, and flourished through the Middle Phrygian period when Phrygians dominated central Anatolia. Dümrek was apparently abandoned in the Late Phrygian or Achaemenid period, when Gordion was still an important economic center. We suggest that a confluence of regional economic and political influences displaced local ritual practices. The evidence from Dümrek suggests that Phrygian, and specifically Gordion, political dominance was supported not only by military force, but also by religion.

Perhaps one of the most important components for understanding and interpreting the surface distribution of sites and artifacts in modern landscapes is the history of how the landscape was formed. Ben Marsh (Chapter 13) discusses the history of the landscape around Gordion over the last 4,000 years based on the physical geography. In the early 1990s, Marsh intensively studied the Sakarya floodplain surrounding Gordion (Marsh 1999). Here he focuses on the adjacent upland areas. One of the more interesting results is the apparent disconnect between upland and lowland evidence. Periods of stability and instability evident in floodplain deposits occur at quite different times from those in the immediately adjacent uplands. His work highlights the importance of studying the geological and physical processes of the larger region to understand the complex nature of land use and landscape evolution.

In the final chapter of Part 3, Ayşe Gürsan-Salzmann (Chapter 14) presents some results of her ethnoarchaeological study of pastoralism and agriculture in the region around Gordion (modern Yassıhöyük). In the second half of the 20th century there was a relatively rapid shift away from a pastoral economy to a more intensive commercial agriculture. Gürsan-Salzmann explores the changing importance of pastoralism vs. agriculture, the local environmental parameters, and the archaeological remains associated with pastoral economies.

PART IV CONSERVING GORDION AND ITS ARTIFACTS

The last part of the book presents some of the ongoing conservation efforts at Gordion. As evidence of past achievements, sites have become "cultural heritage" to be viewed by local people as well as tourists. The economic value of sites in an era of cultural tourism has led to a focus on conservation and an increasing effort to produce museum displays and publications that can be appreciated by a broad audience. In the late 1990s, the Gordion Museum was remodeled and expanded, with American sources funding the reinstallation of exhibits. Museum visitation by Turkish tourists, school children, as well as foreign guests has subsequently increased.

The museum displays would not have been possible without a dedicated team of conservators who stabilize and mend pottery and other artifacts from both old and new excavations (Chapter 16). The conservators' aim is ensure that all finds survive the transition from the site to storage. Every artifact—from painted Attic pots and pieces of sculpted stone to clumps of corroded iron and clay loom weights—is cleaned so that it can be described, drawn, and photographed. Preparation for long-term storage involves not only the application of standard conservation methods but the development of new ones, more appropriate for the field conditions at Gordion.

Ceramics are not only the most ubiquitous item recovered during the archaeological survey, but they are also the most common item found in excavations at Gordion. Only a few of the thousands of sherds excavated are relatively complete or reconstructable vessels, but those that are contain fundamental evidence for understanding ceramic production, food consumption and storage, elite display, and many other aspects of daily life. Conservation of these vessels and their residues is therefore a critical aspect for archaeological analysis.

In Chapter 16, Julie Unruh and Jessica Johnson discuss one of the most important problems for conserving ceramics at Gordion: salts. Salt derived from sediments surrounding ceramics often move into the ceramic fabric over time. After excavation these salts expand and contract as humidity changes, causing the pot's fabric to break apart. Unruh and Johnson describe a new technique for rapid and economical removal of salts, maintaining as far as possible the integrity of the vessels.

As even larger-scale artifacts, sites are increasingly threatened and compromised by looting and expanding population and agriculture. At Gordion, however, the most significant site conservation issues have been tied simply to the exposure of long-buried structures to environmental vagaries: wetting/drying, freezing/thawing, as well as biological agents.

One of the most impressive monuments in the landscape around Gordion is the MM tumulus, previously thought to be the burial place of King Midas. Not only the largest tumulus in the region, it also contained a greater number and richer concentration of luxury goods than any other excavated tumulus in the area. Although named MM after Midas, recent tree-ring or dendrochronological dating of tomb timbers indicate that they were cut around 740 BC, about the time that Midas came to the throne. Thus the tomb is more likely to be that of his father Gordios, built and equipped by Midas but not occupied by him.

Inside the tumulus is one of the oldest preserved wooden structures in the world: a chamber built to house a king and his grave offerings. Rodney Young excavated the tumulus in 1957. By the late 1980s, both the mound and the wooden chamber presented conservation problems. Since the early 1990s, Richard Liebhart and Jessica Johnson have been engaged in conserving this unique structure, with funding from both Turkish and foreign sources. In Chapter 15 they discuss the long history of conservation and preservation efforts for the tomb chamber. Today the wooden structure is not only protected and stable, but is for the first time visible without earlier ugly concrete and wood supports. Even for those who have seen the tomb many times, the new view is spectacular, revealing the massive logs that encase the smooth surfaces of the chamber's interior.

Mark Goodman (Chapter 17) provides a history of the conservation of the Citadel Mound architectural remains excavated by Rodney Young several decades ago. The buildings of the Early Phrygian Destruction level are impressive, but once excavation removed the thick layer of clay that protected them for nearly three millennia, they began to crumble and sag. Long-term exposure of the rock walls to seasonal changes, in addition to their original destruction by fire, has led to the relatively rapid deterioration of the architectural foundations of the Early Phrygian period. Until 2004, Mark Goodman* led team of architectural conservators, architects, and masons who worked systematically across the ruins, protecting standing walls and consolidating the great gateway. This process by itself makes the Early Phrygian settlement plan easier for tourists to see and interpret, and it constitutes the first step in improving site presentation and increasing its value to Turkey.

Gordion has been a center for developing conservation methods. The unique architecture at and around the site provides exceptional challenges for architectural conservation and interpretation. The conservation staff has worked with interns from many international institutions, providing valuable training opportunities for field conservation. Recent work focuses on innovating new conservation techniques without compromising the integrity of the artifact or structure.

In sum, the long-term, ongoing, multidisciplinary studies at Gordion contribute a rich and diverse resource for historians, archaeologists, and conservators. Recent work has redated the Phrygian sequence, with implications for Iron Age development across the region. Artifactual studies detail economic, social, and ritual relationships across western Anatolia from the Phrygian through the Roman periods. We hope this book will serve to broaden understandings of 1st millennium BC and early 1st millennium AD archaeology in the Middle East.

---

* Mark Goodman died suddenly in Istanbul in October 2004. His work made a significant contribution to preserving the site and the meaning of Gordion for future visitors and researchers.

I Excavations, History, and Dating at Gordion

2

GORDION

Explorations over a Century

G. KENNETH SAMS

The site of Gordion was "discovered" in November 1893, when the German Classicist Alfred Körte visited a location on the Sangarios (modern Sakarya) River where engineers working on the Berlin-Baghdad Railroad had reportedly come across "die Reste einer uralten vorgriechischen Niederlassung" (Körte 1897:4). Körte identified the site as Gordion primarily on the basis of what ancient literary sources had to say about the old Phrygian capital, such as its location on the Sangarios River. Most compelling for Körte, however, was how well the geographic location of the site agreed with where Gordion occurs in the itinerary for the march of the Roman general Manlius Vulso against the Galatians in 189 BC, as provided by the Roman historian Livy (Körte 1897:4–18).

Seven years later, in 1900, A. Körte returned to Gordion with his brother Gustav to carry out a single, three-month season of excavation, among the first controlled diggings in central Anatolia (Körte and Körte 1901, 1904). The brothers divided their time between the main settlement mound and burial tumuli. On the mound, they concentrated on a series of trenches on the southwestern edge, reaching levels that were perhaps as early as the 6th century BC. Of the roughly 85 burial tumuli in the vicinity of Gordion, the brothers opened five, named I-V by them and Körte I-V today.

The burials under Tumuli I, II, and V all revealed signs of contact with the Greek world, including imported goods dating the burials from the late 7th century to around the middle of the 6th century BC (Körte and Körte 1904:104–45). In this period Gordion and Phrygia were thought to have been under the control of Lydia, their immediate neighbor to the west, with its capital at Sardis.

Tumuli III and IV were decidedly earlier, belonging to old Phrygian times, the period climaxed by the rule of Midas in the late 8th century BC (Körte and Körte 1904:38–104). Tumulus III was especially rich in furnishings, including bronze vessels and fibulae, handsome pottery both black-polished monochrome and painted, and remains of elegant wooden furniture with inlaid decoration. For the time and for decades to come, the finds from Tumulus III were to represent a singular benchmark for old Phrygian material culture. The finds from the Körtes' work in 1900 were divided between the Imperial Ottoman Museum in Istanbul and the Imperial Museums of Germany in Berlin.

The Körtes' excavations also informed the American investigations that began at Gordion in 1950. During reconnaissance in Turkey in 1948, J. F. Daniel and Rodney S. Young saw Gordion as a strong prospect for beginning excavations.

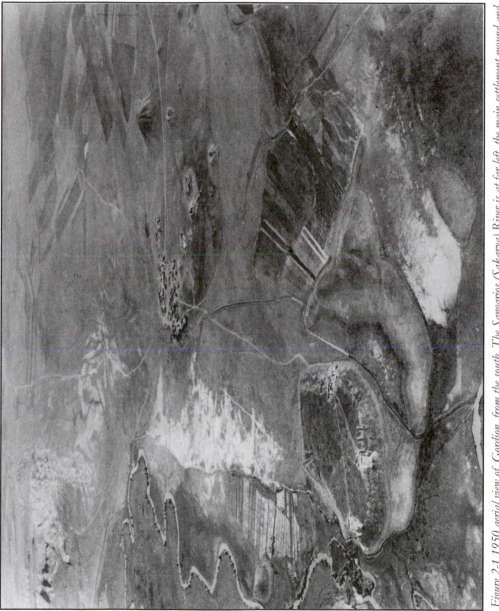

Figure 2-1 1950 aerial view of Gordion, from the south. The Sangarios (Sakarya) River is at far left, the main settlement mound and Küçük Höyük at lower left. The "Midas Mound" tumulus is at upper right.

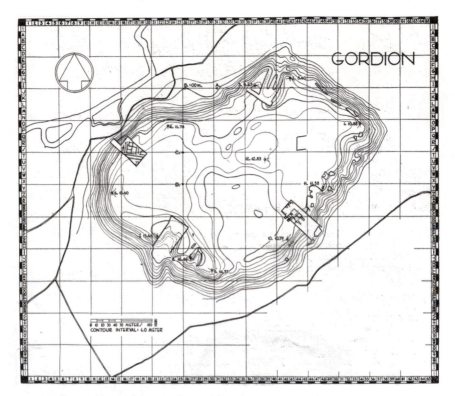

*Figure 2-2 Plan of Main Settlement Mound in 1950, by architect Mahmut Akok.
Trenches made by R. S. Young are at northwest, southwest, and southeast.
Those at southwest and north were made originally by the Körtes*

Daniel died suddenly during the trip. Young, who otherwise would have assisted
Daniel in the project, then gained permission from the Turkish government to
undertake excavations in spring, 1950.

Conducted under the auspices of the University of Pennsylvania Museum,
Young's work at the site continued over 17 seasons through 1973. His excavation
reports are listed in Young (1981:xxxv–vi) and DeVries (1990). He died in 1974
in a traffic accident outside Philadelphia. Young's assistant in the earlier years of
excavations was G. Roger Edwards, who directed the campaigns of 1952, 1958,
and 1962. Machteld Mellink was also a regular participant into the 1960s. Serving
as registrar for almost all of these seasons was Ellen L. Kohler.

Young's (and Daniels') principal motivation in turning to Gordion was
to bring archaeological light to the Phrygians, a little-known people of whose
material culture the Körtes's work had provided intriguing glimpses. Young and
his colleagues learned quickly that the site of Gordion encompassed far more than
Phrygian civilization. The history of settlement in fact extends from the Early
Bronze Age (3rd millennium BC) through the Roman Empire (1st to 4th centuries
AD) and into the Medieval era.

The main settlement mound of Gordion, Yassıhöyük ("Flat-topped Mound"), lies on the present right bank of the Sangarios River (Fig. 2-1). Measuring roughly 500 m east-west and 400 m north-south (Fig. 2-2), the mound is highest in its western portion, where it rises to a maximum of nearly 16.5 m above datum (river surface in 1950). The eastern half is no more than about 13 m high. In the first season the excavators learned the reason for this difference in height: Hellenistic settlement (late 4th to 2nd centuries BC) covers the entire mound, yet only the western half of the mound was settled thereafter during the Roman and later Medieval periods (with Medieval documented in some parts of the eastern half). After the first season, the decision was made to discontinue work in the western half of the mound and to concentrate efforts on the eastern half (the "Main Excavated Area"). For this reason, relatively little is known about the Roman period settlement or, in fact, about the western half of the mound itself (see Chapter 5 this volume).

The periods most extensively investigated during the Young campaigns were thus the Hellenistic and the underlying Phrygian. The earlier Bronze Age strata of the 3rd and 2nd millennia attracted limited attention (Gunter 1991). Their presence was attested by the end of the second season, through a deep and bold sounding made by Machteld Mellink from the top of the mound. Again in 1965 a deep sounding was made below the Phrygian level, while in 1961 the excavators had come upon a stratigraphic fluke wherein the top of an Early Bronze Age mound directly underlies the Phrygian level. The picture of the Bronze Age at Gordion is supplemented by a cemetery of the 2nd millennium BC about 1.5 km to the northeast of the main settlement mound, excavated by Mellink from 1951 to 1953 (Mellink 1956).

The Hellenistic strata at Gordion have proven to be of considerable importance in central Anatolia, primarily because of limited excavations in the region. Excavations revealed an extensive town that was abandoned and in places burned. It is reasonable to link this settlement with the Gordion that Manlius Vulso encountered in 189 BC in his march against the Gauls, a place abandoned by its inhabitants and left full of goods. Numismatic evidence supports the association, since the latest datable Hellenistic coins belong to the beginning of the 2nd century BC. The settlement thus provides a valuable fixed date for the chronology of Hellenistic Anatolia.

The finds from the abandoned settlement afford a microcosmic view of life in Hellenistic Anatolia and of the process of Hellenization that began with Alexander the Great and his conquest of the Persian Empire starting in 334/3 BC. Pottery occurs in great quantity and demonstrates that the dwellers had largely taken on the ceramic shapes found in a Greek house, as seen both in imports and in local imitations (Winter 1984). Terracotta figurines in Greek style—again some imported, some locally produced—were perhaps the objects of household cults of Greek deities (Romano 1995).

From the Hellenistic strata in general come further indications of this hybridized age. Stone weights bear the caduceus emblem of the Greek deity Hermes, god of commerce. Other Greek cults are attested to the Hellenized

Figure 2-3 Old Citadel, Megaron 1 at time of excavation.

Anatolian goddess Kybele, to the Muses, and to Tyche. As known from inscriptions (in Greek script, sometimes with misspellings and grammatical errors), some people have Greek names, others have seemingly odd Greek names, while yet others bear Anatolian or possibly Celtic names (Roller 1987).

A Celtic (Galatian) presence at Gordion in the late 3rd and early 2nd centuries could be implied from the fact that the site was on Vulso's Galatian campaign itinerary and that the inhabitants, by reason of their flight, obviously feared his advance. Yet little by way of material remains had come forth to document their presence archaeologically. That picture changed in 1993 when, in excavations directed by Mary Voigt, evidence for human and animal sacrifice of a seemingly Celtic nature was discovered in Hellenistic levels to the immediate southeast of the main settlement mound (Dandoy et al. 2002).

Beneath the Hellenistic strata lie those representing Gordion during the lengthy Phrygian period, from as early as the 12th or 11th century down to the later 4th century BC and the coming of Alexander. During the 1950s, the excavators gradually saw the basic configuration of the Phrygian period come into focus: two major levels of monumental architecture, an old and a new fortified citadel (see Figs. 2-3 and 2-4), separated from each other by a tremendous clay fill 4–5 m thick. Each citadel had a monumental gate complex at the southeast, the later in fact partly bedded on the substantial remains of the earlier. The lines of the fortification walls are generally similar, although those of the New Citadel extend beyond those of the Old, thus enlarging the fortified area.

Stretches of the walls protecting both citadels have been excavated along the northeast and northwest margins of the main excavated area. At the southwestern edge of the main excavated area, walls flanking a roadway in both citadels appear to have been for fortification (see below).

Much of the Old Citadel (elsewhere herein, Early Phrygian, YHSS 6A) had been destroyed in a great fire that somehow spared the occupants (see Fig. 3-3). Already in 1952 the excavators were aware of this major destruction by fire, revealed in a test sounding. The buildings themselves were relatively well preserved in their lower parts, so much so that it was possible to glean numerous details of construction (Figs. 2-3 and 2-4, Pl. 1). Moreover, most of the buildings affected by the fire were rich in contents that give much information about their use and about Phrygian material culture in general (Figs. 2-6 and 2-7). Sams (1994b) provides an overview of the Destruction Level. By contrast, the overlying New Citadel (elsewhere, Middle-Late Phrygian, YHSS 5-4; Fig. 3-4) suffered greatly at the hands of later inhabitants, who plundered the original (Middle Phrygian) structures of the citadel for building materials. Consequently, excavators uncovering the New Citadel found its buildings in varying stages of preservation: a few courses of walls still standing, walls robbed down to their foundations, foundations themselves robbed out. Further, unlike the Old Citadel, the new one had suffered no destruction that left great deposits of material goods in place.

Given this opposing tale of the two citadels, it is understandable that Young made the Old Citadel, with its monumental buildings preserved by their very destruction debris, the primary goal of excavation. As a necessary consequence of this decision, the New Citadel exists today primarily via documentation, since whatever remained of its original structures had to be sacrificed in order to go deeper into the mound. Exceptions here include sections of the entry complex

Figure 2-4 Old Citadel, Megaron 3 at time of excavation, the largest of the excavated megarons and perhaps the central structure of the citadel.

Figure 2-5 Old Citadel, Unit of Terrace Building after consolidation.

and fortification system, since they lay largely outside the perimeter of the fortifications of the Old Citadel. In 1955, the clearing of the Destruction Level of the Old Citadel (Fig. 3-3) began on a major scale and continued through the 1973 season, Young's last.

The remarkable similarity in the layout of the two citadels was apparent by the late 1950s (see Figs. 3-2 and 3-4). Beyond the entry complexes at the southeast, in each case, lay two large courts—an outer (southeast) and an inner (northwest)—separated by a substantial partition wall. Flanking these courts in both citadels were monumental buildings of megaron type, rectangular structures consisting of an antechamber, or in some cases a shallow porch, opening into a large hall (Figs. 2-3 to 2-4, Pl. 1). The nature of the buildings and their finds suggest that this sector in the Old Citadel was an elite quarter (the Palace Area); the same may have been true for the corresponding sector of the New Citadel.

In both citadels, a street or possibly another court lay to the northeast of the inner court, as indicated by rows of megarons facing onto that open space from the southeast. To the southwest of the courts in both citadels was a second major district, defined by rows of large buildings facing each other across a broad street or esplanade. Those of the earlier citadel took the form of two large, multi-roomed buildings on a terrace, each unit being of megaron plan with antechamber and main hall (Fig. 2-5; see also Fig. 3-2). The multi-room building to the northeast (the Terrace Building) was excavated its complete length of over 100 m by the end of the 1967 season, with eight megaron-type units; it is thus one of the largest buildings known from ancient Anatolia.

Figure 2-6 Old Citadel, view of a unit in row opposite Terrace Building, under excavation.

The contents of both row buildings show that among the principal activities carried out here were textile production and food processing on a massive scale (Burke, Chapter 6 this volume; Figs. 2-6 and 2-7). Who the apparently numerous workers were is not known. The isolation of the row buildings from the Palace Area, with access possible only from either end of the Terrace Building (that from the south controlled by a gatehouse), alludes to a desire for limited communication between the two sectors. In the corresponding sector of the New Citadel (Fig. 3-4), the units that comprise the rows are freestanding rather than structurally one, while a few of the units are not of megaron plan. We do not know whether these buildings continued the function of textile and food production, which again would have required a large work force. One clue that they did may lie in the fact that once again there was a marked separation between this sector and that with the courts and megarons, by substantial partition walls. Further, a New Citadel building partially excavated under Voigt in 1988–89 contained an oven in its basement level,

Figure 2-7 Old Citadel, unit of Terrace Building, with grinding platform.

as did most of the antechambers, or kitchens, of the row buildings in the Old Citadel.

Following the most recent chronology (DeVries et al. 2003), the Old Citadel belongs to the 9th century, with the destruction by fire coming close to 800 BC. The New Citadel, in turn, may have been largely completed by the end of the 8th century, the time of Midas. Unlike its predecessor, the New Citadel, as a fortified entity, had a long life, extending with a variety of major permutations well into the 4th century BC, perhaps even still serving the site when Alexander came in 334/3.

A revelation stemming from the later seasons of excavation under Young was that, from at least as early as the time of the Old Citadel through the life of the New, Gordion existed as a double mound; a street divided the minimally explored western mound from the extensively excavated eastern mound and its Phrygian buildings as described above. In both citadels substantial walls flanked the street; they are now perhaps best viewed as the southwestern fortifications of the eastern mound. When the New Citadel was erected the builders kept the same exterior street level but rebuilt the flanking wall up to the level of the New Citadel. Toward the end of the 4th century BC the decision was made to fill in the valley that separated the two mounds, thus creating the single mound that we see today. This major topographical alteration was carried out in conjunction with the construction of the first of the Hellenistic towns on the consolidated mound (DeVries 1990:400–401).

More recent excavations under the direction of Mary Voigt, which began in 1988, have contributed in many ways to our understanding of Gordion. One important aspect has been the resumption of excavations in the western part of the mound that Young abandoned after 1950. Here, in Phrygian levels contemporary with the New Citadel on the eastern mound, the buildings are primarily domestic, as opposed to the monumental, presumably official buildings, found in the New Citadel. Whether a similar difference in function ensued during the time of the Old Phrygian Citadel is not clear.

Beneath the buildings in question lies 5 m of clay fill, the same as that encountered between the two Phrygian citadels of the eastern mound. In 1993 a small sounding (1 x 4 m) through the clay came to a burned level that could correspond to the Destruction Level of the Old Citadel on the eastern mound (Voigt et al. 1997:4–6). The sounding was too limited to reveal the nature of the burned level; yet here also, as in the post-clay Phrygian levels above, may have been largely domestic settlement contemporary with the grand structures of the old Phrygian citadel.

Herein, then, may lie the reason for two separate mounds at Gordion during Phrygian times: one for official purposes and state-controlled activities, the other domestic, perhaps serving the creature comforts of those involved in the business of the citadel. This, admittedly, is highly speculative, since we know so very little about the western mound in Phrygian times. We do not know, for example, whether the western mound itself was fortified, although the findings from a step trench by T. C. Young in 1994 on the northwestern edge of the mound suggest that it was fortified during the life of the New Citadel (Voigt et al. 1997:4–6; Voigt, Chapter 3 this volume).

Just to the southeast of the main settlement mound lies the so-called Küçük Höyük or Small Mound (see Fig. 3-1). Excavated by Machteld Mellink during the 1950s and 1960s, the Küçük Höyük marks the site of a fortress atop a high bastion, both of mudbrick. Fortification walls extend either side of the bastion, but peter out from erosion in the flood plain of the river considerably short of the main mound. This separately fortified area is now, with the excavations conducted under Voigt, referred to as the "Lower Town."

An unexcavated mound (Kuştepe) to the north of the main mound is probably part of the same outer fortification system, as may be sections of walls found in the present riverbed to the northwest of the main mound. Geomorphological research indicates that in Phrygian antiquity the river ran east of the mound; the river thus revealed land features when it formed its present course (Marsh, in Voigt et al. 1997:23–26; Marsh 1999).

The Küçük Höyük fortress and adjoining walls seem to have been constructed in the late 7th or early 6th century BC, i.e., during the lifetime of the New Citadel. Two earlier periods of defense wall were detected by Mellink. These are now complemented by a substantial terrace and ashlar structure found by Voigt within the Lower Town, a building program that may be as early as the 8th century (see Voigt, Chapter 3 this volume). The Küçük Höyük fortress was destroyed by fire following a siege, an event that, on the basis of imported Attic pottery, can be linked to the march of Cyrus the Great of Persia against Kroisos of Lydia in the 540s BC. At the time of its destruction, fortress occupants were using primarily Lydian, as opposed to Phrygian, pottery, thereby suggesting that the site was a

Lydian garrison. The outer fortifications of which the fortress was a part could have continued to function after the disaster, when Gordion would have settled in as part of the Persian Empire until the coming of Alexander over 200 years later. Beyond lay the Outer Town, a vast, presumably unfortified district to the west and northwest that survey and excavation under Voigt have added to the ancient topography of Gordion (Voigt et al. 1997:8; Voigt, Chapter 3 this volume).

Of the some 85 burial tumuli in the vicinity of Gordion, approximately 35 have been excavated, including the five opened by the Körte brothers in 1900. Excavation of tumuli by the Young team began in 1950, their first year of work (starting with Tumulus A), and continued intermittently through 1969 (ending with Tumulus Z). Since then, three tumuli were the objects of salvage excavations by the Museum of Anatolian Civilizations after attempts had been made to rob them. The excavated tumuli range from the 9th century BC into Hellenistic times, with most in the 9th to 6th centuries, i.e., within the Phrygian period.

Of those belonging to Phrygian times, the interments extending down into the later 7th century were in wooden tombs; then cremation burials without a wooden tomb came into vogue (Kohler 1995; Young 1981). Tumulus burials are relatively rare in comparison with the many people who would have lived and died in and around Gordion during these centuries. The tumuli marked the final resting places of the local elite, royalty and perhaps others of stature within Phrygian society.

The most spectacular of the tombs, opened in 1957, is that under the so-called Midas Mound, an intact juniper and pine construction that is thought to be the oldest, still-standing wooden building in the world (Young 1981:79–190). Recently dated by radiocarbon to around 740 BC, the tomb is thus too early for Midas, an historical figure of the later 8th century, and may be that of his father, Gordias by name, if we accept what later, Classical sources tell us. The burial was rich in grave goods, including numerous bronze vessels and fibulae, and masterly produced inlaid wooden furniture that was surely the exclusive purview of royalty (Simpson and Spirydowicz 1999).

Near the Midas Mound lies Tumulus III, excavated by the Körtes, and a tomb opened by Young in 1956, Tumulus P, the grave of a child (Young 1981:1–77). The last, while again containing elegant inlaid furniture (as did III) also yielded zoomorphic vessels, animal figurines in wood, and a miniature bronze team of horses attached to a chariot, all perhaps playthings for a prince or princess of the Phrygian royal house.

Tumuli III and P have typological affinities suggesting that their dates are similar, falling in the first half of the 8th century, perhaps a generation or so after the destruction of the Old Citadel. Later Phrygian tumuli at Gordion are generally far less grand in their furnishings, as though a pinnacle in the show of disposable wealth had passed.

The excavations at Gordion have given us much insight into the life and changing nature of an ancient Anatolian center. Gordion is of singular importance for the archaeology of Phrygia, where no other site of the period has witnessed such extensive excavation or revealed such a magnitude of monumental architecture and material wealth. In broader perspective, much the same can be said for the archaeology of Central Anatolia in the Iron Age. With few exceptions (Büyükkale-Boğazköy and Kerkenes Dağ), architecture on a scale parallel to that of the Phrygian citadels is poorly attested to for the period.

Moreover, the new, 9th century BC dating for the Old Citadel at Gordion gives its large buildings temporal priority by a century or more over the rise of monumental architecture in the Greek world to the west, which previously was reckoned to be contemporary. With its enormous material wealth, including both local and exotic goods, the great Destruction Level marking the end of the Old Citadel has no equal for the Iron Age in Anatolia or, generally, the eastern Mediterranean.

For the subsequent Hellenistic period, also, Gordion takes on considerable prominence for Central Anatolia, where no other Hellenistic site has been so extensively excavated. Of great chronological significance for the Hellenistic world are the rich deposits of the abandoned level, which can be closely dated to 189 BC and the expedition of the Roman general Vulso. In sum, Gordion easily enters the ranks of major centers in antiquity.

Yet much remains to be brought into focus, such as the western mound and its relationship with the Phrygian citadels of the eastern mound. Future investigation stands to provide us with a more rounded picture of Phrygian Gordion than we possess at present.

3

OLD PROBLEMS AND NEW SOLUTIONS

Recent Excavations at Gordion

MARY M. VOIGT

This chapter briefly summarizes research at Gordion since 1988, setting out the questions we sought to answer and some of our results, providing an example of the ways in which a small-scale re-study project can enhance and supplement data from large-scale older excavations (Fig. 3-1). Many of our questions arose directly from the work of Rodney Young and his colleagues (see Chapter 2 this volume). Other questions and the methods used to address them were new, stemming from the interests of archaeologists trained in anthropology rather than classical archaeology.

For example, in order to infer changes in political and economic systems and to propose factors that influenced such changes, we used generalizations or models derived from a cross-cultural or comparative approach. Documents and the historical narrative constructed from them were considered but were not privileged in the way that they had been by Young. For the most part our goals have been achieved through careful planning and hard work. But like any archaeological project we also posed strategies that failed, balanced by unexpected finds that provided crucial pieces of information.

Our current understanding of the long-term urban settlement at Yassıhöyük/Gordion is based on three different kinds of data: large area clearances made by Rodney S. Young and his colleagues G. Roger Edwards and Machteld J. Mellink between 1950 and 1972 (see Figs. 3-2 to 3-4); small stratigraphic soundings made under my direction between 1988 and 2001; and intensive surface survey conducted since 1987 and currently directed by Lisa Kealhofer. Surface survey and limited soundings have shown that the large mound known as Yassıhöyük and the tall, relatively small mound to the south anchoring a crescent-shaped fortification system (the Küçük Höyük) are surrounded by a low-lying settlement that reached an area of nearly 1 km² when the city was at its maximum size (Fig. 3-1).

BUILDING A NEW RESEARCH PROGRAM: GOALS AND STRATEGIES

In the summer of 1987 a team organized and led by Robert H. Dyson, Jr. (then Director of the University of Pennsylvania Museum of Archaeology and Anthropology), went to Gordion to design a new program of fieldwork at the site. Team members included archaeologists William Sumner and myself and

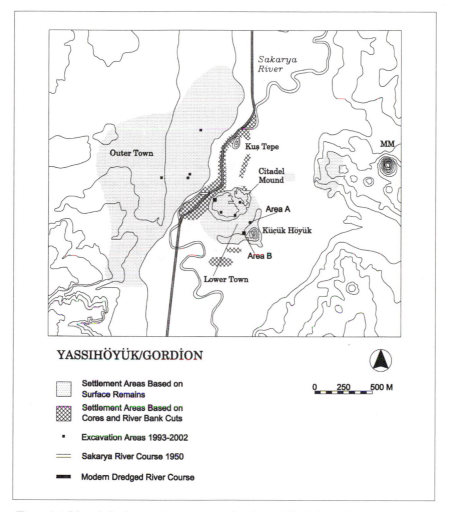

Figure 3-1 Plan of Settlement showing topography of site. The Sakarya River is shown in its modern location, rather than its location during the 1st millennium BC. See Marsh (1999).

architectural conservator and surveyor William Remsen, all of whom had worked with Dyson in Iran as part of the Hasanlu Project.

Excavation at Gordion had stopped with the death of Rodney Young in 1973. Fourteen years later there were good reasons for a new cycle of research. First, Keith DeVries, who had served as Gordion Project Director since shortly before Young's accidental death in 1973, wanted to be relieved of administrative responsibilities in order to concentrate on his own research and writing. Second, Turkish officials were worried about the deterioration of buildings within the Early Phrygian Destruction Level excavated between 1950 and 1972. They suggested a major program of site conservation, as well as

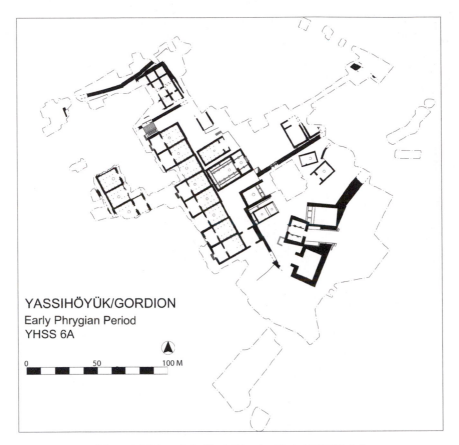

YASSIHÖYÜK/GORDION

Early Phrygian Period
YHSS 6A

0   50   100 M

Figure 3-2 Plan of the Early Phrygian Period/YHSS 6A.

new archaeological fieldwork. Third, Gordion offered an opportunity to conduct research at a large urban site for Sumner and myself who had previously worked on similar sites in Iran.

During a brief three-week season, Remsen mapped the eroded edges of the Main Excavation Area and began to work with G. Kenneth Sams (a member of the Gordion Project since 1967) on the conservation of the Early Phrygian gateway (Fig. 3-2). Sumner walked, biked, and drove the 1961 Gordion pickup truck across the countryside looking for remnants of past human activities. Dyson and I reviewed Young's publications and began work on the Citadel Mound, examining standing architecture and the eroding edges of Young's excavations in order to obtain a basic understanding of building techniques and stratigraphic processes.

In fall 1987, Dyson appointed G. Kenneth Sams as Gordion Project Director, responsible for site and object conservation and the publication of Young's excavations. I was appointed Associate Project Director, responsible for the new

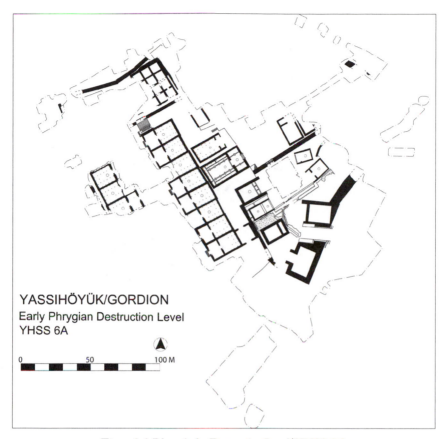

Figure 3-3 Plan of the Destruction Level/YHSS 6A.

excavation and survey, and Sumner agreed to conduct a systematic regional survey of the area around Gordion.

To expand upon the previous interest and expertise within the Mediterranean world, I recruited a team who had worked in Eastern Anatolia and Iran: Robert Henrickson (ceramics), Melinda Zeder (zooarchaeology), and Naomi Miller (paleoethnobotany). I set three primary goals for the initial cycle of new excavation: first, to obtain a detailed stratigraphic sequence with associated ceramic and architectural remains that could be used to supplement and interpret Young's excavations; second, to obtain new information on the economy through the systematic collection of floral and faunal remains as well as manufacturing debris; and third, to obtain regional settlement patterns that would aid in the interpretation of Gordion's political and economic system for each major period of occupation. Work began in 1988, funded by grants from the National Endowment for the Humanities, the National Geographic Society, and private donors.

Figure 3-4 Plan of the Middle Phrygian Level/YHSS 5.

During our first two seasons we defined a sequence covering the period from Middle Bronze Age through Medieval times or ca. 1500 BC to AD 1500. We accomplished this through two soundings: the Upper Trench Sounding which extended from the modern surface to the Early Phrygian Destruction Level (Fig. 3-3), and the Lower Trench Sounding which began at the Destruction Level and extended to the Middle Bronze Age (Fig. 3-5; Table 3-1). In 1990, a season devoted to analysis, DeVries returned to Gordion and agreed to take on the study of Greek ceramic imports from the new excavations, adding them to his much larger corpus from the Young excavations.

A second cycle of excavation began in 1993, funded by the NEH, the Kress Foundation, and private donors, focusing on Gordion as an urban settlement and examining changes in its size, form, and organization through time. Our goal was to obtain an archaeological sample from areas of the site that were virtually unknown, including the western part of the Citadel Mound and the Lower and Outer Towns (Figs. 3-1 and 3-5). At the same time, a Canadian team led by T. Cuyler Young,

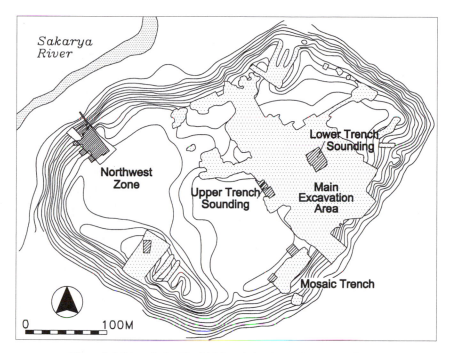

Figure 3-5 Plan of the Citadel Mound showing major excavated areas.

Table 3-1 Historical and Stratigraphic Sequence at Gordion

Phrygian Citadels	Period Names	Approximate Absolute Dates	YHSS Phases
	Early Bronze Age	c. 2500–2000 BC	—
	Middle Bronze Age	c. 2000—1500 BC	10
	Late Bronze Age	c. 1500–12th century BC	8-9
	Early Iron Age	c. 12th century–c.950 BC	7
Old Citadel	Initial Early Phrygian	c.950–900 BC	6B
	Early Phrygian	c.900–800 BC	6A
	Early Phrygian Destruction	800 BC	
New Citadel	Middle Phrygian	c.800–540 BC	5
	Late Phrygian	c.540–330 BC	4
	Early Hellenistic	c.330–mid 3rd century BC	3B
	Later Hellenistic	mid 3rd –mid 2nd cent BC	3A
	Roman	Early 1st–5th century AD	2
	Medieval	13–14th century AD	1

Jr., began work at Gordion, funded by the Royal Ontario Museum, the Social Sciences and Humanities Council of Canada, and the University of Toronto. The regional survey during this phase focused on the area in the immediate vicinity of Gordion. Younger scholars replaced Sumner, who left the project in 1989 when he became director of the Oriental Institute of the University of Chicago (Kealhofer, Chapter 11 this volume).

THE PROCESS OF REINTERPRETATION

We began our research with the assumption that we could not begin to talk about the historical context of the site without a carefully defined relative chronology anchored by absolute dates. The excavation units used to obtain our sequence were different from those used by Young, reflecting ongoing development in archaeological recording and collection techniques. Whereas Young's basic stratigraphic and spatial units were architectural (buildings and building levels), the new excavations used arbitrary rectangular units (operations) with balks between units providing stratigraphic controls. Breaks between minimal stratigraphic units defined within each operation correspond to minor changes in human activities and/or in natural processes. After analysis, these shorter units (representing weeks or months) were grouped into phases, which represented significant periods of time (decades or centuries). For the first time soils were sieved to recover very small items, and samples from each stratigraphic unit were taken for flotation (microbotanical remains).

Ten major chronological units were defined, each characterized by distinctive aspects of architecture, artifact types, and in some cases, floral and/or faunal assemblages (Sams and Voigt 1990, 1991; Voigt 1994). In order to facilitate comparison between old and new data, phase names within the Yassıhöyük Stratigraphic Sequence (YHSS) are those adopted by Young's team (DeVries 1990; Gunter 1991; Sams 1994a); however, we also adopted phase numbers for the new sequence—YHSS 1 through 10—in order to clearly tie the old period names to the new stratigraphic interpretation and to new criteria for period definition (Table 3-1). This distinction is especially important for YHSS 5/Middle Phrygian through YHSS 3/Hellenistic, where better stratigraphic and chronological controls altered our interpretation of Young's data.

Using the new sequence, we set out to address several of the substantive historical questions raised by Young's research and outlined in the *Source* in 1988. Two topics discussed there: the initial appearance of monumental architecture at Gordion, signaling the formation of a powerful Phrygian polity, and the rebuilding of Gordion after the Early Phrygian destruction. New evidence has changed our understanding of the nature and timing of these key events at Gordion.

Problem 1: The Origins of the Phrygian State and Its Chronology

Much of the evidence for the earliest Phrygians at Gordion used to come from historical sources. Writing in the 5th century BC, Herodotus states that Phrygian speakers migrated out of the Balkans into Anatolia (7.73). This event occurred after the Trojan War, according to a lost book by Xanthus of Lydia (a contemporary of Herodotus) cited by Strabo (16.680). During the Dark Age that followed the 12th century collapse of states in the eastern Mediterranean and central Anatolia, the Phrygians established themselves at Gordion, which eventually became their capital. Our excavations in the Lower Trench Sounding provided strong archaeological evidence for the arrival of a new group of people at Gordion in the late 2nd millennium BC. As previously suggested by Sams (1988), the immigrants used pottery with Balkan parallels (Henrickson 1993, 1994; Voigt and Henrickson 2000a, b).

Texts from Greece and Assyria provided evidence for a powerful Phrygian state ruled by Midas and his predecessors in the 8th century BC (Mellink 1991:622 ff.), but no guidance on the emergence of a Phrygian polity. Archaeologically, increased political control and centralization is often indicated by construction projects that required significant inputs of labor (Figs. 3-2 to 3-6). Rodney Young found some evidence for monumental architecture at Gordion, a fortification wall and buildings stratified just beneath the Destruction Level (summarized by Sams 1994a:7–10). Young also found fragments of low-relief sculptures on stone slabs or orthostats that have parallels at Syro-Hittite centers such as Carchemish and Zincirli, built in the late 10th to early 9th century BC (Sams 1989). Sams argued that the Gordion sculptures were later than the eastern parallels, but concluded that the sculptures could be "no later than ca. 800 BC" (1989:453).

The Lower Trench Sounding provided new information on the construction of these early stone buildings (Voigt 1994: 270–72). A series of hard-packed surfaces (YHSS 6B) yielded a lot of construction debris derived from buildings outside of our excavation area. The debris consisted primarily of stone trimming flakes as well as a few shaped blocks; all were of the soft white rock used for the sculpted orthostats. We were extremely lucky to find one piece with a design that could be matched by a wing on one of the sculpted pieces (Sams 1989:pl. 130:2), secure evidence that the orthostats were carved during YHSS 6B.

More information on this early monumental phase was found in 1993 when we again dug below the Destruction Level to explore a wall fragment cleared by Young. We discovered a megaron we nicknamed the PAP Structure (Fig. 3-6), just inside the Early Phrygian gate system (Voigt and Henrickson 2000b). The PAP, gate buildings, and another pre-destruction building built of soft white stone (the Northwest Enclosure) had the same orientation. Based on stratigraphy, as well as building materials, we could now reconstruct a partial plan of the formal buildings of YHSS 6B (Fig. 3-6) that preceded the later palace complex or Destruction Level (YHSS 6A). The absolute date of the YHSS 6B complex was still set by Sams's dating of the associated orthostats to ca. 800 BC which was ultimately tied to a date of 700 BC for the Destruction Level.

When we began work in 1988 one of the few things that most Gordion scholars agreed on was the date of the Early Phrygian Destruction Level/YHSS 6A. This was set at the beginning of the 7th century BC based on an assumed link between the fire and the presence of marauding Kimmerian nomads in central

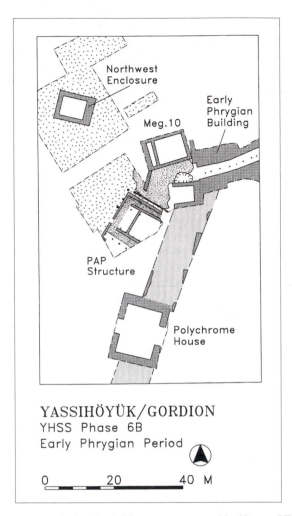

Figure 3-6 Plan of the first Early Phrygian monumental buildings or YHSS 6B.

Anatolia at that time. The dating of earlier and later materials had to be adjusted to accommodate this fixed point, as illustrated by Sams' dating of the orthostats as well as of Early Phrygian ceramics (Sams 1974, 1978, 1989, 1994a).

As we accumulated new data and as older material was re-examined, a 700 BC date became more and more problematic. For example, when Peter Kuniholm, of the Malcolm and Carolyn Wiener Lab for Aegean Dendrochronology at Cornell University, analyzed 256 samples of wood from Terrace Building 2 as part of the stratigraphic sequence, the latest ring dated ca. 861 BC. A gap of more than 150 years between cutting date and the accepted date for the fire was so great that we postulated that the timbers had been reused. The disquieting thing about the early date for TB2A was that it confirmed a pattern set by other dendrochronological determinations from both Destruction Level and pre-destruction buildings (Kuniholm 1988; Manning et al. 2001).

Even harder to accommodate was new information on the subsequent Middle Phrygian/YHSS 5 period, which indicated that: (1) reconstruction started almost immediately after the fire; (2) massive fills were laid over far larger areas than had been thought; and (3) Gordion was at its maximum size during YHSS 5, NOT during YHSS 6A. If the Phrygians' political power had been destroyed by a Kimmerian raid in the early 7th century, who were the rulers that were able to mobilize vast amounts of labor to begin reconstruction, and why were historical sources silent on the large and prosperous city that we had documented archaeologically?

A breakthrough on dating the Middle Phrygian reconstruction level came when Keith DeVries identified a small sherd from a YHSS 5 context within the Upper Trench Sounding as Early Protocorinthian, dating to the late 8th or early 7th century BC. He then linked this sherd with a substantially preserved Early Protocorinthian vessel found in a Middle Phrygian context by Rodney Young. In 1998 DeVries argued that the rebuilding had been completed by at least the early 7th century BC and that the Early Phrygian fire and subsequent rebuilding took place well before Kimmerians were reported in Anatolia.

Just over a year later, Sams noted that no Greek material had ever been found in the nearly two hectares of excavated Early Phrygian Destruction Level. This virtually eliminated the possibility that the imports from Middle Phrygian contexts cited by DeVries were redeposited. In a meeting with DeVries and me in January 2000, Sams suggested that parallels between Early Phrygian pottery and other sites with a secure historical chronology would support a destruction date in the third quarter of the 8th century.

A potential date for the destruction around 750 BC was very important since it placed this event before a time range when radiocarbon dating is imprecise, a period that scientists call the "Hallstatt Disaster." Kuniholm and I then decided to radiocarbon date seeds found on the floor of Terrace Building 2A and reeds from its roof. The seeds, from five different pots including three different plant species (barley, lentil, and flax), produced calibrated dates of 830–800 BC. Reeds from the roof of the building dated 890–815 BC, consistent with the dendrochronological date for the timbers and suggesting a surprisingly early construction before ca. 850 BC.

DeVries and Sams are now conducting a reexamination of artifact parallels for the contents of the Destruction Level buildings excavated by Young (see also Chapter 4 this volume). The results, to date, are consistent with a late 9th century date. Thus, the Early Phrygian destruction is 100 years earlier than previously thought and can have nothing to do with the later Kimmerians. Moreover, YHSS 6A or (in Sams's terminology) the Old Citadel is certainly not the city of Midas, who instead lived in the rebuilt or New Citadel of YHSS 5. Returning to the initial Early Phrygian monumental structures (YHSS 6B), this complex now fits comfortably around 900 BC, the date suggested by its sculptures. We are still waiting for new radiocarbon dates for the Early Iron Age, but the picture emerging is of a relatively rapid rise to power of the Phrygian elite beginning around 950 BC.

Problem 2: The Middle Phrygian Rebuilding

The date and sponsorship of the Middle Phrygian rebuilding phase had long been a problem for Gordion scholars, one reflected by numerous changes in its name. Young assumed that with their capital in ruins, the political power of the Phrygian kings was broken. Having found no pottery earlier than the 6th century BC in good contexts within the New Citadel, Young saw the Persians as sponsors, referring to the rebuilt palace quarter as "the Persian Level" (Young 1955, 1956, 1958). This created a gap of about 150 years between the fire of 700 BC and the arrival of the Persians in Anatolia after 550 BC. As excavation proceeded in the early 1950s, Greek pottery dated to the 7th century BC was found in much later contexts. Young and his colleague G. Roger Edwards postulated some kind of occupation at Gordion, perhaps in the Lower Town; they introduced the term "Lacuna Period" for the time when the Citadel Mound was thought to be abandoned (Edwards 1959).

The recovery of imports dated to the first half of the 6th century BC in primary contexts, within the New Citadel, eventually led Young to reject the Persians as sponsors and to date its constructions ca. 600 BC. He sometimes referred to the rebuilding as the "archaic level" (Young 1960), but retained a preference for "the Persian City." After Young's death, the Gordion publications committee made another change, agreeing to use the term Middle Phrygian period for both the 7th century (that is the Lacuna period), and the construction and occupation of the New Citadel. This terminology emphasized continuities in the layout of the palace quarter between destruction and reconstruction.

New data and DeVries's work on data collected by Rodney Young has produced a radically different picture of the relationship between the fire and the Middle Phrygian building project. Reading through Young's fieldnotes in 1980, DeVries discovered that the face of a retaining wall that confined a thick layer of fill to the southeast of Megaron 1 had been burned, so the fill was laid before the fire (the "Unfinished Project"; DeVries 1990:387–88, fig. 22). This fill or terrace was part of a construction project under way at the time of the fire that can be seen as the first stage in the building of the New Citadel (Fig. 3-3). Thus, the catastrophic fire did not trigger rebuilding but merely interrupted an ongoing process.

Further evidence for the timing of the Middle Phrygian rebuilding project was found in 1989. The stratigraphic section through Terrace Building 2A (Fig. 3-7) shows that after the fire the stone walls were torn down and their blocks thrown into the center of the room before fragile reeds from the burned roof could be disturbed. Once the walls were reduced to a level height, there was erosion and the formation of a hard surface, representing a relatively brief interruption in the building process, a delay between initial leveling and the laying of deep fills and foundations above this particular building. Thus instead of a gap of a hundred or more years between the fire and the start of the Middle Phrygian project, the first stage in reconstruction began immediately (Voigt et al. 1997).

Our exploration of areas away from the Eastern Citadel shows that the Middle Phrygian construction project was not confined to the palace quarter. In 1988,

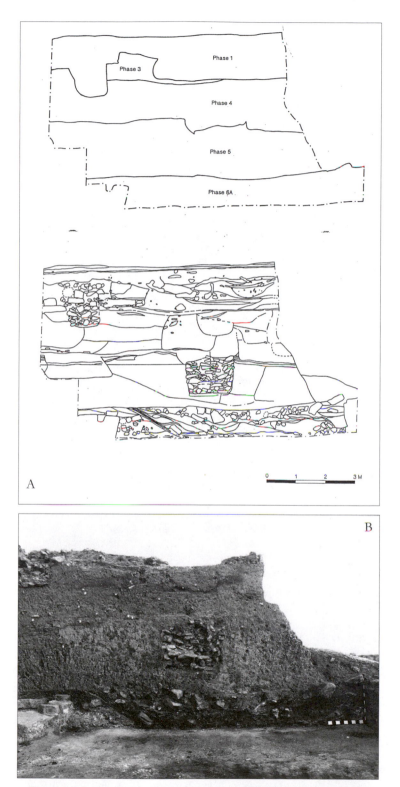

Figure 3-7 Section drawing (a) and photograph (b) showing debris from the Destruction Level/ YHSS 6A and Middle Phrygian/ YHSS 5 rebuilding.

Figure 3-8 Step trench in the Northwest Zone showing depth of the Middle Phrygian/ YHSS 5 fills.

Sams pointed out that deposits found by the Körte brothers in the western side of the Citadel (later incorporated into Young's South Trench) could be interpreted as deliberate fill. This was confirmed when Operation 12, set within the limits of the South Trench, encountered a fill layer beneath Middle Phrygian houses (Sams and Voigt 1990). In 1993 we continued down through more than 5 m of clean fill to a surface with Early Phrygian painted sherds (Operation 17; Sams and Voigt 1995). A step trench in the northwest zone of the Citadel encountered another deep layer of Middle Phrygian fill (Fig. 3-8), this time composed of 3.5 m of clean clay resting on at least 2 m of rubble (Voigt and Young 1999:209, fig. 13).

These two soundings on the western part of the Citadel Mound clearly indicate that the Middle Phrygian building project was far more massive than we had thought. A thick layer of fill was used to create a second high mound to the west, approximately level with the elevated eastern palace complex. A broad street, found outside the western face of the palace quarter wall by Rodney Young, ran between these two elevated areas of settlement (DeVries 1990). We do not yet know how the deep fills of the Western Middle Phrygian Citadel were protected, but there must have been some kind of facing or glacis to prevent erosion. We also have evidence for the kinds of buildings placed on top of the newly created mound. Excavation in 2002 on the northern edge of the Western Mound revealed ashlar buildings with deep rubble foundations that must represent the remains of monumental structures similar in construction if not in plan to those on the Eastern Mound. In the Lower Town, the Middle Phrygian project included not only a fortification system but also a broad terrace along the inner face of the walls on which large-scale stone buildings as well as mudbrick houses were built (Voigt and Young 1999). The timing of specific parts of the Middle Phrygian project is not yet clear, though some information may come from a systematic study of the ceramics recovered from levels immediately above the clay fill.

Problem 3: The Potential of the Outer Town

While much of our research since 1988 has achieved our stated goals, I would like to close this summary with a discussion of things to come. One aspect of our work has thus far been less successful: our attempt to define the nature and date of settlement within the Outer Town. Intensive surface survey established a scatter of pottery over 1 km^2. We had hoped to conduct large area clearances in relatively shallow deposits. Instead, our soundings were limited by current intensive agriculture, modern burials, and a greater depth of deposits than expected. One trench reached well-preserved structures dating to the Late Phrygian period, providing tantalizing samples of pottery that is clearly related to material from Iran. Only one of these soundings reached sterile soil (Operation 22), and again the material was unusual, including complete pots that Henrickson and Sams consider transitional between YHSS 6 and 5 (Sams and Voigt 1995). To avoid some of these problems we tried remote sensing, but neither magnetometer nor resistivity surveys produced comprehensible plans. Agricultural backhoe trenches provided brief unrecordable glimpses of stone wall foundations and courtyards. The archaeological record of this unwalled and almost unknown area of the city is one of our legacies to the next generation of Gordion excavators.

4

GREEK POTTERY
AND GORDION CHRONOLOGY

KEITH DEVRIES

The considerable volume of Greek fine-ware pottery at Gordion gives vivid evidence for a receptive local market and a sustained commercial network through which Greek vases were transported over some 400–650 km of land routes alone (DeVries 1996:447). The pottery also has a key importance to the site as an often sensitive indicator of chronology. By a fortunate coincidence, Greek imports began in the second half of the 8th century BC, not long after the commencement of the "Hallstatt Disaster" in radiocarbon dating (ca. 750–400 BC), a period when radiocarbon determinations lose their precision.

This chapter discusses how the Greek pottery dates several significant contexts at Gordion, from the late 8th century into the late 6th century BC. These years extend from the period of the celebrated King Midas down to the incorporation of Phrygia into the Persian Empire. The contexts include both tumulus burials and occupation deposits.

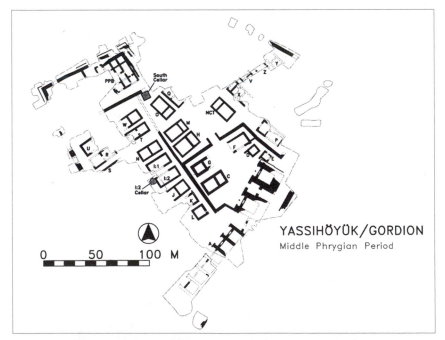

Figure 4-1 Plan of Middle Phrygian level of the Citadel Mound.

THE SOUTH CELLAR AND ITS STRATIGRAPHY

The earliest contexts with Greek ceramics are in the South Cellar, a small squarish structure (5.7 x 5.7 m), which was part of the Middle Phrygian Citadel (Fig. 4-1). It was fully excavated in 1965. In the report for that season, the cellar was interpreted as having been filled in a single operation, datable to the 5th century BC, based on the presence of an Attic red-figure sherd, although the fill was recognized as also containing much earlier material (Young 1966:269). Influential in the interpretation was the experience of the cellar's initial site supervisor, who removed the entire fill of one section without observing stratigraphic distinctions (Gordion Notebooks 114 and 119). Another excavator, who dug the rest of the cellar in three successive trenches, established a sequence of phases for the structure and for its fills (Gordion Notebook 121); her records have made it possible to draw a restored section (Fig. 4-2).

The cellar clearly dated after the beginning of the Middle Phrygian period, for at least part of its north and west walls cut through the original Middle Phrygian surface. Moreover, a pit and a large storage jar lay below the south wall and show that the area of the cellar was previously used.

The cellar originally comprised a single space, but was subsequently subdivided by a partition wall (Fig. 4-2), and the floor level on the south side of the partition wall was slightly raised. The area on the north side of the wall retained its old floor, on which storage vessels were found in situ. In a later phase, that north space was filled in to the surviving top of the partition wall with a soft earth, exceptionally rich in finds. At some point a different, "hard clodded" earth yielding only scanty finds was thrown in on the south side of the wall, as well, over the raised, secondary floor there. Over the top of the partition wall and passing over all the area it had once divided, a fill continued up for ca. 0.30 m and was sealed by a final hard-packed floor. Up to this point, things were clear-cut.

In these contexts there was one piece of Greek pottery: a sherd of a Corinthian Late Geometric kotyle, ca. 735–720 (Fig. 4-3, top), found in the stratum between the original floor and the new, raised floor to the south of the partition. The date, like that of the Early Protocorinthian kotyles discussed below (Fig. 4-3, bottom; Fig. 4-6), is quite secure and rests upon the chronology derived from the foundation dates Thucydides furnishes for Greek colonies in Sicily in combination with the earliest Corinthian pottery found at those sites (Coldstream 1968:322–327; Amyx 1988:397–434; Ridgway 1999).

In addition to the Greek piece, a fragmentary Phrygian lustrous black cup (P 5880) found north of the partition wall showed Greek influence. Its handle imitates a Greek type of the 8th to early 6th century BC.

Another pottery import, from the eastern Anatolian plateau, provides some chronological help: a sherd of an Alişar IV krater-type vessel found with the Corinthian Late Geometric kotyle, not likely to be later than 720 BC. At Gordion, Alişar IV pottery makes its initial appearance not long before the great destruction at the site (Sams 1994a:162–63). The destruction itself can now be dated to the latter part of the 9th century, but not later than 805 BC (DeVries et al. forthcoming). At Boğazköy the ware is known during the Büyükkale II phase, which has been roughly dated to the 8th century BC (Seeher 2000:37–38).

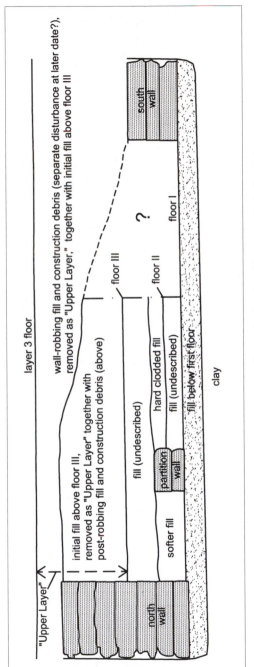

"Upper Layer"

layer 3 floor

wall-robbing fill and construction debris (separate disturbance at later date?), removed as "Upper Layer," together with initial fill above floor III

initial fill above floor III, removed as "Upper Layer" together with post-robbing fill and construction debris (above)

fill (undescribed)

floor III

floor II

?

floor I

hard clodded fill

fill (undescribed)

fill below first floor

clay

softer fill

partition wall

north wall

south wall

Figure 4-2 South Cellar, restored section. Drawn by Carrie Albinger and Katherine Culpepper.

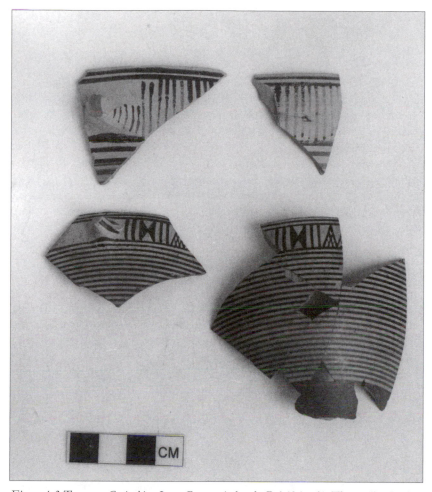

Figure 4-3 Top row: Corinthian Late Geometric kotyle (P 3696 a, b). The smaller sherd is from the stratum between the original floor of the South Cellar and the new, raised floor to the south of the cellar's partition wall. Bottom row: Early Protocorinthian kotyle (P 3241 a. b) from the South Cellar. One fragment is from the Upper Layer and the other from an unrecorded specific context within the cellar.

The phases of the cellar noted up to this point appear to span a fairly short period, for the bronze artifacts in all these contexts are comparable to those in Gordion Tumulus S-1. Part of a bronze belt with a handle similar to that of a belt from Tumulus S-1 was found on the original floor south of the cellar partition, and that was covered over early.[1] In one of the storage jars in situ north of the partition were some of the fragments of a nearly complete belt whose handle resembles another Tumulus S-1 belt.[2] A fibula in the fill with the Corinthian Late Geometric and the Alişar IV sherds closely matches two from S-1.[3] Most of the more than 20 fibulae from north of the partition resemble ones from the tumulus, and none is recognizably later.[4] None of the fibulae from the topmost stratum (the fill below the final floor) is discernibly later than those in the lower contexts, and several also have analogues in the S-1 fibulae.[5]

Above the last cellar floor was what she variously termed the "upper layer" or the "upper fill." This "upper fill" was disturbed by a later partial robbing of the cellar walls, a disturbance which in one area went very deep. The excavator noted that "the highest fill [= upper layer] was mixed...with construction debris of an overlying structure" (Notebook 121:157), which might stem from a separate disturbance. She describes the very different nature of that earth: "fairly heavy and clodded, mixed with many bones" (118).

The abundant Phrygian pottery of the "upper layer" is generally consistent with that of the lower contexts. Moreover, two of the three catalogued fibulae also have counterparts in the lower cellar fills, in Tumulus S-1, or in both.[6] A sherd of an Early Protocorinthian kotyle of ca. 720–690 BC, which joined with sherds from the first excavator's trench (Fig. 4-3, bottom), is close in phase and date to the Corinthian Late Geometric sherd from the fill of one of the first modifications of the cellar.

Along with this early material is a mixture of later artifacts. The latest material includes the abovementioned red-figure sherd, now assignable to the early 4th century BC (P3470), and a rim sherd of a local imitation of an "echinus bowl," a shape starting in Greece ca. 400 BC (South Cellar Context Bag 1). Other material is intermediate, including much of a Hellenizing West Anatolian kotyle of the late 7th or early 6th century BC (Schaus 1992:171, no. 48) and an Attic 6th-century cup fragment (P5800). Tiles and architectural terracottas present ambiguous dating evidence: their manufacture dates to the first half of the 6th century BC (Glendinning, Chapter 7 this volume) but were commonly found in dumps created by a clean-up in the early 4th century BC (DeVries 1990:400).

To summarize, the cellar filling above the highest floor seems to have started fairly early: the late 8th century (the earliest possible date for the Early Protocorinthian kotyle) to the early 7th century BC. A later supplementary filling or a disturbance, e.g., the wall robbing, may have occurred around the early to mid-6th century. New material was introduced early in the 4th century BC, perhaps in connection with the construction of a building above the cellar.

The chronology below the last cellar floor therefore is apt to be no later than the late 8th–early 7th century. The Corinthian Late Geometric in the earliest cellar fill supports, in fact, use before the end of the 8th century, although a single sherd cannot be conclusive. An important find by the first excavator, and thus not assignable to a particular context, is a seal of the Lyre Player group, whose manufacture Boardman (1990) assigns to North Syria and dates to ca. 740–720 BC (Sams and Temizsöy 2000:76, fig. 165). It further strengthens the evidence for a coherent, early component to the cellar's contexts.

THE PHASE OF PHRYGIAN CULTURE OF THE SOUTH CELLAR

The indication of a late 8th to early 7th century BC date for the lower cellar contexts gives a welcome chronological anchor for the wealth of associated

Figure 4-4 Phrygian lustrous black jug with diamond faceting (P 3427), from soft fill to north of the South Cellar's partition wall.

Figure 4-5 Phrygian bichrome painted vessel (P 3278), a sherd of which is from below the final floor of the South Cellar.

*Figure 4-6 Sherd of Early Protocorinthian kotyle (YH 32339.1),
from pit in Building I: 2 cellar. Height 1.8 cm.*

artifacts and to the stage of Phrygian culture they represent. The finds range from such practical items as iron implements to such luxury ivory objects as a stamp seal and a figurine (Young 1966:pl. 74, figs. 5–6). The fine ware attests a high level of craftsmanship at the time. Nearly all the vases were lustrous black ware, and a large number have grooved or relief surface decoration. The most striking ones bear a diamond faceting (Fig. 4-4).

The painted pottery, while rarer, is also notable. While maintaining the Early Phrygian tradition of geometric patterning used at and before the Destruction Level, the patterning became livelier, with a free use of bichrome, which was still fairly rare at the time of the destruction (Fig. 4-5, Pl. 2).

This period of accomplished Phrygian craftsmanship comes at the probable height of Phrygia's political importance under its King Midas, whom Assyrian records show to have been in power during at least the period 718–709 BC.

THE SOUTH CELLAR AND THE DATE OF THE GREAT TUMULUS

One of the most significant aspects of the South Cellar is its implication for the date of the Great Tumulus (MM), which has often been identified as Midas' tomb. As noted above, the fibulae and belts of the cellar correspond to those of Tumulus S-1, which is later than MM. The sequence of tumuli, based on the differing stages of the bronze artifacts, not least fibulae, in each of the burials, is clear: MM, the Mamaderesi Tumulus, Tumulus Z and S-1 (DeVries et al. forthcoming).

Recent adjustments in Anatolian dendrochronology now put the date for the felling of the juniper logs used in the MM tumulus at 740 BC +7/-3, older than the previous determination of 718 BC +1/-1 (Manning et al. 2001; DeVries et al. 2003). The evidence from the South Cellar strongly supports the new date and makes it probable that the construction of the tomb and burial within was not much later. A date around 740 BC would give enough time for the stylistic changes to occur in the artifacts by the time of the cellar, possibly initially used in the late 8th century and being filled in by the early 7th century BC. The old date of 718 BC would be impossibly constricting unless the true date of the South Cellar was considerably later than the manufacture dates of the Corinthian pottery in its fills.

The revised chronology for the tumulus, especially the burial, of course, eliminates the possibility that the occupant was Midas, since the above-mentioned Assyrian records show that he reigned until at least 709 BC.

Middle Phrygian Building I:2 Cellar

Another early context for which Greek ceramics provide dating evidence is a cellar annex of the Middle Phrygian Building I:2 (Fig. 4-1). It was accessible from the main building by a flight of steps cut through the I:2 foundations. Its overall size, ca. 5 m x 5 m, is reminiscent of that of the South Cellar, but its form was less regular. An oven shows that it was a working room. Several floors and remodeling phases indicate a fairly long period of use.

Fibulae from the occupation contexts are comparable to those of the South Cellar and Tumulus S-1.[7] In a pit cutting down into occupation fills was the sherd of an Early Protocorinthian kotyle, very early in that phase and datable to ca. 720–715 (Fig. 4-6).[8] In the cellar's abandonment fill was a Greek or Greek-related sherd of a small dinos with a Greek-looking dark paint overlain by white (Fig. 4-7). It is probably best classified as East Greek Subgeometric and put in the second quarter of the 7th century or a little later.[9] The fibulae of the abandonment fill support a relatively late date, for they have compressed forms with jammed-together mouldings that make them later than the fibulae of the cellar's occupation phase as well those of the South Cellar and Tumulus S-1.[10] They foreshadow the late 7th century fibulae from Tumulus I discussed below.

Tumuli of the Second Half of the 7th Century

A gratifyingly large number of tumuli have Greek pottery from the second half of the 7th century BC or slightly later. Tumulus H contained an East Greek bird bowl of ca. 640–620 BC,[11] Tumulus F a Transitional Corinthian alabastron of ca. 630–615,[12] Tumulus J an East Greek or possibly Hellenizing banded bowl of ca.

Figure 4-7 Greek (? or Western Anatolian?) dinos sherd (YH 32556.4)
from abandonment fill in Building I: 2 cellar.

625–600,[13] Tumulus K-I six apparently Early Corinthian vessels of ca. 620–590,[14] and Tumulus K a banded-rim Ionian cup of a similar date range.[15] The finds from these tumuli, and sporadic finds from the Citadel Mound,[16] document a steady flow of Greek imports soon after the mid-7th century BC.

The very fact that there were regular trade connections is significant. While Assyrian records show that the Kimmerians had been present in Central Anatolia by the 670s BC, they only became a major problem in Western Anatolia, specifically in the Lydian region, by the mid-660s, with crises recurring into the 640s (DeVries et al. forthcoming). Herodotus (1.16) thought that the Kimmerians remained in Anatolia until the Lydian King Alyattes, whose reign began ca. 610 BC, drove them out. But even if they lingered that long, the trade evidence at Gordion indicates some measure of stability was re-established well before. And beyond stability, Tumulus F provides evidence for outright wealth: ivory inlays on a presumably wooden container, a gold earring, and 50 gold sequins once sewn onto a fabric (Kohler 1980:66–67, fig. 11).

Figure 4-8 Phrygian bichrome jug (P 269) from Tumulus H.
Height to rim 21.5 cm. Height to handle 21.7 cm.

In the tumuli of this period there are signs of change in the material culture. Bronze belts have vanished, and fibulae, which had been so abundant in the tumuli from MM through S-1 as well as in the South Cellar, are relatively rare. In fact, there were none at all in the tumuli with Greek pottery, but there were two with advanced, compressed forms in Tumulus I, which is linked to Tumulus J through a tumulus in Ankara.[17] A conservative geometric but bichrome painted pottery style appears to be a hallmark of the period and is embodied on a jug from the excavation of Tumulus H (Fig. 4-8)[18] found in the earth mantle rather than the burial chamber. Its intact state suggests that it was nonetheless a funerary gift for

Figure 4-9 Phrygian dinos (P 636) from Tumulus J. Height 23.5 cm.

that interment. Its patterning is more restrained than that of some pieces from the South Cellar (Fig. 4-5, Pl. 2).

Another style, with an isolated panel decoration, is found in Tumulus J (Fig. 4-9).[19] Isolated panels are common on fragments from the Citadel Mound that lack good, datable contexts and on pottery at other Central Anatolian sites, both Phrygian and non-Phrygian. Tumulus J gives the welcome assurance that the style had begun by the late 7th century BC.[20]

Another major change is in burial practices. While some tumuli still housed inhumations in wooden chambers (H and J), others contained cremations with no chambers (F, K, and K-I).

SECOND QUARTER OF THE 6TH CENTURY

In the second quarter of the 6th century BC, by which time Gordion along with all of Phrygia west of the Halys River had become incorporated into the Lydian empire (no later than 585 BC), another dense sequence of deposits with Greek pottery occurs. By that time, Attic pottery had emerged as a strong competitor to Corinthian ware throughout the Greek world and beyond. Thus its presence, in quantity, at Gordion is not surprising. Its absolute dating is quite closely determinable from the representational style of the earliest surviving olive-oil amphoras that were awarded in the Panathenaic athletic and athletic competitions beginning in 566 BC.

Found in Tumulus K-V (a cremation) were two Attic black figure cups of a type called on the basis of the find location "Gordion cups" (Körte and Körte 1904:140–42, pls. 7–8; Boardman 1974:figs. 108.1–2). They can be dated to ca. 570–560 BC,

Figure 4-10 Attic black-figure Gordion cup (SF 96-269) signed by Sondros as maker, from dump deposit on the Western Citadel Mound. Height 9.4 cm. Rim diameter 15.3 cm.

on the Panatheniac criterion. One is signed by Kleitias as painter and Ergotimos as maker, who were the collaborators on the most celebrated of all Attic black figure vessels, the François Vase.

A clay floor of the Middle Phrygian Building M (Fig. 4-1) contained numerous fragments of an Attic black figure amphora (P2074), which von Bothmer has put stylistically between the Tyrrhenian Group and Lydos and has dated to 560–550 BC (Edwards 1959:26, pl. 65, fig. 4; Gordion Notebook 74, 125 and section, 131). Approximately contemporary with it is a large dump deposit on the Western Citadel Mound (Chapter 3 this volume). The material was thrown into a pit cut down into both a Middle Phrygian structure and trenches that robbed out that building's walls. The dump thus was well after the structure's abandonment.

The deposit yielded a huge volume of Phrygian coarse and fine pottery, a lesser amount of Lydian, and a still smaller amount of mixed Greek pottery, comprising (at a minimum) Attic, Corinthian, and East Greek. Among the Attic is a late Gordion cup bearing the name of Sondros as maker (Figs. 4-10 and 4-11); a likely date is 560–550 BC (Brijder 2000: 554–557). Previously known Sondros cups are all very fragmentary; the Gordion find is the first to preserve figured decoration and the overall form.

The rest of the Attic pottery is consistent with that mid-century date. A black-figure krater attributable to the painter Lydos belongs to what Tiverios defines as that artisan's middle phase and dates "from 555 to just before 540" (Fig. 4-12; Tiverios 1976:85),[21] while an Attic black-glaze olpe dates ca. 575–550 BC (Sparkes and Talcott 1970:77, 253, nos. 247–249; Gordion YH 54211). A Corinthian aryballos and two kotyles have a Middle Corinthian character (A. Brownlee, personal communication).[22] In the lowered Middle and Late Corinthian

Figure 4-11 Detail of interior of cup in Fig. 4-10.

chronology urged by Tiveros, they would fit the dates of the Attic finds (Tiverios 1985–86:79–80).

The Greek pottery, with its consistent, tight dating of the Attic pieces, and, in all probability the Corinthian, provides a close date for the abundant, associated Phrygian material as well. The Phrygian fine pottery is overwhelmingly gray to

Figure 4-12 Attic black-figure column krater (P 4563a, b; P 5415; YH 51501); the two lower fragments are from dump deposit on the Western Citadel Mound.

Figure 4-13 Phrygian jug from dump deposit on Western Citadel Mound (SF 96-332).

black ware, but it includes a nearly complete painted jug (Fig. 4-13), whose decoration strikingly demonstrates the persistence of geometric patterning at this relatively late date. The one advanced aspect is the panel-like framing of the decoration.

The deposit also reveals a change in the manner of fastening garments. As discussed above, fibulae became scanty by the second half of the 7th century. Fibulae are completely absent from the dump despite the great volume of material; instead, bronze pins are present.

Figure 4-14 Attic black-figure Lip Cup (P 2304) from burned floor inside a gate of the circuit wall around the Lower Town.

OUTER CIRCUIT WALL AND THE PERSIAN CONQUEST

Immediately east of the Citadel Mound lay the Middle and Late Phrygian Lower Town, which during part of its early history had been protected by Gordion's outer circuit wall. That fortification was the scene of military action, as is shown by arrowheads embedded in its mudbricks and by a siege ramp that was erected against a high fortress incorporated into the wall. The assault was evidently successful, for a fire swept most of the fortress, and there was further burning in areas to the inside of the one known major gate of the circuit. In destruction contexts in the latter zone were fragments of Attic Little Master cups, including the lip-cup illustrated in Fig. 4–14. Accepted dates for the production of the Little Master class are ca. 560–525 BC (Brijder 1996: passim; Brijder 2000: 549, 557–68), and the Gordion cups fall early in the overall sequence.[23]

Since the 1980s, excavators at the Lydian capital of Sardis have also come across dramatic evidence for military action. Destruction contexts there, too, include Attic Little Master cups (Greenewalt et al. 1995:18, fig. 20; Greenewalt and Rautman 1998: 490–92), and they are again early, pointing to a mid-century date, as does other Attic poetry from those deposits. Attacks at both sites at the same period are only explicable as occurring during the Persian conquest of the Lydian Empire in the 540s. Thus Gordion and Sardis together give a general substantiation to the absolute dating for that phase of Attic pottery, previously based on stylistic evolution, although allowing for a possible slight downward adjustment.

*Figure 4-15 East Greek perfume flask (T 1), in the form
of a kore figure, from Tumulus A. Height 26.8 cm.*

TUMULUS A

Tumulus A (a cremation), the excavation of which began on the first day of the first season of the University of Pennsylvania Museum's work at Gordion, was, ironically, the most luxurious deposit ever found at the site, containing gold and electrum jewelry, a silver mirror, and ivory objects (Kohler 1980:67–69). An East Greek terracotta perfume container in the form of a young woman ("kore") suggests a date of ca. 540–530 BC for the burial (Fig. 4-15; Romano 1995:13–14, no. 27). The date is supported by a fragmentary Greek ivory figurine (Sheftel 1974:27, fig. 2a). Confirming the decline of fibulae and their traditional forms is the presence of a single fibula of an unrecognized type (B 1439).

The date of the tumulus in the very early years of Persian domination is significant, for it is near the very end of the sequence of known pre-Hellenistic tumuli at Gordion. With the consolidation of Persian rule in Anatolia, Daskyleion and Kelainai were made the capitals of the two Persian satrapies governing Phrygia. The now minor status accorded Gordion corresponds both to the cessation of tumulus burials and to the overall eclipse of monumental architecture on the Eastern Mound in the Achaemenid period (the Mosaic Building, discussed in Chapter 7 this volume, being an exception).

Gordion hardly lacked economic vitality in the Achaemenid period, however. Voigt's work documents industrial activity, Lawall (1997) has found that a steady importation of Greek wine begins in the late 6th century, and the commerce in Greek fine ware increased. In addition to the dates that such pottery continues to give during that period, it serves as an index of the site's prosperity despite its new, secondary role.

CONCLUSIONS

Greek pottery is an invaluable guide throughout the periods considered here, dating the artifacts with which it is associated. It establishes that production of the lustrous-black facetted ware occurred in the late 8th or early 7th centuries; previously the ware had lacked good chronological definition and was dated as late as the 5th century BC. The Greek dating evidence also shows that the widespread isolated panel style of Phrygian painted ware had begun by the late 7th century. Furthermore, it documents and dates changes in fibulae, not least the decline in their use.

More broadly, the contexts in which the Greek pottery appears, and for which it furnishes the dates, shed light on Gordion's cultural and political history. The South Cellar gives evidence for a particularly high standard of craft production during the era of Midas. The tumuli of the latter half of the 7th century BC indicate that Central Anatolia was more flourishing at the time than we might otherwise suppose from Herodotus's account that Kimmerians were still present. Finally, the Greek imports in the latest pre-Hellenistic tumuli tie the end of the monumental burial tradition to the Persian establishment of political centers elsewhere in Phrygia, when Gordion took on a new but still notable character.

NOTES

1. South Cellar belt: B 1605. Tumulus S-1 belt: Caner 1983: pl. 77, G1; Kohler 1995, fig. 52, I. The rest of the South Cellar belt was found in a nearby pit in that floor.

2. South Cellar belt: B 1604. Tumulus S-1 belt: Caner 1983: pl. 77, G4; Kohler 1995, pl. 66B.

3. Caner 1983, pl. 50, 783A and 783B (Tumulus S-1) and 784 (South Cellar).

4. The published ones are Caner 1983, nos. 518, 619 (cf. 615 from Tumulus S-1), 692, 771 (cf. 783B from S-1), 776 (cf. same), 826 (cf. 818 from S-1), 864 (cf. 854 and 854B from S-1), 1059 (cf. 1070 from S-1), 1062 (cf. 1070 from S-1), 1099, 1119, 1122 (cf. 1126 from S-1).

5. The published ones: Caner 1983, nos. 675 (cf. 664I from Tumulus S-1), 826 (cf. 818 from S-1), 848 (cf. 843 from S-1), 1018, 1119 (cf. 1127 from S-1).

6. Caner 1983, nos. 449 (cf. 418 and 430A-431 from Tumulus S-1) and 1061 (cf. 1062 from lower in the cellar and 1070 from S-1). The third: no. 950.

7. SF 521 (YH 32811), SF 522 (YH 32817), SF 614 (YH 32848).

8. The wall flares out more broadly (in the Late Geometric manner) than it does on the EPC kotylai, Coldstream 1968: pl. 21, d-f, but the foot has more of the EPC profile than do those of the advanced LG kotylai of Coldstream: pl. 19, j-f.

9. Callipolitis-Feytmans 1970: 105 for the beginning of the East Greek small dinos production and cf Coldstream 1968: 330 for the context. Eilmann 1933: Beil. 35, 14 for added white.

10. SF 448 (YH 32848), SF 450 (YH 32074).

11. P 286. Kohler 1995:TumH 2, pp. 48-49, pl. 27B-D.

12. P 291. Kohler 1995:1980: 66, fig. 8.

13. P 591. Kohler 1995:TumJ 35, 68, pl. 39A.

14. Körte and Körte 1904:133-134, fig. 117.

15. P 4930. Unpublished.

16. Especially important because they come from the early part of the overall period considered here are two bird bowls, P 1488 and P 2057, which M. Kerschner places in the third quarter of the 7th century (pers. comm., July 28, 1996), and fragments of Middle Wild Goat I oinochoai (jugs): P 3579 (ca. 640-625 BC) and two sherds, P 1265 and P 2728, from probably the same oinochoe (very late in MWG I, ca. 630-625 BC).

17. Caner 1983:no. 522, pl. 40 and no. 697C, pl. 46 (the I fibulae). Mellink 1990:140 (Ankara tumulus).

18. P 269. Kohler 1995:TumH 18, p. 51, pl. 28J.

19. P 636. Kohler 1995:TumJ 36, 68-69, fig. 27D, pl. 39B.

20. Another Gordion tumulus, Tumulus B, has two nearly complete vessels with isolated panels. A Lydian lekythos puts the tumulus into the sixth century. (Kohler 1995: pls. 8C and pl. 10D-g; G. Gültekin, pers. comm. 2002).

21. Two sherds of the krater, P 5415 and YH 51501, are from the dump, while two others, P 4653 a-b, are from the Eastern Citadel Mound.

22. P 210, YH 54238 and YH 54242.

23. A formative phase of lip-cups dates slightly earlier, ca. 565–560, than that of the standard Little Master cups in the analysis of Brijder, who has the normative cups begin ca. 560. The palmette decoration of the lip-cup of Fig. 4–14 suggests a date of ca. 560–550.

5

RECONSTRUCTING THE ROMAN-PERIOD TOWN AT GORDION

ANDREW GOLDMAN

In 25 BC the Roman Emperor Augustus (27 BC–AD 14) annexed a large swath of central Turkey to create the Roman province of Galatia. To facilitate the administration of this new territory, three cities were founded at the largest Galatian tribal centers, Ancyra, Tavium, and Pessinus (modern Ankara, Büyüknefes, and Ballıhisar, respectively). Although Gordion had a legendary reputation by Roman times, it was not chosen to become a major center, having long since declined from its position of regional dominance. Indeed, the geographer Strabo (ca. 64 BC–ca. AD 21) describes the former Phrygian capital as having been reduced in his day to a mere village, if slightly larger than those around it (Strabo 12.5.3). Gordion had become one of many small communities along the Ancyra-Pessinus highway amid the Galatian highlands.

It is small wonder, then, that Roman Gordion has until recently failed to receive significant attention. Strabo's widely accepted description of the Roman-period settlement provided little incentive to pursue further investigation. After a brief exploratory sampling of the Roman-period strata by R. S. Young in 1950, excavations were quickly re-directed to areas of the Citadel Mound beyond the Roman town's periphery, where pre-Roman levels were more readily accessible (Young 1951). The impressive pre-Roman remains have garnered the lion's share of resources and research at Gordion, and the late habitation levels were treated with the casual disregard common to other major Anatolian Bronze or Iron Age centers, such as Boğazköy, Kültepe, and Acemhöyük. For nearly 50 years the modest discoveries of Gordion's Roman-period inhabitants thus remained unanalyzed and unpublished, quietly tucked away in storage depots.

ROMAN GORDION: HISTORICAL AND ARCHAEOLOGICAL SIGNIFICANCE

Since 1993 we have witnessed a resurgence of interest in Roman Gordion, as scholars have become increasingly aware of its potential to shed light upon provincial dynamics in Roman Galatia. The primary impetus for this change was the publication of Mitchell's *Anatolia* (1993), a landmark study that heightened interest in the economic, political, and cultural development of central Anatolia during the Roman Imperial period. Mitchell's work opened a new dialogue about complex socioeconomic phenomena such as urban growth and consolidation, the expansion of the regional economy, and patterns of rural settlement and land ownership. Such issues have rarely been addressed for Rome's Anatolian provinces, and Mitchell's detailed models, formulated largely on the basis of the surviving literary and epigraphic sources, have sparked much discussion and debate about Roman Galatia.

The chief criticism that can be leveled at Mitchell's work is the virtual absence of archaeological data in support of his theses. The fault rests not with Mitchell but with the dearth of excavations at Roman-period sites in the Galatian hinterlands. Although the former urban centers of Roman Galatia have received some attention, Galatian town and village sites have lain virtually untouched. Over the past several decades steady increases in population and agricultural activity in central Turkey have affected such sites adversely. The rapid disappearance of these smaller sites is diminishing our opportunity to recover evidence of their organization and development. Such circumstances are doubly disturbing since sites elsewhere across Turkey are also disappearing, reducing potential comparanda in a country where scant evidence exists for the physical organization or material culture of such communities. The lack of archaeological data in the rural districts of Galatia and adjacent provinces has hindered our study of Roman-period settlement, and we must view current models for Galatia's development and organization with caution in light of the limited body of material evidence upon which they are based.

Excavated Roman-period material at Gordion can address this lacuna, and analyzing it gives us the first opportunity to detail the social and economic dynamics of Galatia's rural landscape. The town is exceptional as the only excavated settlement of its date, size, and rural status in central Turkey, as well as one of the few excavated Roman-period towns in Anatolia.

Gordion was located on a major east-west highway linking Ankara and the Black Sea region to the northeast with Pessinus, Colonia Germa (modern Babadat), and the Aegean provinces to the southwest. The presence of this road—still partially visible to the east of Gordion—facilitates the study of trade patterns on both local and interregional levels. In addition, Gordion's location near the nexus of the three urban *territoria*, thus at some distance from the influence of these major provincial centers, provides an excellent environment for measuring the impact and extent of Romanization in rural Galatia.

Finally, the town's extended period of occupation, from the early 1st century AD until at least the early 5th century AD, allows us to study long-term change in the settlement's size, organization, and economic activity. Comparison of observed changes with events known to us through the surviving historical sources permits an investigation of the impact of wider regional developments on local conditions.

Although the analysis of excavated material from the Roman-period occupation strata began only in 1996, results from this ongoing work have already produced important contributions to our understanding of both Roman Gordion and the Galatian province. Following a general reconstruction of the town's history, discussion centers on an analysis of the middle Imperial phase of town's occupation (Phase 3), a roughly 50-year period during the Flavian and Trajanic eras (ca. AD 70 to 120). This particular phase is contemporaneous with a critical era during which a well-documented program of wide-scale regional development was set into motion by the Roman emperors and their subordinates (Broughton 1938; Magie 1950; Mitchell 1993). A broad range of literary, epigraphic, and numismatic sources relates directly to this crucial stage of Galatia's provincial development, the details of which will be discussed briefly below. This phase is the most widely explored and most extensively studied stratum of the town, providing the best archaeological data to inspect the historical models in some detail.

Historical sources have inherent limitations, and their silence on certain issues raises numerous questions. For example, to what extent, if any, did the Roman-sponsored initiatives of the 1st century AD affect the economic and cultural fabric of Galatia's non-urban communities? Did administrative, military, and economic developments across Galatia have a measurable impact on life in the rural hinterlands? Is it possible to detect a noticeable increase in Romanization within the countryside, beyond the immediate range of the province's capitals? Potential answers to such questions lie within the archaeological finds from Roman Gordion.

HISTORICAL CONTEXT OF GORDION PHASE 3 (FLAVIAN AND TRAJANIC ERA)

Before turning to the archaeological data from Roman Gordion, an overview of the province during the late 1st and early 2nd centuries AD is essential. According to textual evidence, Galatia during the Flavian and Trajanic periods witnessed political, military, and economic reorganizations on an unprecedented scale. At the accession of Vespasian in AD 69, Galatia had been a province for nearly a century, its territory slowly expanding as Augustus and his successors annexed and appended adjacent regions. Although Galatia stood as the eastern frontier in Anatolia for four decades, the province enjoyed comparative peace during the 1st century AD. Because Galatia contained no legionary forces, a governor of lower political status was normally selected to administer the territory.

The local economy appears to have been based on both agricultural and pastoral production; Pliny the Elder and other ancient authors praise the high quality of the region's barley, its sheep, and woolen products (Broughton 1938). The province always possessed few urban centers, and until the Neronian period, civic coinage was minted in limited quantities.

Nero's Parthian War (AD 54–66) in eastern Anatolia resulted in significant changes in the defense and administration of Galatia in the subsequent early Flavian era. Vespasian saw the need for a stronger, permanent frontier zone in Anatolia, after the incursions of the Alani tribesmen and a revolt in neighboring Pontus during the civil wars of AD 68–69. Permanent legionary bases were therefore constructed in eastern Cappadocia, along the Euphrates River at Satala and Melitene. By AD 72 the whole of Anatolia to the west of the Euphrates lay within the Empire's borders. Vespasian further consolidated Roman administrative and military control by annexing the remaining client kingdoms in Anatolia in AD 75. The districts of Pontus, Pisidia, Isauria, Phrygia, Lycaonia, and Paphlagonia were included in the expanded province, a massive unified command that ancient writers referred to simply as Galatia.

Ancyra remained the chief metropolis of the province. To oversee a smooth transition within Galatia, Vespasian dispatched governors of proven loyalty, most of who had served previously as *legati* under his direct command or had past experience in dealing with Eastern affairs (Mitchell 1993). Among other duties, these governors or their direct subordinates upgraded the provincial highway network across the newly enlarged province. Preserved milestones from Galatia, Cappadocia, Pontus, Pisidia, Paphlagonia, Lycaonia, and Armenia Minor attest to these enormous building programs (Mitchell 1993). The improvement of the Ancyra-Pessinus highway was among these projects that facilitated the rapid deployment of the army, its supplies, and communications. Such projects also stimulated local and interregional commerce, as suggested by the increased output of bronze coinage among the cities of Galatia.

This chain of events, gleaned from the literary, epigraphic, and numismatic sources, is interpreted as a major effort by the Flavians to improve infrastructure, administration, defense, and prosperity. While the exact speed, scope, and impact of these events is debated, these developments clearly mark an important developmental phase for Galatia (Mitchell 1993).

PRELIMINARY RESULTS FROM THE YOUNG/VOIGT EXCAVATIONS (1950–2002)

Portions of the Roman-period town have been explored in three separate areas on the Gordion Citadel Mound (Fig. 5-1). Young excavated two sectors of the community in 1950, on a bluff in the Northwest (NW) Zone overlooking the river, and in the Southwest (SW) Zone, where the Körte brothers had excavated several trenches during their 1900 field season (Körte and Körte 1904). In the late 1960s and early 1970s, Young's team uncovered a third area at the northeastern corner of the settlement. Beyond a series of small trash pits and the occasional stray coin find, no evidence for Roman habitation was discovered in the Main Excavation area.

The NW Zone, where R. S. Young excavated a 24 x 40 m trench, is the largest area of the settlement exposed and is thus the focus of this chapter. M. M. Voigt and T. C. Young's resumption of excavation in that area between 1995 and 2002 uncovered two earlier phases of the settlement, so a total of four Roman-period building phases (Phases 1-4) are now recognized in the NW Zone (Voigt et al. 1997; Sams and Voigt 1997, 1998).

Analysis of the first two phases is currently under way. Dating of these two phases remains tentative, but together they appear to span ca. AD 0 to 70/75, roughly from the early Julio-Claudian to the onset of the Flavian period. Evidence from these two early phases and contemporary ceramic finds from the eastern Citadel Mound indicate that the town rapidly expanded during this early phase, nearing its largest extent of ca. three hectares, covering no more than one-third of the Citadel Mound. Such limited dimensions lend credence to Strabo's description of the site as a village during the early 1st century AD.

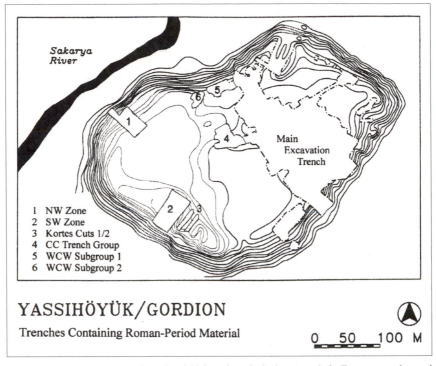

1 NW Zone
2 SW Zone
3 Kortes Cuts 1/2
4 CC Trench Group
5 WCW Subgroup 1
6 WCW Subgroup 2

YASSIHÖYÜK/GORDION

Trenches Containing Roman-Period Material

0   50   100 M

*Figure 5-1 Plan of the Gordion Citadel Mound, with the location of the Roman trenches and
the approximate perimeter of the settlement at its largest extent.
Plan by S. Jarvis; revised by A. Goldman.*

The phase of interest here is Roman Phase 3, dated via the ceramics, lamps, and stray coin finds to ca. AD 70/75–110/120 (Goldman 2000). Roman Phase 3 of the NW Zone proved to be well preserved, and Young's 1950 excavations revealed three separate structures lining a cobble-paved, colonnaded street (Fig. 5-2). Building 1, to the north, possessed a peristyle courtyard and at least two subsidiary rooms, the largest of which was partitioned by a mudbrick wall. Voigt's excavations of the earlier phases of Building 1 revealed that the peristyle plan was a new one, replacing the simple, open courtyard of Phases 1 and 2. Simultaneously, a rectangular room to the southwest was partitioned off to form a space accessible only from the cobbled street (Fig. 5-3). A similar double-roomed suite was located in Building 2, just to the east. These detached rooms were probably small shops (*tabernae*), a common feature of towns across the empire. No such rooms have been identified thus far in the earlier Roman strata, suggesting that more complex subdivisions of space, for both private and commercial reasons, occurred during the Flavian/Trajanic period.

Roman Phase 3 also witnessed the building of colonnades and sidewalks along the paved street 6 m wide. These colonnades were constructed using stone from pre-Roman structures, and over a dozen plinths and stone bases were discovered *in situ* along the street (Fig. 5-4). The three surviving stone bases indicate that the columns

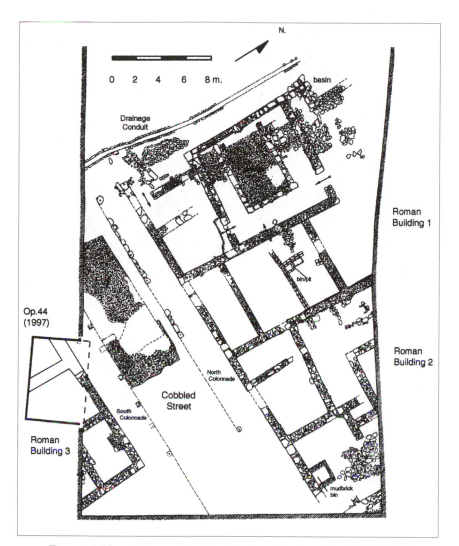

Figure 5-2 Plan of Roman Phase 3, with colonnaded street. Plan by E. B. Reed; revised by A. Goldman.

were either fully or partially made of stone drums and probably topped by wooden architraves. The colonnade would have presented a rather rustic display to an urban dweller: red and gray stone was used interchangeably, column placement varied up to 0.75 m, and no attempt was made to place opposing columns symmetrically across the expanse of the street. The inhabitants sought to convey the image of a proper Roman public venue lined by typical columnar façades. The colonnade's presence demonstrates not only the development of a more sophisticated manipulation of public space during Roman Phase 3, but also that significant resources were committed to constructing the outward trappings of an urban center in a rural Galatian setting.

Figure 5-3 Isolated street-side room in Building 1 (Roman Phase 3),
probably a shop (taberna). *Courtesy of Gordion Archives.*

The ceramic and numismatic assemblages further support the view
that prosperity increased in Roman Phase 3. Recent analysis of Phase 1 and 2
ceramics has confirmed that red-slipped fine wares—commonly referred to as
Eastern Sigillata (ES)—appear for the first time in large quantities during Phase 3.
These ES fine wares include an imported Cypriote vessel with the characteristic
nicked rouletting, barbotine "webbed" cups popular in the Roman West (Fig. 5-5),
and popular Flavian forms such as vertical rim dishes (Fig. 5-6) and cups. While
no evidence of production has been found to date at Gordion, analysis of the
fine wares associated with Phase 3 is currently under way to determine whether
manufacture took place locally. Preliminary compositional matches of the wares
suggest some trade links with the Levant (Goldman and Grave in prep.). The
larger issue of the production and dissemination of Roman-period fine wares in
Galatia is yet to be addressed (Hayes 1997:54).

The Gordion fine wares, however, most closely resemble those found in the
Pontic region rather than in western or southern Anatolia. Since imports make
up only a small percentage of the excavated assemblage, it appears that much of
the pottery is of Galatian manufacture, perhaps from one of the province's urban
centers. The development of local Galatian ceramic industries and the growing
circulation of red-slipped wares would tie in well with the increased commercial
activity suggested for the Flavian and Trajanic eras (Mitchell 1993).

Coins provide additional evidence for the growth of economic activity at
Gordion during Phase 3. Although one hoard of 22 coins was unearthed in 1973
(Hoard X, dated via rare issues of the emperor Galba to ca. AD 69–70), most

Figure 5-4 Roman Phase 3 colonnaded street, with gutter and cobble-paved surface.
Courtesy of Gordion Archives.

are stray coin finds of Galatian issue (DeVries 1990:405–6). Low denomination bronze pieces of the Flavian and Trajanic periods dominate the more than 80 Roman-period coins recovered. Comparatively few later issues from the Severan through Theodosian eras are present. It is difficult, of course, to say anything certain based on such a random collection. If the coins reflect a representative sample of circulating currency, then the frequency of Flavian and Trajanic issues might indicate an increase in commercial transactions at Gordion. Such a view would correspond with our understanding of the regional economy during this period, when improvements to the province's infrastructure and the burgeoning output of civic coinage are likely to have bolstered local markets.

If the interpretation of Roman Phase 3 is correct, then the site's physical and commercial development appears to correlate with the imperial initiatives of the Flavian period. Road building activity played a role in this new prosperity, for roads facilitated the movement of currency, labor, and trade goods. Gordion would have benefited from its location on a highway linking several administrative

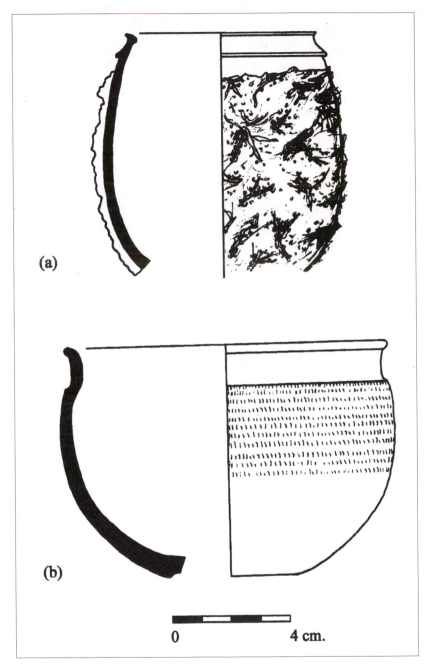

*Figure 5-5 "Webbed" barbotine cup (a) and Cypriote Sigillata cup (b).
Drawn by A. Goldman.*

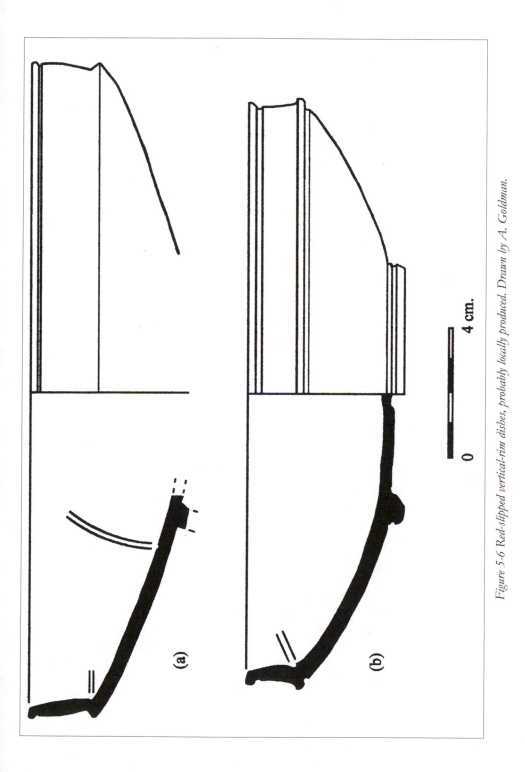

Figure 5-6 Red-slipped vertical-rim dishes, probably locally produced. Drawn by A. Goldman.

centers. Some suggest that Gordion should be equated with Vindia or Vinda, a posting station (*statio*) on this highway listed in the Antonine Itinerary. The distance between Gordion and Colonia Germa corresponds exactly to that listed in the itinerary, placing Vindia or Vinda in the immediate vicinity of Gordion (French 1978; Mitchell 1993). Although no present evidence confirms this identification, Gordion's role as a local administrative center would explain many of the developments discussed here.

Whatever the precise causes, inhabitants of this small rural settlement embraced the benefits that accompanied Galatia's new provincial status. They built peristyle-plan houses, erected columnar porticoes, set up shops, used more coins, and imported increasing quantities of such high-quality goods as fine pottery. A growth in prosperity seems to occur in conjunction with or immediately following the Flavian imperial initiatives, indicating that parts of rural Galatia prospered during the reorganization and upgrades documented within the literary and epigraphic sources (Mitchell 1993).

Roman Phase 4, the final Roman stratum currently recognized at the site, was relatively lengthy, from ca. AD 110/120 to the mid- or late 4th century. Strong continuity in ceramic forms from Phase 3 to 4 in the NW Zone indicates that any break in habitation was comparatively short. About 0.5 m of fill separates the two building phases, and finds from the underlying fill, including Trajanic coins and a Broneer Type 24 lamp, date Phase 4 rebuilding to the first quarter of the 2nd century AD.

It is tempting to equate the end of Phase 3 with the major earthquake of AD 110 which, according to Jerome and Orosius, leveled the three capitals of Galatia (Broughton 1938) and required the reconstruction of the imperial temple at Pessinus (Waelkens 1986; Mitchell 1993). A large mass of degraded organic material found in 1997 in the Phase 3 fill of Building 3, perhaps debris from a thatch roof, could be evidence of this earthquake, as might a crushed skeleton discovered entombed within Building 1 Phase 3 debris.

Little can be said at this time about the function of the Phase 4 buildings, a series of closed structures built either atop or slightly offset from the Phase 3 buildings. Preservation in Phase 4 was exceedingly poor, with significant disturbance caused by over 60 early Byzantine stone cist graves (ca. 4th–5th centuries AD), wall-robbing activities, medieval pits and numerous subterranean tandor-style ovens (ca. 11th–14th centuries AD), and military entrenchments from the Battle of the Sakarya in 1921.

However, significant modifications in the town plan are apparent: structures in the southern half of the NW Zone trench were never rebuilt, while portions of those to the north of the street (Fig. 5-2) adopted new plans with squared rooms. The western rooms of Building 2 were transformed into a paved alley with a central drainage conduit, producing a more dispersed settlement plan than that of Phase 3. These changes, in combination with the negligible presence of imported objects, coins or fine ware pottery, appear to indicate that activity declined or changed significantly in at least this portion of the town during Phase 4. Habitation certainly ceased by the late 4th century AD, at which time the western half of the excavated area was converted into a cemetery. It seems probable, then, that the town experienced some decline in population and economic activity during this final phase of Roman occupation.

CONCLUSION

Much work remains in our investigation of Roman Gordion. Future excavation and analysis is certain to further our understanding of life in the town and, by extension, the nature of provincial dynamics in the rural hinterlands of Roman Galatia. It is already clear that Strabo's portrait of Gordion as a small village, while perhaps valid during his own lifetime, is less applicable to slightly later periods, when a more sophisticated town plan was imposed upon the settlement and an influx of coinage and high-quality goods occurred. While Gordion never did regain the economic and political clout that it wielded in pre-Roman times, it was hardly the unsophisticated country hamlet that Strabo suggested.

II Interpreting the Finds from Gordion

6

TEXTILE PRODUCTION AT GORDION AND THE PHRYGIAN ECONOMY

BRENDAN BURKE

The legends of King Midas of Gordion and his incredible wealth are well known from Greek and Roman sources. While finds of gold are rare at Gordion, finely crafted metal vessels, objects of ivory and alabaster, and intricately carved wooden furniture attest to the wealth of the Phrygian elite. Workshops for the manufacture of such elite goods have not been located securely from the excavations at Gordion. Within the Citadel Mound, however, the most definitively located craft activity is the manufacture of Phrygian textiles. This chapter demonstrates that a centrally organized textile industry was a major feature of the Phrygian royal economy at Gordion and that it was an important resource for the Phrygian elite during the Early Iron Age (ca. 9th century BC).

The site of Gordion provides an ideal opportunity to study the organization of a well-developed textile industry and how this craft functioned in the political economy of 1st millennium Anatolia. The scale of production is indicated by the large quantity of textile tools found in standardized workshop units, in the Terrace Building, and in the Clay Cut structure.

CONTEXTS OF PRODUCTION

Defined by courtyard surfaces and internal enclosure walls, the excavated portions of the Early Phrygian Citadel Mound are divided into two principal zones, the residential quarter with large freestanding megaron structures and the industrial area located on a high terrace toward the southwest (Fig. 6-1). We can map cloth production activity from the excavated remains in these two parts of the Gordion mound.

Elite Residential Quarter

The eastern half of the main excavation area at Gordion is thought to be the residential quarter of the elite because of the elaborate nature of the megaron buildings and traces of luxury goods found within. Megaron 3 is by far the most impressive of all the buildings at Gordion, and it is the best candidate for a royal residence. Its large size required two rows of interior support posts along the side and back walls, presumably supporting a balcony. This building contained the most luxurious items, including carved ivory furniture inlays, fine bronze and clay vessels, wooden furniture, a deposit of gold pieces that may be unstamped coinage, and also fragments of woven textiles which are associated with the furniture in this room (Bellinger 1962; DeVries 1980b:35; Ellis 1981).

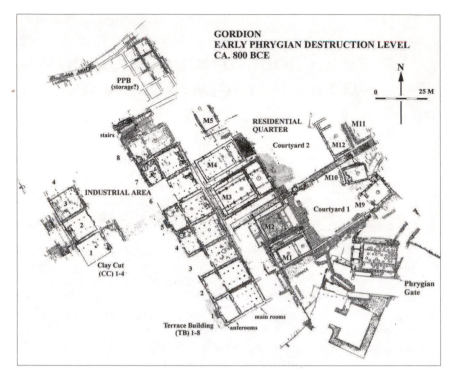

Figure 6-1 Detailed Site Plan, Early Phrygian Destruction Level, 9th century BC.

In Megaron 4 there were about 25 spindle whorls and an indeterminate number of loom weights (tools of cloth production) in the main room along the rear wall. Behind Megaron 4, in a storeroom similar to that behind Megaron 1, were found approximately 75 doughnut-shaped loom weights.

North of Megarons 3 and 4, buildings of an earlier phase of the Citadel Mound, dating to the beginning of the Early Iron Age, were excavated. These structures went out of use well before the destruction of the Citadel Mound in the late 9th century BC and were found mostly emptied of their contents. Referred to as Megarons 6, 7, and 8, the buildings (not shown in Fig. 6-1) contained cooking installations and equipment related to cloth production, similar to the later Terrace Building and Clay Cut structures to the west but on a smaller scale (DeVries 1980b:35).

The Industrial Area

Most of the evidence for weaving and spinning comes from the Terrace Building and the Clay Cut structure. These buildings were constructed on an extensive raised terrace approximately 1 m high, behind the back walls of Megarons 1-4 (Figs. 6-1 and 2). This terrace created restricted access between the elite quarter and the industrial

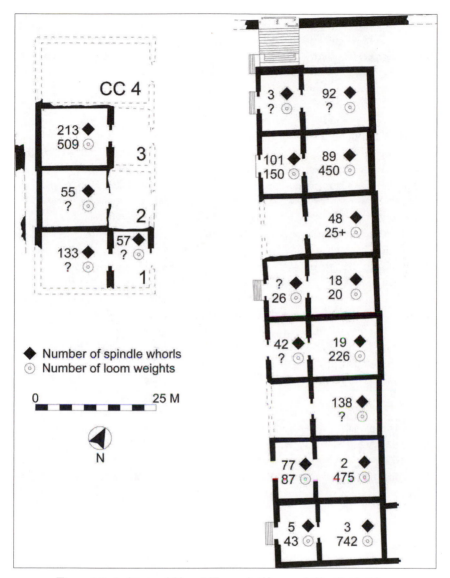

Figure 6-2 Architectural Plan of Terrace buildings and Clay Cut buildings.

sector and could only be entered from either end. Twelve individual megaron units have been excavated to varying degrees in these two buildings (TB 1-8, CC 1-4), and all had the typical megaron form, with a single stepped entrance leading to an anteroom which often contained cooking installations. The back room, or main hall, usually had grinding platforms along the back wall and large numbers of loom weights, spindle whorls, and other textile equipment (see Fig. 2-7).

The individual workshop units or rooms measured approximately 11.5 m wide. The anterooms were about 7 m deep and the main rooms measured 13 m long, for a total length of 20 m for each megaron unit—fairly massive dimensions. The buildings were of different-colored sandstone and limestone, with courses of stone, wood, and mud brick.

The Terrace Building was excavated to its full extent of 105 m, revealing 8 workshop units (TB 1-8) of nearly identical megaron plan. On each side of the workroom there is a row of postholes and another row along the back wall. These rows of posts would have supported a second story wooden gallery that surrounded the room on three sides, roughly ∏-shaped, similar to the arrangement of Megaron 3. These workshop units provided a separate working quarter for cloth and food production on a very large scale inside the fortification walls of Gordion.

Twenty meters to the southwest, across a broad street, was the parallel building named the Clay Cut, or CC. The layer of clay placed over the Early Phrygian Destruction Level by the Middle Phrygian rebuilders gave the conventional name to this excavation area in the Clay Cut. The CC building was identical to, though a mirror image of, the Terrace Building, with megaron units composed of an anteroom entered from the north and a main room behind. Unlike the Terrace Building, the exact length of the entire CC building is not known since only portions of four megaron units have been excavated (CC 1-4). The rooms of the CC are nearly identical to the TB, as are the general characteristics of the finds inside, leading us to conclude that the CC was most likely the same length as the TB.

These two parallel buildings were planned and constructed together late in the Early Phrygian period during an ambitious building program in the 9th century BC. It is thought that the workshop buildings were built at the same time because they rest on the same terrace fill and the sidewalls of each room are aligned to the midpoint of the workshop unit across the street. This line would also continue through the center of Megaron 4.

PRODUCTION EQUIPMENT

Textile equipment, food-processing installations, and large quantities of pottery were the primary finds from the workshop units. Evidence for cloth production is plentiful, including clay spindle whorls, loom weights, knives, and other tools made of ivory, bone, and wood. All of the workshop units contained some loom weights and spindle whorls (Fig. 6-2). Over the three decades that the CC and TB were excavated, the discovery of massive numbers of relatively plain loom weights and spindle whorls was not unexpected, and some of the excavation notebooks do not record the number of tools in detail. During the excavation of TB 4, for example, R. S. Young noted, "We finish digging the burned fill...[finding] more whorls, doughnuts and iron knives. To recount in detail would be tedious" (Gordion Notebook 67, p. 78 [1957]).

Figure 6-3 Spindle whorls.

Spindle Whorls

Before weaving, all fibers must be spun into thread. Fired clay spindle whorls are attached to the ends of wooden spindles, providing a flywheel for drawing out and spinning wool or linen fibers. Over 1,000 whorls were collected from the Early Phrygian destruction level at Gordion. Most are plain and date to a fairly restricted period of time, the Early Phrygian Destruction Level of the late 9th century BC (Fig. 6-3). None of the whorls from the Terrace and Clay Cut buildings showed signs of distinctive decoration; most examples were asymmetrical, bi-conical whorls, with smooth surfaces, and some had a mica slip. Even though many of the whorls were severely damaged by fire, some revealed traces of organic temper

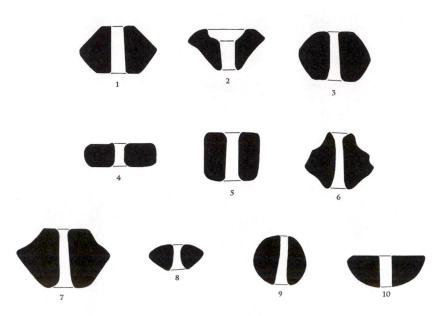

Figure 6-4 Cross-section drawings of spindle whorls.

in a standardized fabric. Ten different types were distinguished based solely on the shape and profile of the whorls to analyze variation (Fig. 6-4). Style and decoration vary little, suggesting that these whorls were not crafted as individual personal objects, but belonged instead to a centrally controlled industry.

The whorls from the Early Phrygian Destruction Level at Gordion range in weight from very light (less than 10 g), to so large that some could have functioned as light loom weights (about 100 g or more). On average, they weighed 24 g. The lighter whorls were probably used for the spinning of finer thread, although ethnographic studies suggest that experienced spinners can spin fine thread with a broad range of weights (Parsons 1972:65, 1975). Heavier whorls were more likely used to ply two or more threads together, suitable for heavy textiles. There is some evidence for individual assemblages of spindle whorls within the workrooms, such as the five whorls found in a carved wooden box in CC 3, which probably made up a spinner's kit (DeVries 1990:386–87, fig. 20). This room also had the largest number of spindle whorls—187—for any of the workshops.

Some whorls were found stored in ceramic vessels along with metal needles and knives. These clusters are particularly interesting because they reflect the spinning kits of individual workers. The measured weights covered a broad range, suggesting that the Phrygian spinners used a variety of weighted whorls for different qualities of thread, as is revealed in some of the textile fragments. One set of thirteen whorls ranged from 3 to 38 grams (YH33698 Small Find #592).

Figure 6-5 Loom weights.

However, whorls of another set found together (pot YH33668) were similar in weight, 10–14 g (YH33643 Small Find #591).

In the fourth Terrace Building unit, only 19 spindle whorls were found, but their average weight, 35 grams, is much greater than those from other rooms. The central location of this room along the terrace, and the heavier whorls found inside, suggests that the spinning here involved the twisting together of finer threads into thicker yarns, a process known as plying. Possibly, the spinning of finer threads was located in adjoining rooms, such as TB 3, and threads were brought to TB 4 for plying. Heavier thread would be suitable for weaving strong cloth, which Phrygian textile finds at Gordion demonstrate was often two-ply.

Loom Weights

Once thread was spun it could either be attached to loom weights and used as warp (the vertical threads on a standing loom) or used as weft (the horizontal threads). The most common type of loom weight found at Gordion is referred to as the "doughnut" type because of its round shape and large central hole (Fig. 6-5). Other shapes occur in nearly every occupation level but none in such large numbers as the Early Phrygian "doughnut."

Catalogued examples vary in quality of preservation. Most of the weights were made of sun-dried clay from the banks of the Sakarya River, and only some were preserved accidentally in the fire that destroyed the Citadel Mound in the early 9th century BC. Straw was mixed in with the pebbly clay to give the weights integrity when suspended. Only a small percentage of the recorded loom weights from Gordion were available for study, as most had either been discarded or had

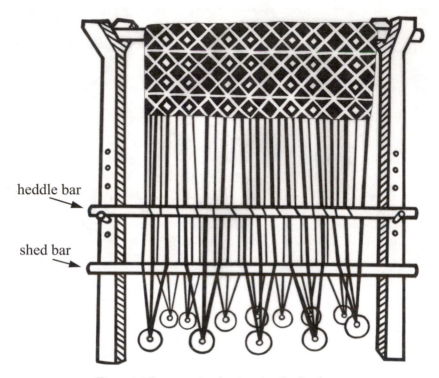

heddle bar

shed bar

Figure 6-6 Reconstruction drawing of a Gordion loom.

later deteriorated in storage. At least 2750 doughnut-shaped loom weights have been identified through the excavation notebooks although the total number of Early Phrygian weights was probably much higher.

The shape of the Gordion loom weights suggests that warp-threads were directly attached to the unfired clay weights, through the central hole (Fig. 6-6). Some sets of weights found in the Terrace Buildings were found in one or two rows, as if the loom was still standing at the time of destruction. Seven weights in a group of 49 from CC 3 even had threads attached to them when they were excavated (DeVries 1990:387).

Excavation in the anteroom of TB 2 produced 87 typical doughnut-shaped, clay loom weights (average weight 557 g), with the majority ranging from 400 to 700 g. These weights are heavy compared to other loom weights found throughout the Mediterranean and Near East. The 400 loom weights found in the Loom Weight Basement at the Minoan palace of Knossos, for example, averaged only 155 g (Burke 1998:68). The heavy weights at Gordion suggest thick warp threads and, consequently, heavy-duty textiles. While some of the spindle whorls from Gordion are lightweight, presumably for fine thread, most probably this thread would have been used for supplemental wefts or decorative additions to woven textiles rather than warps.

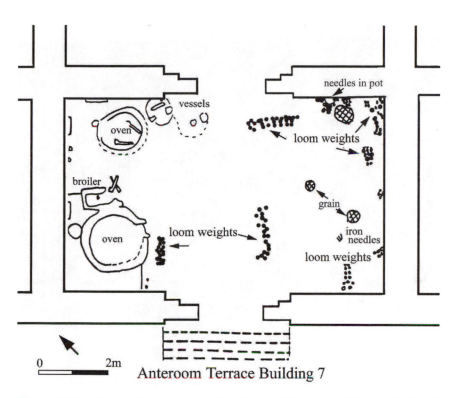

Figure 6-7 Plan drawing of the contents and installations of the anteroom in Terrace Building 7.

In the anteroom of TB 7 (Fig. 6-7), three sets of weights were found in rows, one with 21 doughnut-shaped weights in a line about 1.59 m in length, giving us a good idea of the width of the textiles woven on this loom. As noted by DeVries, the central part of the anteroom would have been a logical place for looms, perhaps standing perpendicular to the doorways so that there would be a good source of natural light but traffic flow would not be impeded (DeVries 1980b:39, 1990:385; Gordion Notebook 156: p. 114).

Based on the distribution throughout the TB and CC structures, it is estimated that one loom used between 20 and 40 weights, which were divided into two rows for one warp shed. If we estimate 15 threads tied to each loom weight, in two rows of 20 loom weights each, that would mean that these looms were producing textiles with about 600 warp threads (approximately 1.5 m wide) of an indeterminate length.

The total number of loom weights—2,743—is only an estimate, since many weights were not collected or fully recorded. Yet, if we assume that each loom used 40 loom weights, and some looms could certainly have used fewer, we can estimate that there could have been about 70 looms in use in 18 different rooms at the time of destruction. These looms would have been distributed over the 11

Figure 6-8 Gordion comb and textile.

excavated main rooms and the 7 anterooms of the TB and CC structures. If we reconstruct a complete CC structure with a total of 8 rooms, like the parallel TB structure, and we include all of the unexcavated anterooms, we have 32 rooms, which suggests at least 125 looms in the industrial area. Some of the weights found were in storage and we should not imagine all of the weights in use at one time, but the number of looms demonstrates a concentration of weaving activity unparalleled at any other site in the eastern Mediterranean.

Weaver's Comb

Other tools indicate the production of cloth at Gordion, including a unique weaver's comb from the anteroom of TB 2 (Fig. 6-8; YH33701 Small Find #583), found during excavations directed by M. Voigt (Voigt 1994). The thoroughly charred remains of a toothed weaving implement in the form of a wooden comb was found blackened with unwoven warp threads adhering to one side and woven textile on the other. The comb had a plain top and sides with a slightly curving row of teeth. It is very fragmentary, but it is quite possible that this tool is the earliest known reed or textile comb used to keep the warp threads separate and to push the weft threads down during weaving. It could have been used on a warp-weighted loom or for band weaving. The relatively small size of the object from Gordion, approximately 6 cm wide, suggests that it was used for making small, decorative bands.

Metal Objects

Iron needles of different sizes and shapes are common, indicating a variety of tasks including stitching of fine cloth, working heavier materials like leather, and over-casting. The needles' eyes, though often obscured by rust, seem to have been made by pulling the needle to a point and then bending it down against the shaft making a thin loop, or eye, in the shape of an elongated oval (McClellan 1975). The self-soldering character of iron makes this the preferred method for making needle eyes.

Many bronze and iron knives were also found in the Terrace and Clay Cut buildings (Fig. 6-9). They often occur with spindle whorls, needles, and ceramic vessels. The knives are either straight or have a slightly concave shape and an interior sharp edge, and range in length from about 8 to 12 cm. The knife bases often have pegs for hafting them to wooden, bone, or ivory handles. Many of them were found in the northern workroom units—TB 7, 8, and CC 3—which together produced at least 26 knives. While food preparation is one possibility, they may also have been used to cut the knotted threads of carpet weaves. The shape and size of these blades is appropriate to a hand-held tool used for cutting wool thread. The earliest indications for pile-carpet technology come from a special type of bronze knife found in women's graves in the Sumbar Valley, east of the Caspian Sea, dating to the late 3rd millennium BC (Barber 1991:171 n. 10; Böhmer and Thompson 1991; Khlopin 1982).

Figure 6-9 Gordion knives.

Another indication of knotted carpets at Gordion comes from Megaron 2, which is decorated with one of the earliest known pebble mosaics from antiquity (Fig. 6-1 and see Pl. 1). Multi-colored river stones were laid in a wide variety of patterns which are also found in other examples of Phrygian art (Böhmer 1973). These various patterns seem to be imitating Phrygian carpet designs, providing a vivid image of the types of textiles that could have been produced at Gordion (Young 1965:13).

TEXTILES AND FOOD

Located alongside the textile production equipment were grinding platforms, hearths, ovens and bins which would have supplied food to hundreds, if not thousands, of people. Grinding platforms with saddle querns and kneading trays were present at the back of all but two main rooms (TB 1 and 2). One or two round dome ovens of brick and clay, a U-shaped construction of crude brick presumably for broiling, and a round stuccoed hearth were typical installations in the anterooms (Fig. 6-7).

In addition to baking and roasting, certain types of sipping vessels and finds of sprouted barley suggest that beer was brewed at Gordion. Side-spouted sieve jugs, known as beer mugs, had built-in tubes that would filter floating husks from the brew. Phrygians drinking beer through a long spouted jug were commented on by the Greek poet Archilocus (DeVries 1990:386; Sams 1977:108–15, 1994a:74–76). Other food remains from the Terrace Building and Clay Cut included wheat, lentils, hazelnuts, and cornelian cherries, as well as butchered cattle (DeVries 1990:386–387).

The concentration of textile tools and food processing equipment for large-scale production within the Terrace and Clay Cut buildings and inside the fortification walls indicates that large numbers of workers were actively clothing and feeding many people. The heavy-duty cloth that these weavers made, possibly knotted carpets in some cases, would likely have been supplied to large groups of Phrygians, perhaps even to the Phrygian military, who would have also depended on supplies of food and beer from the palace.

CONCLUSION

Archaeological evidence from Gordion demonstrates that cloth production and food preparation were the major activities in the Terrace and Clay Cut Buildings at the time of the Early Phrygian destruction. As Mellink (1991:629) stated, "The organization reflected in the citadel plan is one of a privileged society preparing for war and siege…The Phrygians show themselves heirs to a long tradition, to which Trojans of Troy II and VI belonged and to a branch of which, on the other side of the Aegean, the Mycenaeans were also indebted."

Although at Gordion we lack administrative records such as the documents found in Aegean palaces, Phrygian textiles most likely had a similar function to Aegean cloth, acting as both a medium of exchange and as a prestige good. The volume of spindle whorls and loom weights of a fairly standardized shape found in a central workshop quarter inside the walls of Gordion indicates cloth made on a massive scale for distribution directed by the ruling elite. The large size of the doughnut-shaped loom weight implies that the woven textiles were strong and durable.

Rodney Young, director of Gordion 1950–1974, stated in a preliminary report: "The rooms of the Terrace Building, with evidence of all kinds of different activity in each…suggest nothing but a large and disorderly apartment house in which each family carried on its manifold daily activities in its own room or suite of rooms" (1960:242–43).

When Young made this statement only three of the TB rooms had been excavated. With succeeding work, it has become clear that Young was mistaken; the evidence from the TB and CC does not reflect individual households. The repetitive finds of textile tools and food production equipment document a large workshop quarter where laborers were producing cloth and food for the Phrygian elites. With the massive data produced from the Young excavations and continuing work at the site, we have been able to broaden our understanding of Phrygian economy and culture, demonstrating that the production of goods, including textiles, was of vital importance to the Phrygian ruling elites like Gordios and his son Midas.

7

A DECORATED ROOF AT GORDION

What Tiles are Revealing about the Phrygian Past

MATT GLENDINNING

A half-century of digging at Gordion has brought to light a dazzling array of Phrygian architectural terracottas known to laymen as roof tiles. After pottery, clay tiles are probably the most abundant artifacts at the site, and their recovery and analysis has been a persistent theme in the exploration of Gordion. Brushing aside the dust of ages to reveal a tile molded in relief and still brilliantly painted can be exciting and rewarding. At once architectural and artistic, the tiles offer a glimpse of Phrygian building styles and decorative tastes and provide clues about the site's history.

Those who have dug at Gordion also know that the terracottas can be confusing. They are more likely to be found discarded in late trash dumps than they are associated with their original buildings. Fortunately, even scattered parts of a tiled roof share certain characteristics, and these allow some sense to be made of a large, disparate body of material. As an illustration of recent approaches to studying the Gordion tiles, this chapter brings together six previously unrelated types of tile that once formed a single, highly decorated roof system.

RECOVERY AND PREVIOUS RESEARCH

Clay roof tiles were probably invented in the Greek city of Corinth, where they were first used to cover the Temple of Apollo early in the 7th century BC. The new type of roof improved on traditional thatch and mud techniques by being both water- and fireproof. Tile technology soon spread to other Greek sanctuaries and had reached Sicily, south Italy and Etruria in the west, and Ionia in the east, by the last quarter of the 7th century BC. The Phrygians of central Anatolia were using tiles by the first half of the 6th century (Glendinning 1996a, 1996b; Le Roy 1967; Robinson 1984; Roebuck 1990; Wikander 1988, 1990; Winter 1993).

Archaeologists first became familiar with ancient Phrygian tiles thanks to the work of Alfred and Gustav Körte. Excavating in 1900 along the southwest edge of Gordion's Citadel Mound (see Fig. 3-1), the brothers recovered a few fragmentary tiles. Although their reconstruction of a tiled building (Fig. 7-1) is untenable—mistakenly combining tiles of different fabric, size and design—the illustration nevertheless conveys the exuberant decoration typical of Phrygian architecture (Körte and Körte 1904:153–70).

The six types of tiles presented here come from the excavations of Rodney S. Young between 1950 and 1973. His teams recovered massive numbers

Figure 7-1 Körte and Körte (1904) tiled building reconstruction.

of terracottas, especially in early seasons along the southeast edge of the mound. Young's assemblage included many well-preserved examples, and while repetitive pieces were often discarded, several thousand tiles are still preserved. The quantity of recurring types suggests that the tiles were mass-produced for use on numerous buildings within the fortified Middle Phrygian settlement (Fig. 7-2).

The date, design, and location of the tiled roofs have always been a matter of debate. In what is still a major reference work, for example, Swedish scholar Åke Åkerström (1966) dated some of the Gordion tiles to the late 6th century and others to the late 5th, while more recent work suggests a significantly earlier chronology (Isık 1991). Uncertainty surrounds the Gordion tiles due to the way they are often studied. Earlier research often treated the tiles as isolated works of art, an approach that allowed unrelated stylistic dates to be assigned to pieces that may once have belonged to the same building. A more holistic method is adopted here, in which the tiles are first identified as interrelated components of actual roofs, based on shared characteristics such as fabric, form, size, decoration, and archaeological context. Serving as a set of cross-referencing variables, these features provide the most reliable information about how the tiles were originally used.

Current research thus approaches the terracottas with new questions. Which ones worked together to form actual roofs? What do the tiles' stratigraphic contexts suggest about date of manufacture and use? How do tiles elsewhere in Anatolia compare to those at Gordion? And what do the tiles tell us about developments at Gordion?

Figure 7-2 Plan of Middle Phrygian settlement, Gordion.

The Tiles

Close inspection of the corpus of Gordion tiles (ca. 4,000 pieces) reveals a group of 613 fragments related by fabric, dimension, design, and decoration. Six tile types are involved: pans, covers, ridge tiles, raking simas, lateral simas (gutters), and pendent frieze plaques—all together the fundamental components of a tiled roof system. The group can largely be identified by eye alone: the relief work is crisp, the red, white, and black paint particularly well preserved, and the fabric characterized by numerous inclusions and a well-defined transition between the gray core and red surface oxidation. Among the clays commonly used for tiles at Gordion, the distinctiveness of this one has been confirmed by thin section analysis.

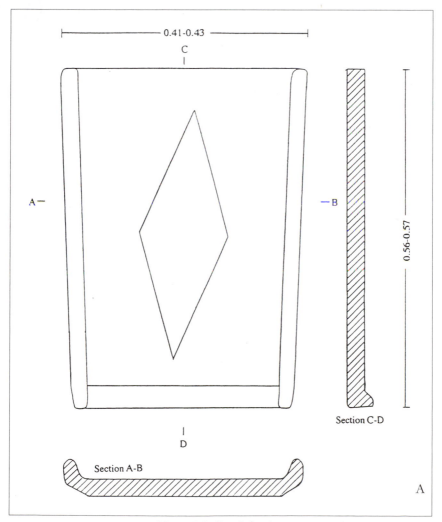

Figure 7-3a Pan 1 drawing.

Figure 7-3b Pan 1 photograph.

Pan Tile

A pan tile (Fig. 7-3a and b) functioned like a modern shingle by shedding water down the slope of a pitched roof. Raised side borders prevented lateral seepage. Overlapping of one tile to the next in a vertical row was achieved by tapering, and downward slipping was prevented by rabbet flanges on the front underside. The tile is painted white and adorned with a red diamond at its center and a red band at the front edge.

Cover Tile

Cover tiles (Fig. 7-4a and b) also functioned in vertical rows, overlapping so as to protect the seam between horizontally adjacent pans. This series matches the previous pans in size and decoration. The double pitch of the quadrifacial exterior forms an angle of 110°. At the back end is a semi-circular flange designed to fit over the front edge of the next higher pan, there to be overlapped by the next higher cover.

Ridge Tile

Ridge tiles (Fig. 7-5a and b) were designed to protect the apex of a double-pitched roof. This variety can be associated with pan 1 and cover 2 on the basis of decoration (red lozenge on a white background) and shape (quadrifacial exterior, 110° peak). The width can be estimated at ca. 50 cm and the length along the ridge at ca. 44 cm. It is not clear from preserved pieces how the tiles joined. Judging by the angle at which the rim of the side opening passes through the wall of the tile, these ridge covers sat atop a roof sloping at ca. 15°.

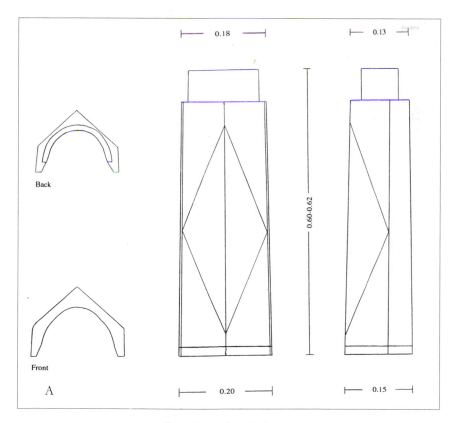

Figure 7-4a Cover 2 drawing.

Figure 7-4b Cover 2 photograph.

Raking Sima

The raking sima (Fig. 7-6a and b), essentially a pan tile with one side border heightened, prevented water from dripping over the gable edges of a double-pitched roof. This series consists of a pan like Figure 7-3 attached to a vertical plaque (the sima) 19–20 cm high, 52–53 cm long and 3 cm thick. The flat sima face is divided into four panels filled alternately with a double-S scroll and floral star in relief, painted white, red, and black. The pan element is ca. 44 cm wide and 58–60 cm long, including an overlapping flange at the front end. The pan is decorated with a red lozenge on a white background.

Lateral Sima

The lateral sima (Fig. 7-7a and b), a pan tile with a raised front gutter, shed water over the edge of a pitched roof by channeling it through a spout. In this series, a pan identical to Figure 7-3 is joined in front by a vertical sima 20–22 cm high, 44–46 cm wide, and ca. 3 cm thick. The sima is decorated with an upper register of eight "tongues" molded in relief and with a variety of painted motifs (*dipinti*) flanking the spout below, all in red, white, and black. The U-sectioned spout projects at an angle of 10° below the sima face and often bears a painted lozenge on its underside. Five corner pieces preserve parts of the attached raking sima (Fig. 7-6).

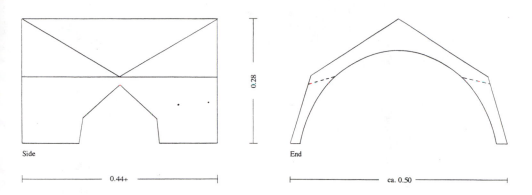

Figure 7-5a Ridge tile 3 drawing.

Pendent Frieze Plaque

The pendent frieze plaque (Fig. 7-8a and b) was not, strictly speaking, part of the roof. It consists of a rectangular or square plaque attached at its top to a horizontal shelf. The tiles were designed to protect a squared beam, e.g., string courses in the half-timbered walls commonly used by the Phrygians. The tile face bears a variety of decorations, either painted or in relief, such that a horizontal series formed a repetitive frieze. Figure 7-8 is adorned with two registers of molded relief: a row of five square lozenges tangent at their points above six pairs of double-S scrolls. Both lozenges and scrolls are alternately red and black against a white background. Iron or bronze nails secured the frieze panels to their underlying beam.

Decoration

These six types of tiles come from different archaeological contexts and did not all belong to the same building. Indeed, the survival of five corner sima pieces virtually guarantees that the 613 fragments in the group represent at least two roofs. But as *types* related by fabric, dimension, and decoration, the six tiles can be taken as representative components of a functioning roof system and reconstructed as shown in Figure 7-9.

Superficially, the roof is of the so-called Corinthian style, i.e., it employs flat pan tiles and pitched covers. But the similarity with Greek roofs goes little further. Those familiar with Lydian material will note a close resemblance to the colorful mock-up tiled structure at Sardis (Pl. 3), the product of replication experiments by Eric Hostetter (1994). The modern eye is immediately struck by the extravagance of such roofs, with their bright colors and dense ornamentation. Gordion's tiled skyline must have been dazzling.

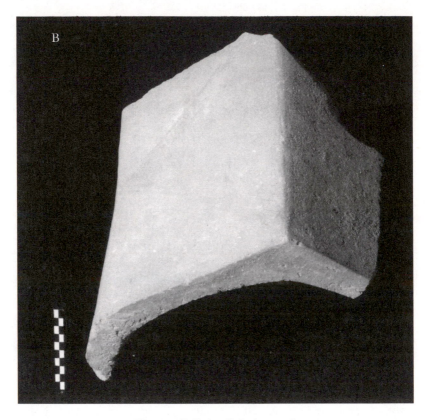

Figure 7-5b Ridge tile 3 photograph.

Rich adornment was typical of the Anatolian tile tradition. Friezes—repetitive bands of decoration—were especially common, typically serving as raking or lateral gutters or the sheath of horizontal beams. Nearly 20 varieties of frieze survive at Gordion. Some carry geometric motifs common in Phrygian art, others figural designs with a distinctive Near Eastern flavor (Glendinning 2002). Painted pans and covers formed broad swaths of decoration across the roof, e.g., lozenges, chevrons, stripes, or a checkerboard (Glendinning 1996c:165).

Phrygian tiles tend to be adorned with motifs drawn from the realm of Mediterranean minor arts, e.g., small objects of wood, metal, ivory, bone, or cloth (Winter 1993:233, 235–36). The star, double scrolls, and tongues in Figures 7-6 to 7-8, for example, are closely paralleled in Greek metalwork and textiles. A preference for such patterns may stem from the Phrygians' early history: they had migrated into Anatolia from Thrace during the Dark Age that followed the collapse of the Hittite Empire around 1200 BC. Admittedly, nothing is known about these putative wanderers in this early stage of their history, but their artistic traditions, like those of later migratory groups (e.g., Celts, Vikings),

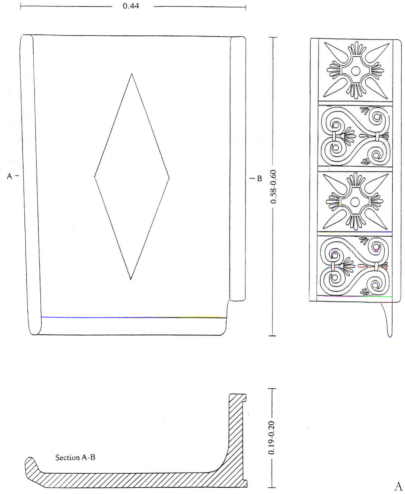

Section A-B

A

Figure 7-6a Raking sima 4 drawing.

Figure 7-6b Raking sima 4 photograph.

probably focused on minor arts that could be easily carried, stored, and traded. Designed to cover small objects, nomadic decorative vocabulary often makes use of repetitive, compartmentalized, and geometric designs, precisely the kinds of motifs the Phrygians chose for their tiles. Tiles makers in the 6th century were able to draw on a rich heritage of designs to adorn their buildings (Glendinning 1996c:210–12).

The influence of textile designs was especially strong. Lozenges repeating across the pans and covers give the impression of a tent or canopy, much like the patterned ceilings of some Etruscan tombs. In earlier days, before adopting roof tiles, the Phrygians may have used textiles in their buildings. For example, the series of rock-cut façades in the Phrygian Highlands is thought by many to mimic the look of textiles in Phrygian architecture (Barnett 1975:430; Dinsmoor 1975:66; Glendinning 1996c:212). The roof in Figure 7-9 could well reflect such older traditions of architectural embellishment using fabrics. And the terracotta frieze in particular could be a descendant of decorative, woven bands of cloth, of the sort still to be seen encircling the yurts of central Asiatic tribesman. Both Dinsmoor (1975:66) and Akurgal (1955:92) compare the Phrygian Highland façades to movable tents. The yurts of central Asiatic nomads indicate that portable tents can be highly ornamental: patterned "belts" wrapped around the outside (adding centripetal force to the wooden frame), together with decorated, overhanging fringes (as for an awning) suggest ways in which the frieze format could have derived from such a context. Instructive examples are on display in the Ethnographic Museum in Istanbul.

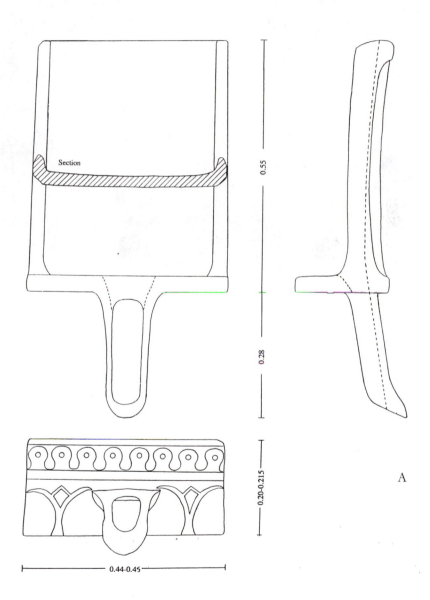

Section

0.55

0.28

0.20-0.215

0.44-0.45

A

Figure 7-7a Lateral sima 5 drawing.

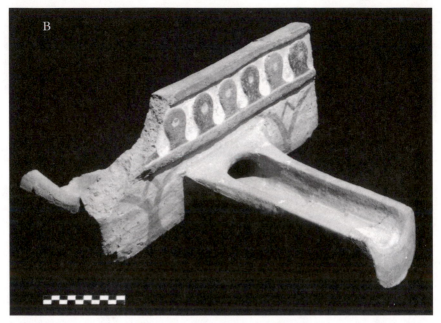

Figure 7-7b Lateral sima 5 photograph.

Design

The richness of Phrygian tile decoration may explain the art historical focus of earlier studies. But elements of design and typology are equally important, and comparisons elsewhere reveal much about Gordion's connections to other areas.

The pan and cover tiles look essentially Greek (Corinthian), but certain features are distinctly Anatolian, such as overlapping by tapering on the pans, and the specific type of rear flange on the covers. The best parallels come from the Lydian capital, Sardis, where tiles nearly identical in size, shape, and decoration have been recovered from stratigraphic contexts dated ca. 550 BC or earlier (Glendinning 1996c:47–49, 61–66; Ratté 1994:365–370). Sardis also has several varieties of raking sima like Figure 7-6, some dated before ca. 550 BC that are remarkably close in dimensions and decoration to Gordion 4. Other examples come from Miletus and an unknown site thought to be located in southwest Anatolia. Lateral simas like Figure 7-7 have been found at Sardis, Düver, and Miletus, while pendent frieze plaques shaped like Figure 7-8, but with different decoration, are known at two other inland sites, Düver and Pazarlı (Glendinning 1996c).

The Gordion roof, or variations on it, thus seems to have been a popular model in Anatolia, since components have been recovered at a number of sites. Secure contexts indicate that the design was in use by the first half of the 6th century BC at Sardis. The similar roof at Gordion is probably contemporary.

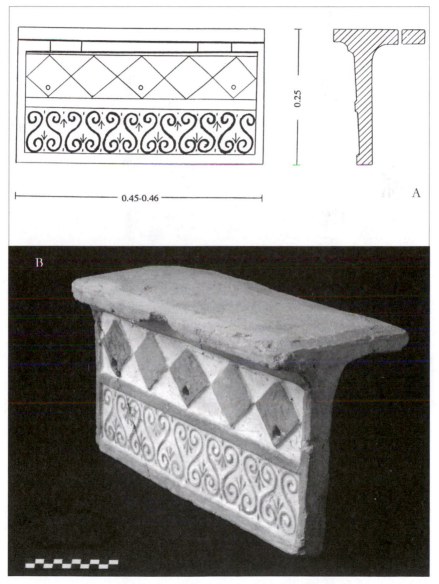

Figure 7-8 Pendent frieze 6 drawing (a) and photograph (b).

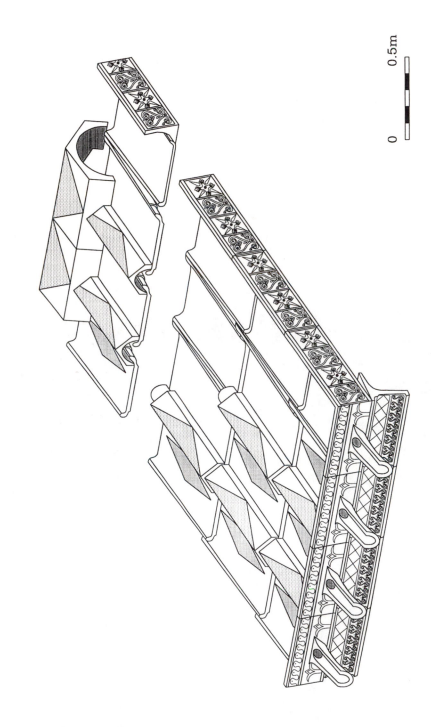

Figure 7-9 Decorated tile roof drawing, Gordion.

0   0.5m

Although parts of the roof reflect Greek inspiration, overall the system varies considerably from Greek models and thus offers a glimpse of Phrygian craftsmen working within their Anatolian setting. Gordion tile makers were clearly engaged with contemporary Anatolian trends, and the tiles' efficient design and crisp workmanship testify to a competent Phrygian tradition. Corroborating the evidence of ceramics, small finds, and recent excavation, therefore, this tiled roof contributes to a picture of late Middle Phrygian Gordion as a prosperous, cosmopolitan, and well-connected regional center (DeVries 1988; Sams 1979a, 1979b; Voigt et al. 1997).

The roof points to a particularly close association with the Lydians. This is partly to be expected: terracottas at Sardis and Gordion are among the best preserved—thus most readily comparable—in Anatolia. However, the similarities run deeper than mere typology. Parallels of structural design are also abundant: rear lugs and a drip molding on the pans, the geometry of the cover tiles and their odd rear flange, and an uncanny similarity of the stars and scrolls on the raking sima. Such parallels are pervasive and involve not only decoration but also the way the tiles were designed, thus revealing more than casual affinities between the two sites.

It is notable that tile technology seems to have arrived at Gordion in the late 7th or early 6th century BC, exactly when significant quantities of Greek and Lydian pottery also began to reach the site. Since the Gordion terracottas exhibit no change over time in respect to design, style, size, or decoration, it can be assumed that tiling was imported to the site as an already developed tradition. In the absence of evidence pointing elsewhere, it seems logical to conclude that the Gordion tile tradition was formulated under Lydian influence (DeVries 1997:20–21; Glendinning 1996c:1–2, 14, 180–217; Sams 1979a:8–9).

This issue bears directly on problems at the heart of recent Gordion investigations: the history of the Middle Phrygian citadel and the nature of Lydian influence at Gordion. The conventional view has long held that after a widespread destruction around 700 BC, Gordion was garrisoned by Lydian soldiers and the main citadel rebuilt under Lydian sponsorship in the first half of the 6th century. The tiles would fit that scenario perfectly, but it is no longer tenable. Recent work by Mary M. Voigt, Keith DeVries and G. Kenneth Sams suggests a 9th century BC date for the massive destruction, with the Middle Phrygian rebuilding coming in the 8th (see Chapters 2–4, this volume; DeVries et al. 2003). The Middle Phrygian citadel had stood for more than a century before tiled roofs were introduced to the site.

Nevertheless, the roof reassembled here still enables us to speak with assurance of Lydian influence at Gordion. Lydian-trained tile makers, equipped with expert technological know-how, probably worked or taught at the site in the early 6th century. They would have brought with them the essential methods of manufacture, including procedural details of mold making, fashioning, painting, and firing, and they shared decorative ideas. Historical and archaeological considerations suggest that the Lydians expanded into central Anatolia in the early 6th century BC. The tiles may help substantiate the commonly held theory that Lydians occupied Gordion at that time.

CONTEXTS

Finally, a brief word about contexts. Recognizing these six tiles as parts of a single roof design allows us to identify patterns in the archaeological record. Although the stratigraphy at Gordion is notoriously complex, making older excavation notes difficult to follow, the picture is fairly clear for these tiles. The field notes suggest that many of the 613 known fragments were recovered from the floors of three distinct structures.

The first, Building A, was an enormous Middle Phrygian structure that was renovated in the 5th century BC; tiles were found resting on its new floor (Young 1951:6–10, fig. 1, 1953:9, 14–17, 1955:1–2). Sherds found below the floor included Gordion P 55, identified by Keith DeVries as part of a complex-form rhyton from the workshop of the Sotades Painter, ca. 470–460 BC. Many other terracottas were found scattered across the patterned pebble floors of the so-called Mosaic Building (see Mosaic Trench in Fig. 3-4), which replaced the two southwest units of Building A when the latter was renovated. The date is debated. Mellink (1988:228–29) placed the Mosaic Building in the 6th century, but reports that the excavator dated it ca. 475–450 BC. A date contemporary with the renovation of Building A is suggested since the floors of both structures lie at precisely the same level, over the same reddish, gravely fill. The third structure was the Painted House, a small, cellar-like room nestled between two larger neighbors in an area of the citadel called the Inner Gate Court (see Fig. 3-4). Decorated with figural paintings in Greek style, the building has been dated variously between the late-6th and mid-5th century BC (DeVries 1990:392; Glendinning 1996c:27; Mellink 1980:93; Young 1955:9).

It was mainly the Mosaic Building context that led Young and thus Åkerström to date many of the Gordion tiles to the 5th century BC. But the picture can now be clarified: these six specific tiles were probably used not only there but also on two other structures built or modified in the 5th century, Building A and the Painted House. The significance of this discovery is unclear, but it might signal some connection among these buildings (whose functions are unknown), especially the Mosaic Building and the Painted House. Both were unusual (for Gordion) in architectural plan, and both were adorned with wall mosaics of clay pegs. One wonders if the identical roofs helped express some linked purpose for the buildings.

While the tiles of Figures 7-3 to 7-8 may well have been used as late as the 5th century, several factors suggest they were manufactured in the 6th century BC. First, firm parallels at Sardis consistently fall within the first half of the 6th century. Second, in several places around Building A examples of tiles 1-6 were found *below* the 5th century floor (i.e., in earlier levels). And third, the floors of all three buildings were found strewn with other tile types, some belonging to a different roof design known to have been used at Gordion in the first half of the 6th century (Glendinning 1996a). Why tiles from two roof designs were found mixed together remains a mystery, but similarities in size, design, and workmanship suggest that they are all contemporary.

Summary

The preceding discussion highlights a classic hazard in archaeology, the recycling of sturdy, long-lived, and reusable artifacts. Rodney Young had correctly identified the tiles' *depositional* contexts, and thus Åkerström and others cannot be faulted for following Young's lead in assigning the tiles to the 5th century. Indeed, continuing excavation at Gordion will no doubt uncover more tiles like Figures 7-3 to 7-8, which in all likelihood will be found stranded on 5th century floors or scattered in 4th–3rd century trash layers.

But recent work, applying new methodologies, is changing our understanding of the Gordion terracottas. As most experts now recognize, a study of terracottas should begin with a study of roofs, not of individual pieces or motifs. Identifying all the known components of a roof—through factors such as fabric, shape, decoration, and context—is a crucial first step that should precede any attempt at interpretation.

At Gordion, reassembling the tiles into a coherent roof enhances their potential usefulness for archaeologists. Figure 7-9 and Plate 10, for example, allow discussion not merely of isolated motifs but of an entire decorative program, in which the influence of the minor arts, especially textiles, is evident. Mundane details of shape and design reveal close connections to the Lydian capital, Sardis, thus helping to date the Gordion tiles and to clarify the history of the site. And the archaeological contexts of all six tile types give us some idea of where the roof was used, inviting speculation about the relationship between various buildings or parts of the citadel. Architectural terracottas thus can tell us much about the past, and they remain an important component of Phrygian studies as work at Gordion continues.

Catalogue

1. Pan Tile. Figures 7-3a and b. Gordion Inv. A 110. Building A, Trench J, Layer 6. Fieldbook 22:95; Åkerström 1966:147, Plate 81:1. Gordion, museum depot. L. 0.570, back W. 0.410, front preserved W. 0.320, H. side borders 0.085, L. flange 0.075, Th. 0.025-0.030. 82 extant fragments.

2. Cover Tile. Figures 7-4a and b. Gordion Inv. A 141a. Building A, Trench J, Layer 6. Fieldbook 22:95; Åkerström 1966:147. Gordion, museum depot. L. 0.615, L. cover proper 0.550, back W. 0.180, front W. 0.200, back H. 0.130, front H. 0.150, Th. 0.025-0.040. 48 extant fragments.

3. Ridge Cover Tile. Figures 7-5a and b. Gordion Inv. A 86. Building A, Trench F, Layer 4. Fieldbook 12:71. Gordion, museum depot. Est. L. (along ridge) 0.44, est. Diam. 0.50, preserved H 0.250, Th. 0.030-0.060. 12 extant fragments.

4. Raking Sima. Figures 7-6a and b. Gordion Inv. A 205. Trench TBT-6b, south end, level 5. Fieldbook 93:151; Åkerström 1966:140-141, 147-148, Plates 69:3-6, 83:2-3. Gordion, museum depot. Preserved L 0.416, preserved W 0.180, W. flange 0.070, H. 0.190, Th. 0.027. 120 extant fragments.

5. Lateral Sima. Figures 7-7a and b. Gordion Inv. A 164. Trench NCT-A9, Layer 5. Fieldbook 53:138; Åkerström 1966:147-148, Plates 83:1, 83:4. Ankara, Museum of Anatolian Civilizations. Preserved L 0.470, L. spout 0.280, W. 0.457, H. sima 0.200, H. pan edge 0.075, Th. 0.025. 123 extant fragments.

6. Pendent Frieze Tile. Figures 7-8a and b. Gordion Inv. A 227. Trench TB-E2S2, Level 3. Fieldbook 100:198; Åkerström 1966:142, 148, Figure 41:7, Plates 72:4, 85:1-2. Gordion, Museum. W. 0.457, H. 0.249, Th. 0.030, D. shelf 0.185. 233 extant fragments.

8

GLASS VESSELS FROM GORDION

Trade and Influence Along the Royal Road

JANET DUNCAN JONES

The glass vessels recovered from fifty years of archaeological investigation at Gordion make up one of the most extensive bodies of early luxury glassware from datable contexts. This remarkable body of material, long under-appreciated outside the world of ancient glass studies, illuminates significant aspects of the commercial, technological, and cultural interchange between East and West Asia in the 1st millennium BC. Several of these finds hint forcefully at a tradition of glass production in Asia Minor, possibly Phrygia itself, from as early as the 8th century BC.

The Gordion corpus currently comprises over 500 diagnostic fragments of glass ranging in date from as early as the mid-8th century BC to early Roman imperial times. All the major glass forming technologies known from the ancient world are represented: molding, core-forming, and blowing. Molding and core forming were the earliest glass vessel-forming technologies and the most important until the advent of glass blowing in the mid-1st century BC. These early, labor-intensive techniques produced luxury trade wares, primarily unguent bottles and table wares, in limited quantities, for elite patrons.

Ancient Gordion in this period lay in the contact zone between the civilizations of the Near East and the Mediterranean. This chapter focuses on the ways in which finds at Gordion from two specific early glass-forming industries—the manufacture of vessels on a core and the production of colorless molded vessels—shed light both on key periods in the evolution of glass production in the ancient world and on the economic and cultural relationship of Gordion to other Near Eastern states and to the Greek world in the 1st millennium BC. A full study of the glass vessel finds from Gordion is currently in preparation.

EARLY CORE-FORMED VESSELS

Gordion has yielded over 170 fragments from glass vessels made by the core process. Core-forming, the earliest glass technology devised exclusively for the production of glass vessels, first appeared around 1500 BC in northern Mesopotamia. In this method, a core composed of a combination of clay, mud, sand, and an organic binder was affixed to the end of a metal rod and shaped into the form of the inside of the body of the vessel. Molten glass was either wound or dipped onto the core and was smoothed evenly over it by repeated reheating and rolling on a stone slab in a process called marvering. Decoration was

Figure 8-1 Wide-bodied core-formed alabastron. Collection of the Corning Museum of Glass, acc. no. 59.1.65. Height 16.8 cm. Photo permission of museum.

added by trailing threads of contrasting colors around the body, marvering them, and combing them into a pattern, most commonly zigzag, festoon, or feather patterns. Rims, handles, and bases were applied separately after reheating. The rod was removed and the vessel cooled slowly (annealed) to prevent stress cracking. Finally, the core was scraped out, leaving a rough interior surface.

This technique produced small, sturdy, thick-walled bottles. Ancient core-formed vessels are often well preserved or broken into large pieces that preserve a sizable portion of the vessel profile. The shape of a vessel depended upon the period in which the vessel was produced. The early (2nd millennium BC) core-forming workshops of Mesopotamia produced small pear-shaped (piriform) and globular bottles (Fig. 8-1). Mesopotamian workshops of the 1st millennium BC produced pointed and cylindrical bottles as well. In the Mediterranean, the earliest two phases of production fashioned core-formed vessels in smaller versions of Greek ceramic shapes.

Figure 8-2 Core-formed bottles, Mediterranean Class I: B. Representative bottles from the Collection of the Toledo Museum of Art. Left to right: TMA acc. nos. 1923.162, 1923.150, 1923.105, and 1923.339. Height 12.2 cm (acc. no. 1923.150). Gift of Edward Drummond Libbey. Photo courtesy of museum.

Two types of core-formed vessels from Gordion point toward key moments in the diffusion of glass-making technology from Mesopotamia into the Mediterranean world. The earliest core-formed vessel found at Gordion is a wide-bodied alabastron with yellow festoon thread decoration on a dark blue body (Pl. 4). The vessel, neither entirely Mesopotamian nor entirely Mediterranean in type, seems to represent a transitional type. It has the wide body profile of a Mesopotamian alabastron, but the handles and rim are closer to styles that later emerged in Mediterranean glass production. The vessel appears to capture the period in the 7th century BC when the core-forming technique first appeared in the west and just before the halt of Mesopotamian production. Murray McClellan (1984:25) has suggested that the Gordion alabastron might be a missing link—a very early transitional product of an eastern Mediterranean core-forming workshop.

The vitality of the early stages of glass production in the Greek world is exemplified at Gordion by over 100 fragments of high-quality core-formed bottles. These belong to the first major group of glass vessels produced in workshops in the eastern Mediterranean from the late 6th to the late 5th centuries BC (Grose 1989:110–13) (Fig. 8-2). As noted above, vessels of this industry were imitations in miniature of Greek ceramic forms, primarily the amphoriskos, alabastron, aryballos, and oinochoe. The ground color of the vessels is primarily opaque dark blue or opaque white with opaque white, yellow, or turquoise blue thread decoration.

These core-formed glass vessels were created as containers for perfumed oils. At Gordion they served a function similar to the Attic lekythos, the premier retail perfumed oil container of the period, which was also actively traded between Greece and Persian-dominated Asia Minor in this period (DeVries 1977:545).

Research on Attic pottery from Gordion and elsewhere within the Persian Empire has shown that Attic ceramic workshops of the 6th to 5th centuries BC catered actively to Persian customers and that one-third of all the Attic pottery recovered consisted of lekythos fragments (DeVries 1977:544). Because the demand for perfume and for elegant perfume containers was more characteristic of eastern than western cultures of the time, the presence of quantities of Attic lekythoi and Greek core-formed glass vessels at Gordion suggests that the strong local demand was fueled by the perfume-loving Persians who controlled Asia Minor at the time and by their local imitators (DeVries 1977:545).

DeVries, who studies the Attic pottery at Gordion, suggests that low prices indicate that lekythoi were shipped wholesale to perfumers who filled them in local shops as part of the retail perfume trade (DeVries 1977:545; Chapter 4 this volume). Similarly, glass bottles may have been brought in quantity from a production center such as Rhodes, which was well known in this period both for its perfume industry and its production of core-formed bottles of the same type found at Gordion. Production of this early group of Mediterranean core-formed vessels ceased by the end of the 5th century BC (Grose 1989:115).

EARLY MOLDED GLASS AT GORDION

The technique of making glass vessels by molding in closed multi-part molds arose over half a millennium after core-forming techniques. In this process, glass, either molten or cold, was introduced into a mold that was heated until molten glass filled the cavity of the mold. Rim, handles, and foot were added separately to the hot vessel. The vessel was then annealed. The cooled body of the vessel was finished by cold-working processes such as drilling, cutting, and polishing (Grose 1989:45). The earliest molded glass vessels found in quantity are drinking cups and bowls of the late 8th through 7th centuries BC from northern Mesopotamian sites such as Nimrud, Khorsabad, and Kuyuncik (Grose 1989:75). Production of these vessels in the Near East all but ceased in the period after the fall of Assyria in the late 7th century but reemerged in the 4th century in what appears to be a conscious revival of earlier forms and techniques (Ignatiadou 2004:183).

The earliest and most notable glass find from Gordion, a nearly complete colorless mesomphalic phiale found in Tumulus P, dates from the earliest period of production of molded glass vessels (Fig. 8-3a and b). The bowl was found in a fragmentary state inside a bronze bowl. It was most likely shattered when bronze bowls stacked on tables in the southwestern corner of the tomb fell to the floor under collapsing roof beams (Young 1981:8).

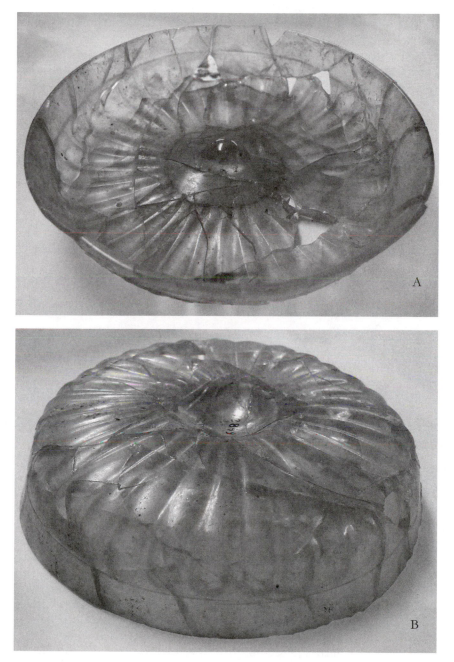

Figure 8-3 Interior (a) and exterior (b) views of molded colorless mesomphalic phiale from
Tumulus P. Diameter 15.4 cm. Gordion inv. no. 4000 G206.

The phiale, more than 1 cm thick in some places, is decorated with a petal motif on both the exterior and the interior surfaces. On the exterior, 32 molded convex petals of varying widths radiate from a central shallow concave omphalos. This design is mirrored on the interior by 32 concave petals radiating from a large shallow central disk upon which a tall solid omphalos knob has been molded. Because the circumference of the interior disk is greater than that of the exterior omphalos, the interior petals begin farther out from the center of the vessel than the exterior petals. The interior petals may have been first molded, then deepened and further defined with a rotary grinding tool (von Saldern 1959:26).

The overall effect of the bowl is markedly light and graceful. Special attention appears to have been paid to the optical effects of the interaction between interior and exterior decoration by giving strong definition to transitional zones. For example, a line is incised around the exterior of the cup at the level of the tips of the interior petals, and shallow grooves have been cut to define the lower ends of the interior petals. Particularly striking is the way in which the rim has been fashioned so that the interior of the bowl gives the sense of an open, flaring profile, while the exterior profile appears straight-sided and constrained.

The phiale is one of the earliest colorless molded vessels known. It derives from a period in glass production when, in addition to opaque or translucent colored glass in imitation of semiprecious stones, transparent colorless glass in imitation of rock crystal was first produced (von Saldern 1970:210). The fact that it is decorated on both the interior and exterior, unlike later glass bowls with molded decoration, points toward the influence of prototypes in metal (Barag 1985:67). The bowl has traditionally been attributed to a glass workshop in northern Mesopotamia, possibly around Nimrud, where there is a concentration of finds of molded vessels dated to the late 8th and 7th centuries BC. These vessels are mostly hemispherical bowls in green glass, some with cut or ground decoration (von Saldern 1970:211).

The Gordion vessel, however, stands apart from the majority of these finds with respect to the high quality of its colorless fabric, its mesomphalic shape, its decoration, and the consummate skill with which it was fashioned. The only close parallel in glass from Mesopotamia is a fragment of a colorless mesomphalos bowl with molded petal decoration on both exterior and interior in the British Museum attributed generally to "British Museum excavations in Mesopotamia" and dated to the late 8th to 7th centuries BC (Barag 1985:66–67, no. 42). There is as yet no certain evidence that either vessel was produced in Mesopotamia.

Given the lack of good parallels in glass from Mesopotamia, it is tempting to consider whether the bowl could have been a more local product. Gordion itself had developed a vigorous metalworking tradition by this period, influenced to varying degrees by Neo-Hittite and Assyrian workshops. Highly skilled local artisans produced distinctive mesomphalos bowls in bronze with petal or ribbed decoration as well as other vessels and objects related to drinking, but these large bowls have a different type of petal motif and a different overall sense of proportion from the glass bowl.

Figure 8-4 Molded colorless bowl with Phrygian-style petal decoration.
Gordion inv. no. 7177 G283. Max. dim. 7.8 cm.

Figure 8-5 Bronze omphalos bowl with Phrygian style petal decoration from Tumulus MM.
Gordion, inv. no. B881 / MM73. Photo courtesy of the museum. Diameter 17.8 cm.

Figure 8-6 Molded colorless phiale with petal decoration. Collection of the Toledo Museum of Art. acc. 79.74. Photo courtesy of the museum. D. 17.3 cm

Particularly exciting in this regard is the recent identification of a second molded bowl from an early, possibly mid-8th century BC, context that addresses more directly the question of glass production in Anatolia in this period (Fig. 8-4). Six adjoining lower body fragments of thick colorless glass survive from a large shallow vessel. Like the bowl from Tumulus P, this vessel is decorated with a molded petal motif on both the interior and the exterior surfaces. In this instance, however, the design is a distinctly Phrygian version of the petal motif well known from a group of bronze bowls found in Tumulus MM (Young 1981:131–41)(Fig. 8-5). On the interior surface of the bowl are portions of five concave petals with rounded bases and portions of three background petals. The background petals taper to a point where they are overlapped by the rounded foreground petals. The same petals appear in convex form on the exterior of the vessel.

This second early molded glass bowl from Gordion, in a distinctively Phrygian style, brings the possibility of early molded glass production in Phrygia tantalizingly closer. Perhaps it is more than coincidence that this bowl provides only the second-known parallel to the technique of the *phiale* from Tumulus P. Further work, including much overdue chemical analysis of these fragments, should provide interesting revelations about the role of Phrygia in the earliest period of molded glass production.

MOLDED VESSELS IN THE "ACHAEMENID STYLE"

Gordion came under Persian control from the mid-6th century until 333 BC. The lasting cultural influence of Achaemenid Persian control in Asia Minor is suggested at Gordion by 15 fragments of high-quality molded glass vessels in the so-called Achaemenid style from 4th and 3rd century BC contexts. These fragments come primarily from the types of drinking vessels preferred by

Figure 8-7 Molded colorless kalyx with petal decoration. Diameter 10.6 cm. Collection of the Archaeological Museum of Rhodes, inv. no. G733. Courtesy of 22nd Archaeological Ephorate of Greece (Dodecanese, Rhodes).

the Persians – the wide shallow phiale (Fig. 8-6) and the deep kalyx (Fig. 8-7) decorated with combinations of rays, petals, almonds, or grooves (Grose 1989:80–81).

The phiale was not a new form in Asia Minor. As discussed above, there had been active local production of a distinctively Phrygian version of the Near Eastern phiale, primarily in metal but also in pottery at Gordion and other sites of Phrygian Anatolia from at least the 8th century BC (Young 1981:234). A new wave of these vessels in metal, probably in ceramic and, perhaps, in molded glass, likely accompanied Persian governors and bureaucrats on their way into Persian-controlled western Asia Minor from the 6th century BC on. That the elegance and fine workmanship of these vessels caught the attention of Lydians and Greeks among others is suggested by the number of regional workshops that began to provide local elites with their own versions of these wares in metal, ceramics, and glass. At Sardis, the terminus of the Persian Royal Road, there was a thriving industry in so-called Achaemenid-style ceramic bowls (Dusinberre 1999:73). Rhodes clearly was the site of a workshop producing phialai and kalykes in glass from the early 4th to the early 3rd centuries BC (Triantafyllides 2000b:30). A second important center of production was located in Macedonia (Ignatiadou 1997:114).

The Gordion examples seem to fall into two categories. First, a group of high quality vessels represented by nine fragments at Gordion from drinking bowls of elegant craftsmanship. This fabric is colorless with a slightly greenish tint and very few bubbles or impurities and has a strong resistance to weathering.

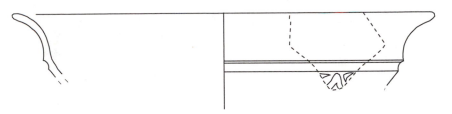

a. Gordion inv. YH 52596

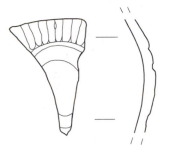

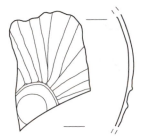

b. Gordion inv. 504 G33   c. Gordion inv. 12866 G400

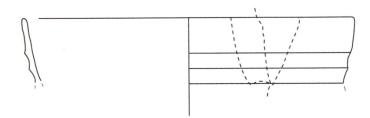

d. Gordion inv. YH 53340

Figure 8-8 Fragmentary molded colorless bowls from Gordion, scale 1:1; dimensions:
a. diameter 18.0 cm, b. max. dimensions 4.82 cm × 3.29 cm,
c. max dimensions 5.10 cm × 4.10 cm, d. diameter 14.0 cm.

Some of the fragments of this group are decorated with petals or almonds. The most impressive example is a fragment from the Voigt excavations from a large diameter phiale (Fig. 8-8a). The fragment, decorated with petals, comes from a bowl very close in dimension, decoration, and quality to intact bowls of uncertain provenance now in the Toledo Museum of Art (cf. Fig. 8-6) and in the Corning Museum of Glass. An interesting fragment in this group from a straight-walled vessel of smaller diameter has three distinctive, wide, horizontal grooves on the

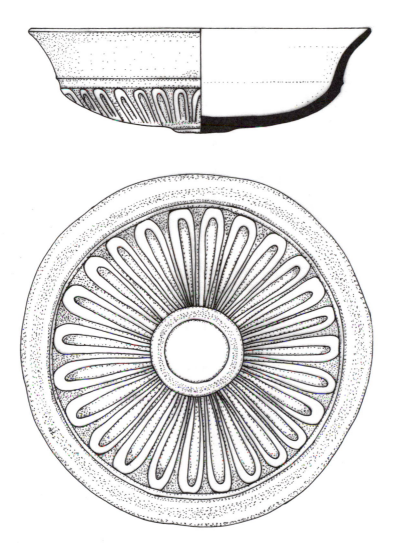

*Figure 8-9 Molded colorless phiale with petal decoration. Diameter 13.0 cm. Collection of the
Archaeological Museum of Rhodes, inv. no. Y870. Drawing by Vicky Skaraki.
Courtesy of 22nd Archaeological Ephorate of Greece (Dodecanese, Rhodes).*

upper body (Fig. 8-8d). Such horizontal fluting is common on Achaemenid-style
metalwares (Miller 1993:116). The best parallel for the Gordion grooved fragment
appears to come from excavations at the Mausolleion at Halicarnassos (Ignatiadou
2004:191–92). None of the Gordion fragments come from contexts earlier than
the second half of the 4th century BC.

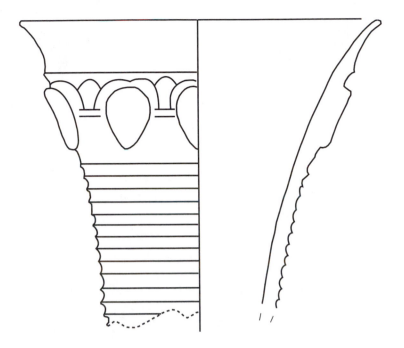

Gordion Inv. 1595 G81

Figure 8-10 Molded colorless beaker with decoration of almond bosses and horizontal fluting. Diameter 9.4 cm. Scale 1:1. Gordion inv. no. 1595 G81.

High-quality colorless vessels, such as those from which these fragments come, were long assumed to have been products of Persian workshops. However, there is no clear evidence for production of colorless glass vessels in the Persian heartland and, except for a cache of vessels at Persepolis, most examples come from Asia Minor and the eastern Mediterranean region. They are more likely to have been products of Persian-influenced workshops in the western satrapies or particularly skilled regional traditions working in the long-lived Achaemenid style (Grose 1989:81). Triantafyllides asserts that such vessels were likely made in several regional centers in the eastern Mediterranean marked by rich metal-working traditions; he cites Gordion along with Ephesus as possible centers in Asia Minor (Triantafyllides 2000a:201). The relative concentration at Gordion of fragments from high-quality molded colorless vessels supports the notion that Phrygia played an important role in this second period of molded glass production.

A second group of 4th century BC molded vessel fragments from Gordion has clear affinities in style and fabric with vessels in the Achaemenid style produced in workshops on Rhodes. These are made of a lesser quality glass that is more vulnerable to weathering. Two fragments (Fig. 8-8b and c) from the bases of

Figure 8-11 Molded colorless beaker with decoration of almond bosses and horizontal fluting from Derveni. Diameter 11.1 cm. Collection of the Archaeological Museum of Thessaloniki, inv. no. B45. Courtesy of museum.

petal-type bowls with raised disks encircled by grooves are similar in execution to Rhodian-made phialai (Fig. 8-9). The second fragment (Fig. 8-8c) may come from a vessel decorated with a white lotus design such as that seen on a bowl from Nippur from a tomb dated to the Achaemenid period (Barag 1968:17–18, figs. 1–3) or on a Hellenistic bowl in the British Museum thought to be from Canosa (von Saldern 1959:39, figs. 22 and 23).

Gordion, then, may have been both producer and importer of molded colorless glass vessels in this period. Scientific analysis of fragments from both categories of vessel should reveal more on this subject.

THE MACEDONIAN CONNECTION

The best known of the Gordion molded vessels in the Achaemenid style is a partially preserved beaker with a flaring rim and tapering body (Fig. 8-10). Almond-shaped bosses decorate the upper body; there are thirteen preserved horizontal grooves on the lower body down to the break. This remarkable vessel,

Figure 8-12 Core-formed amphoriskos, Mediterranean Class II: G. Height 11.9 cm.
Collection of the Toledo Museum, acc. no. 1923.96. Courtesy of museum.

made of three joining fragments, is related to a better-preserved vessel from Grave
B at Derveni (Fig. 8-11) and to a silver cup of similar shape in the Ashmolean
Museum said to be "found in Erzerum" (Vickers 2000:261).

This vessel and its Macedonian sibling draw attention to a third period of
exchange and influence when eastern style vessels of western manufacture like the
beaker above found their way eastward to Gordion. In this case, the vessels came
possibly as the result of the migration of a group of Celts known as the Galatians,
who migrated southeast into Anatolia from Macedonia in the 3rd century BC. The
Galatians had invaded Macedonia and settled there for a generation in the early 3rd
century before migrating into Asia Minor, arriving at Gordion sometime just after
the middle of the 3rd century BC (DeVries 1990:402).

There is also evidence that the Galatians transported with them examples
of a particular class of core-formed glass vessel produced in this period that
consisted of small, dark blue unguentaria with a spool bases or amphoriskoi with

Figure 8-13 Core-formed amphoriskos, Mediterranean Class II: G.
Gordion inv. SF88-133a-e.

base knobs (Jones 1995:28–29). Concentrations of finds of core-formed vessels of this group point to centers of manufacture in Italy and Macedonia (McClellan 1984:79, 322–25). Bottles of this period had been considered rare in western Asia until a cluster of at least six identifiable bottles of this type similar to one from the Toledo Museum of Art were identified in late 3rd to early 2nd century BC contexts at Gordion (Jones 1995:27) (Fig. 8-12). One amphoriskos was recovered, together with coins of Macedonian and Thracian issue and other luxury items from the floor of a house burned during the sack of Gordion by the Romans in 189 BC (Jones 1995:32) (Fig. 8-13). Thus, glass vessels of Macedonian manufacture, like the Gordion molded beaker and the core-formed amphoriskos, along with the coins and other luxury items, may have been transported to Gordion by Celts in the mid to late 3rd century BC.

CONCLUSION

Recent work on the core-formed and molded glass vessel fragments from Gordion has focused on the important insights this material provides into key moments in the exchange of glass luxury items, vessel styles, and manufacturing techniques between the Near East and the Mediterranean world:

•A fragmentary wide-bodied core-formed alabastron appears to serve as an early indicator of the movement of a new glass-forming technology westward in the 7th century BC. A century later, a sizeable assortment of fragments from core-formed vessels made in imitation of Greek ceramic shapes reveals an eastern appetite for the vessels made with the new technology in the west.

•Two mid-8th century BC molded colorless bowls seem poised to reshape our conception of how and where the early production of molded glass vessels evolved. Four hundred years later, fragments of molded colorless bowls of similar profile reflect both an intense renewed interest in eastern styles and practices and the development of local industries, perhaps one in Phrygia, to answer a growing regional demand for eastern-styled wares.

One might imagine a 4th century BC scenario in which impeccably groomed Persian governors of western satrapies sported perfumed oils from small, colorful, glass bottles of Rhodian manufacture while local elites set their tables and drank their wines from transparent Persian-styled petal bowls of local manufacture. Luxury glasswares based on technologies and styles from the east, manufactured at western centers such as Rhodes or Macedonia or Gordion, formed part of a rich consumer discourse that traveled back and forth along the major east-west highways of Asia Minor. Traces of this multi-tiered and enduring exchange survive in the material record from Gordion.

9

A Preliminary Report on the Human Skeletal Material from Gordion's Lower Town Area

Page Selinsky

The site of Gordion is perhaps best known for the Tumulus MM burial excavated in 1957 and initially believed to be that of the legendary King Midas (but recently redated, see Manning et al. 2001). Other tumuli and cemeteries have yielded a skeletal collection that stretches from the 17th century BC to at least the 4th century AD. Little is known about the occupants of the excavated burials because few studies of the Gordion skeletal material have been conducted (Bostancı 1962; Çiner 1971; Prag 1989). Published work has focused primarily on the burial goods and practices rather than the skeletal remains (Anderson 1980; Goldman 2000; Kohler 1995; Mellink 1956; Young 1981).

This chapter presents preliminary results from an anthropological study of the human skeletal remains excavated between 1993 and 1995 from the Lower Town area of the site (see Fig. 3-1) (for a more detailed description of the excavation see Voigt et al. 1997). The skeletal material in the Lower Town cemetery sheds light on lifestyle, health, and mortuary practices in Later Hellenistic and early Roman periods. Most intriguingly, evidence of human sacrifice may also confirm historical records documenting the invasion of central Anatolia by a Celtic people.

DESCRIPTION OF SAMPLE

Fifty individuals were represented in the skeletal sample from the Lower Town. Their distribution in time periods and age groups is shown in Table 9-1. The skeletal data combined with the archaeological evidence suggests that the function of the Lower Town area changed significantly between the Later Hellenistic and Roman phases (Voigt et al. 1997). For example, among the 20 individuals recovered from the Later Hellenistic phase (late 3rd to 2nd centuries BC), only one was from a formal interment. The other 19 were not buried but either placed in a deep pit or found on a surface sometimes mixed with large amounts of animal bones (Dandoy et al. 2002; Voigt et al. 1997). In contrast, by the early part of the Roman period (c. 1st to 2nd centuries AD), the Lower Town area was being used as a formal burial ground, with 24 inhumation and two cremation burials.

The Later Hellenistic skeletons are from a critical time of transition in the site's history (Voigt et al. 1997), when a Celtic people known as the Galatians is reported to have overrun Gordion (Livy 38.12–27). Until recently, there was some dispute about the identification of a specifically Galatian archaeological presence

Table 9-1 Lower Town Sample Distribution

Time Period	No. of Individuals	Age Category[1]	No. of Individuals
Later Hellenistic	20	Infants (0–3 years)	9
Roman	26	Children (3–12 years)	8
Medieval-Modern[2]	1	Subadults (12–20 years)	7
Undated[3]	3	Young Adults (20–35 years)	12
		Middle Adults (35–50 years)	9
		Older Adults (50+ years)	5

[1] These commonly used age categories (Buikstra and Ubelaker 1994; White 2000) are based on osteological criteria. In the case of a skeletal age estimate straddling two categories, the individual has been assigned to the most appropriate age group based on skeletal development.

[2] Only limited skeletal data for this individual will be presented as a single specimen cannot be considered representative of a population and since the archaeological context makes it impossible to date more firmly than between the 12th and 20th centuries AD.

[3] These individuals will not be discussed as they cannot be assigned to a specific time period.

(DeVries 1990; cf. Winter 1988), but it appears that the Later Hellenistic individuals from the Lower Town were sacrificed according to Celtic tradition. This material represents the first such evidence for Celtic ritual practices found in Anatolia.

The Roman specimens from the Lower Town are the only burials excavated at Gordion from the early period of Roman occupation. Data collected from these burials can be integrated with previous research (Bostancı 1962; Çiner 1971) on 3rd and 4th century AD Roman postcranial elements from Gordion. However, these studies are biometric in nature and not comparable with the information presented in this preliminary report. Nonetheless, current and past research combined make the Roman skeletal remains from Gordion one of the more fully studied Turkish collections from this period.

Although much has been published on human skeletal remains of greater antiquity from Anatolia, comparatively few studies have been done on collections from classical times (e.g., Angel 1951; Özbek 1991; Sevim 1995). As interest in bioarchaeology is ever increasing, this study will become part of a larger body of osteological research characterizing the past populations of Anatolia.

Paleodemography

Paleodemography uses age and sex data derived from past populations to try and reconstruct demographic profiles which, in turn, are used to make interpretations about health and mortality. This section outlines the methods used to make sex and age estimations on the Gordion sample and presents the comparative data. The skeletal sample from the Lower Town is small and represents only a portion of the population of living individuals from which it came. However, this is not unusual: when dealing with archaeological populations, multiple variables impact the representativeness of skeletal samples, and some degree of sample bias is unavoidable (see Waldron 1994; Wood et al. 1992). Nevertheless, these variables must be taken into consideration when doing paleodemographic reconstructions.

Age Estimation

Age can be estimated for all individuals, both mature and immature. In the case of immature individuals, estimations are often very accurate because they are based on developmental changes (e.g., tooth formation and eruption) which are under tight genetic control (Ubelaker 1989; White 2000). Age determination in adults is far more complicated as no tightly regulated developmental processes occur. Instead, adult aging techniques are based on highly variable degenerative changes in the skeleton. These include alterations in various areas of the pelvis (Brooks and Suchey 1990; Meindl and Lovejoy 1989) and cranium (Meindl and Lovejoy 1985), as well as more general measures of advancing age such as tooth wear (Brothwell 1989, Buikstra and Ubelaker 1994) and arthritic changes in the spine and other joints (Stewart 1958).

Sex Determination

The accuracy of sex determination is largely dependent on the state of preservation of a specimen and also the age of the individual. For instance, individuals under the age of 18 do not consistently show marked sex differences (Ubelaker 1989). Methods used to determine the sex of individuals included standard techniques relying on differences in skeletal morphology (Buikstra and Ubelaker 1994; Phenice 1969) and more general criteria, based on size and overall robustness of the skeleton (Bass 1995; Ubelaker 1989).

Results

Looking at the age data for the Lower Town populations (Fig. 9-1), some differences are apparent. The Roman sample has a more expected paleodemographic profile with a high percentage of infant remains (27%), whereas the percentage infants in the Later Hellenistic group is markedly lower (5%). This could be due to taphonomic processes (natural forces including decay, burial, and erosion that affect the preservation and condition of the remains of living organisms) and sample bias, as infant bones are smaller and more delicate than those of older individuals (Guy et al. 1997). Cultural practices could also have been a factor, such as different burial customs for infants. Overall, the Roman mortality profile is more like what is to be expected in an archaeological sample (Ubelaker 1989).

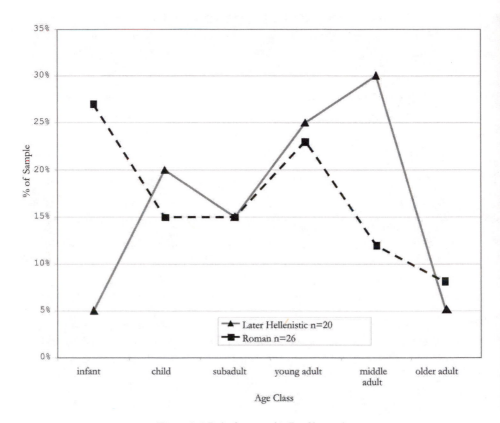

Figure 9-1 Paleodemographic Profile graph.

In the Lower Town, only 22 skeletons from known periods were mature enough and complete enough to be sexed. Of these, nine were female and thirteen were male. The distribution of females and males between the various phases at Gordion is shown in Table 9-2. It is notable that the ratio of males to females is more evenly distributed in the Later Hellenistic sample than the Roman. This pattern, along with the underrepresentation of infants and children, has been observed at presumed Celtic ritual sites in Britain (Wait 1995).

Paleopathology

Paleopathology is the study of patterns of disease and trauma in past populations. Understanding the pathologies present in archaeological populations helps in the reconstruction of diet, occupational hazards, and living conditions.

The most frequently recorded pathologies in the Lower Town skeletal sample are those common to most archaeological populations, such as arthritis, dental disease, fractures, dislocations, and porotic hyperostosis, which is indicative

Table 9-2 Distribution of Sexes by Time Period

	Female	Male
Later Hellenistic	6	7
Roman	3	5
Medieval-Modern	0	1
Total	9	13

of anemia and most often occurs during infancy and childhood (Stuart-Macadam 1985, 1992). However, some of the Later Hellenistic skeletons also bore injuries that suggested interpersonal violence supporting the archaeological interpretation of the Later Hellenistic skeletal sample as the result of Celtic ritual practices. Traumatic pathologies of this sort were not present in the Roman specimens.

Evidence of Ritual Activity

Though the skeletal evidence of trauma is not abundant, the correlation of archaeological and historical evidence for a Galatian presence at Gordion adds to the interpretation. All but one of the Later Hellenistic skeletons were found in unusual contexts. For example, the skeletons of two adult females (YH 47397, 47398) were found in a deep pit with the comingled remains of two children (YH 45050). Large grinding stones lay across the upper body of one of the women (YH 47398). This type of burial context has parallels from other Iron Age sites in Europe and has been interpreted as resulting from ritual activity (Cunliffe 1997; Wait 1995).

The remaining individuals were deposited on a surface rather than buried. The bones showed signs of having been exposed to the elements, such as cracking and bleaching. Another indication that the remains were left close to the surface was the presence of carnivore tooth marks on many of the skeletons. Most convincing was the fact that the skeletons were often found in atypical postures, intermingled with animal bones, and that most deposits consisted of the remains of more than one individual. In some cases, the skeletal elements appeared to have been carefully arranged.

The clearest example of sacrifice-related trauma was one of the female individuals from the pit burial (YH 47397), aged 30–45, who had sustained two depressed cranial fractures. This woman also had a broken rib on her right side. There were no signs of healing for any of the fractures, indicating that she died shortly after these injuries. These types of trauma are often indicators of interpersonal violence (Lovell 1997), as was almost certainly the case here.

Other evidence of violent trauma included a spiral fracture of the left thigh bone (femur) found in a mixed deposit (YH 42653) containing three individuals and a large quantity of animal bone. The femur most likely belonged to an adult

Figure 9-2 Photograph of skeletal assemblage YH 35741. Courtesy of Gordion Archives.

male aged 40–44. The pattern of fracture indicates that the bone was fresh when the break occurred, meaning shortly before or after death. To fracture the femur in such a manner would have required great force such as that from a violent direct blow or a fall from a height (Lovell 1997).

The skeletal assemblage (YH 35741) shown in Figure 9-2 perhaps best demonstrates the careful arrangement of skeletal elements both human and animal. This group consists of the articulated skull, mandible, and first two vertebrae of an adolescent of indeterminate sex aged 15 years +/- 36 months. Another individual, represented by a heavily weathered partial left pelvic bone, was a male aged 20–35. The skull of the adolescent shows signs of weathering, but not to the degree as the pelvis, which was probably exposed on the surface for a longer time. Also found with the human remains were the skull, femur, and pelvis of a dog.

The placement of a human cranium with the first two vertebrae in anatomical position is enough to suggest decapitation. In this case, the vertebrae were also damaged, furthering the belief that the head may have been cut off. Based on archaeological context as well as physical examination, it seems probable that the adolescent was decapitated, after which the head was placed on the surface upon which the adult male pelvis was already lying exposed. The human remains give the appearance of having been carefully arranged with the dog skeleton.

None of the remaining Later Hellenistic skeletons from the Lower Town showed tangible skeletal evidence of a violent death. However, the careful arrangement of skeletal elements from multiple individuals, including children, the association of the human remains with animal bones, and the presence of wood in the foramen magnum of one specimen (YH 40816) suggest something other than normal peaceful burial. Other Celtic sites in Europe with similar evidence lend support to the interpretation of ritual sacrifice (Brunaux 1988; Wait 1995).

Conclusion

These data provide insights on the past inhabitants of Gordion and demonstrate the intimate relation between biology and culture. For example, the Later Hellenistic and Roman skeletal groups had different paleodemographic profiles. The large number of young and middle-aged adults in the Later Hellenistic sample is most likely due to a bias in the sample, but a bias which was caused by the cultural practice of ritual sacrifice rather than taphonomic processes. By comparison, the Roman skeletons are the result of conventional burial practices and more likely reflect the population structure.

Although well-documented in classical literature, previous arguments for a Celtic incursion at Gordion were based on convincing but limited archaeological and linguistic evidence (DeVries 1990; Voigt 2003). The Later Hellenistic remains discussed here provide significant new support for a Galatian presence at Gordion, and the archaeological contexts demonstrate similarities to European Celtic populations. The contrast between the Later Hellenistic and Roman skeletal samples demonstrates distinct evidence of different mortuary and religious customs, suggesting a dramatic shift in the practices of the groups inhabiting Gordion between these two phases of the site's history.

10

THE LOCAL POTTER'S CRAFT AT PHRYGIAN GORDION

ROBERT C. HENRICKSON

Through ideology and behavior, society shapes the pottery assemblage and craft as surely, if not as directly, as do the potters. These artisans have a repertoire of skills which changes over time and must adapt to local materials. Vessel function influences vessel form as well as material choice and preparation. For example, diet and preferred methods of food preparation affect the characteristics of a cooking pot (Arnold 1985; Rice 1987). The specific sequences of forming and finishing methods used derive from the local craft tradition, so technological differences and changes may have cultural or socioeconomic implications.

Reconstructing and understanding the technology underlying the local potter's craft at Phrygian Gordion in the earlier 1st millennium BC provides a baseline for evaluating subsequent continuity and change. This chapter will be on the pottery of daily life, the core of the local craft, rather than the finer wares. Pottery recovered from the Early Phrygian Destruction Level (YHSS 6A, late 9th century BC) provides the focal corpus, supplemented by material from YHSS 5 (8th-6th centuries BC).

The basic unit of analysis is the "ware": a recurring combination of distinctive attributes including color, temper ("inclusions"), forming and finishing methods, firing, characteristic vessel forms, and types of decoration. This is parallel to the way Americanists define "type" (Rice 1987).

GENERAL CHARACTER OF PHRYGIAN CERAMICS

Grey wares became the predominant core of the local pottery industry during the Early Phrygian period (YHSS 6, 950–800 BC) and lasted until the end of the Hellenistic period (YHSS 3, 330–150 BC). These included not just utilitarian vessels but most of the finer ones. They constitute ca. 80% of the rim sherds and vessels in Early Phrygian (YHSS 6B-A) contexts on the Citadel Mound and in contemporary and later tombs (cf. Sams 1994a:33–35; Kohler 1995; Young 1981); in Middle Phrygian contexts grey ware frequencies rise to 85% or more (Henrickson 1993, 1994; in prep.). Under Lydian, Persian, and Hellenistic hegemony (late YHSS 5, YHSS 4–3), grey wares still made up >50% of the assemblage, particularly for the utilitarian wares, as the local craft tradition continued.

Among the grey wares, fine wares (5–10% by sherd counts, depending on context) have no visible temper, and exterior surfaces are slipped and usually well finished. Common wares (>50–80%) have medium grit inclusions (maximum diameter <0.5 mm). Forming methods depend on the size and shape of vessels, and simple surface treatments predominate (usually wet smoothed, often self-slipped). Coarse and cooking wares (10-20%) are similar to common wares but have larger grit (maximum diameter <1–2 mm) and usually less careful surface finishing (cf. Sams 1994a:31–40). Common wares are the focus of the following discussion which moves from materials to the tools and working methods of the potters—the technology of the craft—to the organization of production, and finally to how the craft began to change under outside influence.

MATERIALS AND RESOURCE EXPLOITATION

Clay and fuel are potters' major resource requirements. Various suitable clays are available in the vicinity of Gordion. Instrumental neutron activation analyses (INAA) of both ceramics and clays from around Gordion reveal similarities in chemical composition and confirm local pottery production.

The similar chemical compositions of fine, common, and coarser wares indicate that the same clays were used for all. Natural inclusions were left in the common and coarse ware pastes but removed from the finer. At any given time, two to three primary sources supplied most clay (Henrickson and Blackman 1996; in prep.). In the Early-Middle Phrygian periods (YHSS 6–5), local potters used both non-, moderately (<1%–5% calcium), and even highly calcareous (15% or higher) clays (Henrickson and Blackman 1996; in prep.).

Fuel for firing could include dung, agricultural waste, or brush (Matson 1966). Some ash could be used in preparing clays, particularly in refining clay for fine wares. The addition of dung to raw clay could improve its working properties (Rye 1981). Although materials needed for painted decoration might not be available locally, the quantities needed would have been limited and easily transported.

ARCHAEOLOGICAL EVIDENCE OF TOOLS AND WORKSHOPS

Potters' tools would have been few and simple, with many perishable or makeshift. Most can be inferred from a study of the vessels and sherds themselves and from reports on traditional potters (e.g., Güner 1988; Rye and Evans 1976). Only one YHSS 6-5 kiln (Johnston 1970) and no workshops are known.

Potters at Gordion used true potters' wheels to throw small vessels (max. dimension <30 cm); they often hand built and finished larger vessels on turntables (slow wheels or tournettes; Henrickson 1991, 1993, 1994). The wheel assembly was likely wooden; the pivot stone might look like a door socket.

Modification of the initial shape might involve "paddle and anvil"—a wooden paddle applied to the exterior against a rounded cobble on the interior face. Trimming, shaving, and cutting would require a sharp edge, but bone or even wood could suffice. Some sherds with worn edges may have been used as scrapers. Pebbles with smoothed or polished areas may be burnishers used for smoothing and compacting surfaces. Reeds, sticks, or bones could incise decoration, but formal stamped or impressed decoration required manufactured stamps (Sams 1994a). Production of some fine ware vessels involved elaborate moulding (Henrickson et al. 2002).

CERAMIC ANALYSIS

Ceramic vessels are the end product of a production process—a series of decisions and actions—each influencing or constraining all subsequent ones. Every forming and finishing method leaves characteristic traces both within the fabric and on the surfaces. Primary forming, the initial shaping, leaves traces both within the fabric and on the surfaces. Secondary forming, the modification of the basic shape, may alter some traces within the fabric and leave new ones on surfaces. Surviving marks on surfaces tend to result from finishing activities such as smoothing. Linking specific residual traces on sherds and vessels to forming and finishing methods aids in reconstructing production sequences (Rye 1981).

A wide variety of different forming and finishing sequences can yield a specific vessel shape and size (Henrickson 1991; Van der Leeuw 1993). In addition, traditional potters use various forming and finishing methods in specific sequences for different sizes of even one vessel shape (e.g., Güner 1988; Rye and Evans 1976). Therefore, the analyst should reconstruct sequences for each vessel shape and size. At Gordion, the Early-Middle Phrygian ceramic craft differs markedly from that of the Bronze Age (YHSS 10–8; Henrickson 1995b) and Early Iron Age (YHSS 7; Henrickson 1993, in prep.; Voigt and Henrickson 2000b).

Forming and Finishing

The Early Phrygian ceramic assemblage consists of fairly standardized vessel shapes and sizes (Sams 1994a; Johnston 1970). Each size of a given shape had a distinctive sequence of forming and finishing. The general relationships among size, shape, and forming method are summarized in Figure 10-1. Production of jugs/jars illustrates the variety (Figs. 10-2 to 10-5), similar to that for other such shapes as pots or bowls.

Small jars or jugs (maximum diameter and height <20–25 cm) were usually thrown on a potter's wheel (top, Fig. 10-2). Depending on the proportions, initial forming in two pieces (neck and body) might be necessary.

Medium jars (maximum diameter and height < ca. 35 cm) were hand built using coils or strips of clay butted onto a slab base on a turntable (bottom, Fig. 10-2). The lower body was left thick to resist the stresses from forming the upper body. Secondary shaping of the body required a curved tool to thin the sides, regularize the shape, and increase the diameter slightly by pushing outward from the inside. The neck and rim, added after the body had partially hardened, were finished as the vessel rotated on a turntable; then the entire outer surface was smoothed, sometimes resulting in a self-slip. Grooves might be incised on the upper shoulder and a handle added. Scraping the interior, often rather carelessly, reduced wall thickness (cf. large widemouth pots, Figs. 10-2 vs. 10-3).

Large storage jars (max. dimensions ca. 35–80 cm) were built onto a slab

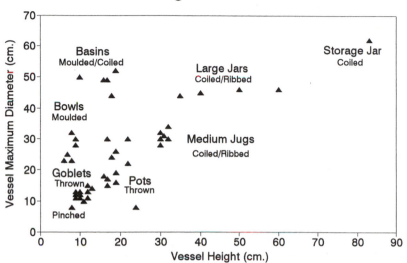

Figure 10-1 Relationship of vessel size to primary forming methods (YHSS 6A).

base (Fig. 10-4). Construction may have consisted of coils added and then drawn upward (see beveled joins). Periodic horizontal breaks mark construction episodes; separate coils are not always identifiable. Forming increments decreased in height in the upper body in order to reduce stress on the partially hardened lower body.

Oversize storage vessels (*pithoi*) exhibit coiled construction on a layered slab base (Fig. 10-5 [YHSS 5]). Rounded cross-sections of individual coils are identifiable in vertical breaks; surfaces of individual coils are easily visible in long horizontal breaks. Horizontal breaks at 12–15 cm vertical intervals mark construction episodes of roughly four coils' height. Deep finger-strokes working the coils of the neck together are also clear. Interior and exterior smoothing marks indicate use of a turntable in finishing (Hampe and Winter 1962, 1965; Henrickson 1995a; cf. Voyatzoglu 1974).

Different yet contemporary methods of making a specific shape and size may mark the work of different potters or workshops. For example, compare the differing construction of two large YHSS 6A carinated bowls (Fig. 10-6). Both had moulded bases and coiled upper bodies, but the transition from moulding to coiling phases is much lower in one than the other.

The decoration and finish of grey common wares were generally simple. Often wet smoothing left enough fine clay on the surface to yield a self-slip. A thin final micaceous slip or wash, producing a silvery sheen, was characteristic in the Early Phrygian period (Sams 1994a:32–33) and later. Burnishing could provide a finer surface, often on limited areas, or it could consist of isolated strokes. A finely burnished surface

*Figure 10-2 Forming methods for small (top two) and medium jars (bottom) (YHSS 6A).
Scale 10 cm.*

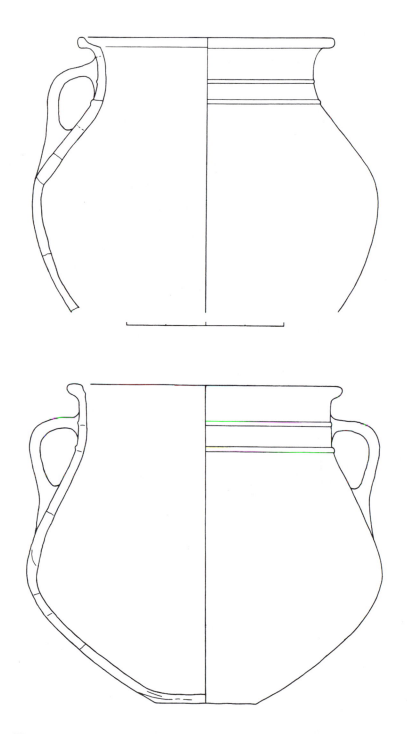

Figure 10-3 Forming methods for medium wide-mouth pots (YHSS 6A). Scale 20 cm.

may conceal a coarse and poorly compacted fabric. Some fine ware vessels exhibit a high burnish or polish, which can be a special type of slip (see below). Common ware vessels may have incised, stamped, or painted decoration (Sams 1994a).

Firing

A combination of technological factors may account for the dominance of reduction firing during the Early-Middle Phrygian (YHSS 6-5) and later periods. It may be slightly more fuel-efficient, minimize problems with clays (especially

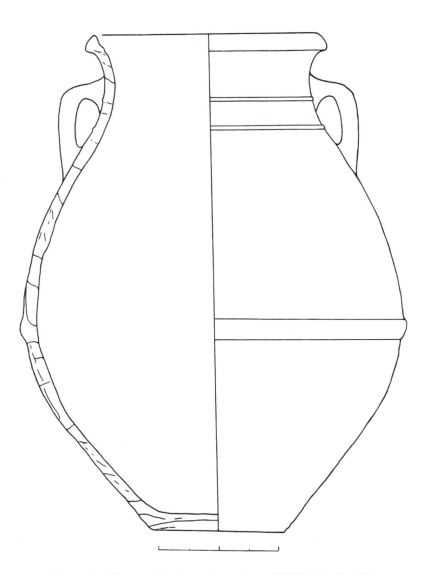

Figure 10-4 Forming of a large wide-mouth jar (YHSS 6A). Scale 20 cm.

calcareous ones), and could help mask color variations resulting from the diverse clay compositions used (Rye 1981; Rice 1987). Cultural factors such as color preference could also contribute.

Refiring experiments indicate that the original firing temperatures were a rather modest 700–800°C, which would not require use of a formal kiln. Traditional potters often fire pottery at such temperatures without a permanent structure ('kiln') (Güner 1988; Rye and Evans 1976). Only the lustrous black fine ware (see below) would require the closer control of temperature and atmosphere, which a kiln provides. The only known YHSS 5 kiln (Johnston 1970) has an interior diameter of <1 m, adequate only for firing small vessels.

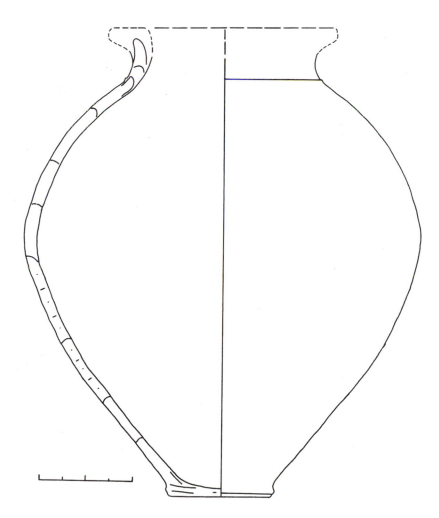

Figure 10-5 Forming a pithos (YHSS 5). Scale 20 cm.

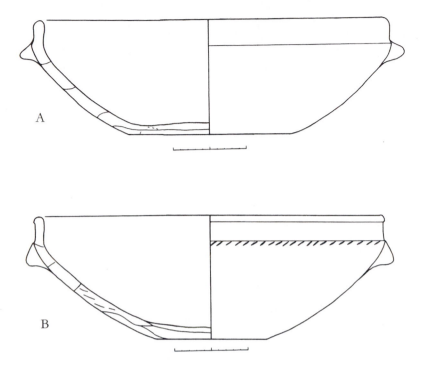

Figure 10-6 Two different ways to make basins (YHSS 6A). Scale 10 cm.

Special Wares

A brief survey of other, more specialized, or elaborate local wares (based on INAA data) provides evidence for the breadth of potters' working knowledge.

Diverse buff wares, ranging from relatively coarse to fine with slipped and burnished surfaces, demonstrate competence in oxidation firing. Sams (1994a) has distinguished distinct styles of painted decoration in the Early Phrygian period, likely representing at least separate workshops. Several varieties of bichrome and polychrome painted decoration are known, mostly from the Middle Phrygian period. The most elaborate consists of an overall burnished red slip which defines white-ground panels with black and red geometric or naturalistic designs (e.g., Sams and Temizsoy 2000: Figs. 82–84; Kohler 1995:Frontispiece, 1–10 [TumB 15–16; pl. 39 TumJ 36]).

Two distinct varieties of oversize storage jars (pithoi) are known from early YHSS 5 contexts; chemical composition data show that both are local. One variety is rather coarse grey to brown and poorly fired (Fig. 10-5). The second has a coarse orange yet well-fired fabric which was used only in ledge rim jars; some have apparent capacity marks incised on their shoulders (Edwards 1959:265, Fig. 9-10; Henrickson 1995a).

Lustrous black fine ware is perhaps the technological height of the local craft (see Chapter 4 this volume, Fig. 4-4 for illustration). Shapes often copy metal vessel prototypes (cf. Young 1981:pl. 60–61). The paste is very fine, without visible inclusions, and uses clay from the same sources as the grey common and coarse wares. Forming involved either throwing or moulding, depending on vessel shape and decoration. The glossy black finish generally shows no discrete burnish or polish marks and has a silky-smooth feel. The apparently polished surface is actually a sintered slip achieved by altering the chemical composition of the fine clay slip so as to lower its vitrification temperature (Henrickson et al. 2002). Such manipulation of the clay composition shows a craft thoroughly familiar with the properties of local clays and flexible enough to avoid dependence on a specific clay composition (either calcareous or non-calcareous was suitable).

Organization and Scale

Combining various lines of evidence we may infer the organization and scale of pottery production at Gordion in the Early–Middle Phrygian periods. The vessels exhibit relatively standardized shape and size groupings. The limited number of distinct clay compositions implies the exploitation of relatively few sources. Thus the nature of the assemblage itself, in the light of ethnographic parallels, indicates specialist potters working in a limited number of workshops (Blackman et al. 1993; Henrickson 1993, 1994; Peacock 1982).

Sams has proposed potential Early Phrygian production groups. First, he noted (1994a:187) that "the potting establishments themselves...remain elusive, and the closest link to them comes perhaps with the consignments of bowls and other shapes, including several production groups." For example, bowls found stacked together (up to 28 per group) and resting on the remains of wicker baskets demonstrate the movement of large numbers of single vessel forms into the city (Sams 1994a:3, 6, 42–43, 187, pl. D1-2, E1). Second, distinctive styles of painted decoration define likely production units (Sams 1994a:134–174). Likewise, since they must be stamped before the clay hardens impressions from a single stamp on multiple storage jars may mark products from a single workshop (Sams 1994a:42–43, 46).

The INAA chemical composition data provide some indication for the potential breadth of vessel repertoires produced by individual workshops and the minimum number of local workshops. While a single clay source might have been exploited by more than one workshop, we may begin to estimate minimum numbers of producers (workshops) since the clays available locally are diverse (Henrickson and Blackman 1996; in prep.). When varied vessel sizes and shapes have a single clay composition, it suggests that an individual source/workshop made a range of shapes and sizes. Conversely, if individual contemporaneous exemplars of a specific vessel form and size exhibit different compositions, they are likely from different sources/workshops.

INAA data for 70 individual vessels from the anteroom of Terrace Building 2 in the Early Phrygian Destruction Level (YHSS 6A; cf. Fig. 10-1) and 90 from a terminal Middle Phrygian (YHSS 5 [ca. 550 BC]) trash pit suggest that the minimum number of workshops is limited at any point in time (Henrickson and Blackman in prep.). In both cases, no more than two or three distinct clay compositions encompass the great majority of the vessels. Despite the technological and cultural continuity linking these two corpora, each shows exploitation concentrating on different clay sources. Composition data also demonstrate that a variety of vessel forms and sizes (small to large jars, pots, and bowls) employ similar clay, so individual workshops likely produced a range of utilitarian pottery.

Ethnographic studies indicate some specialist artisans may concentrate solely on production of very large storage jars and work independently of other potters (Blitzer 1990; Hampe and Winter 1962, 1965; Voyatzoglu 1974). Since the clay composition data for these storage jars is similar to that of other pottery (Henrickson and Blackman in prep.), more than one workshop may have exploited a single clay source.

A noteworthy pattern is the relatively limited use of the calcareous Sakarya River clays available around Gordion during the Early Phrygian (YHSS 6) period, this marking a distinct break with patterns of the Early Iron Age industries. Early Phrygian workshops, or at least their clay sources, may have lain elsewhere in the valley (Henrickson and Blackman 1996; in prep.). As the city grew during the Middle Phrygian (YHSS 5) period, so did its demands. Ceramic composition from YHSS 5 contexts suggests more intensive use of clays likely found in the immediate area of Gordion.

The Middle Phrygian period also offers abundant data on varied socioeconomic contexts throughout the city (Voigt and Young 1999). The Citadel Mound contexts include a building in the elite quarter (Operations 1–2), an upper-class residential area (Operation 17) on the southwestern edge, and an area of uncertain status in the northwest (Operations 29-36). Along the city wall in the Lower Town, excavation in Area A revealed part of a monumental terrace. In the Outer Town, almost 500 m from the Citadel Mound, a small sounding (Operation 22) yielded part of a semi-subterranean room. Ware frequencies are comparable for all areas, even for lustrous black fine ware, although large pieces of orange coarse ware jars emerged only in the elite service buildings. INAA composition data indicate that the same clays were used in pottery from all areas, so presumably the same workshops supplied all areas and social strata of the city. Potters, particularly those producing common rather than fine wares, may have been independent of direct state control in ancient state societies (Costin 1990; Stein and Blackman 1993), although their situation at Gordion remains ambiguous.

RESPONSE TO FOREIGN IMPACT

In the late 7th or early 6th century BC (late YHSS 5), Gordion fell under Lydian control. A wide range of characteristic Lydian pottery is found in all areas of the city, from the elite quarter on the Citadel Mound to the Outer Town (fine buff paste and painted decoration [monochrome to polychrome]; see DeVries 1990:Fig. 27; Sams 1979a; Sams and Temizsoy 2000:Figs. 105–112). Local copies or adaptations however, are relatively uncommon. "Fruitstands" are a notable exception (top, Fig. 10-7). Local potters copied the general shape (wide shallow dish on a cylindrical shaft with a flaring base) but used local slipped and burnished grey common ware; pattern burnishing reproduced the overall design of the Lydian

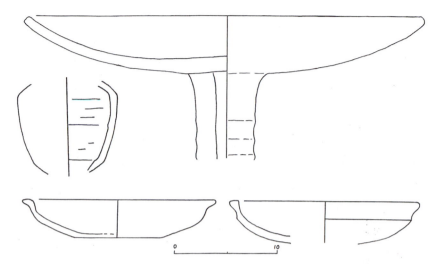

Figure 10-7 Local gray ware adaptations of Lydian and other prototypes (YHSS 5). Top, local gray ware Lydian-style fruit stand. Bottom, flattened rim bowl, non-local style made of local gray ware. Left side, local gray ware lekythos.

geometric painted motifs. The alien prototype was thoroughly assimilated into the local craft. Likewise, small bowls with extended or flattened rims are adopted from a non-local tradition but produced in grey (bottom, Fig. 10-7). Yet the most common Lydian vessel forms—lydions, small cups with handles, and bottles (lekythoi) (Sams 1979a)—were rarely made locally (local lekythos left side, Fig. 10-7).

The limited copying of only a few foreign types and the very heavy assimilation they exhibit suggests the strength of the local YHSS 6-5 craft tradition and its resistance to change. This contrasts with later periods (YHSS 4-3, Persian-Hellenistic periods) when local fine wares were generally buff, often with painted decoration, and copying of foreign vessel forms became common (Henrickson 1993, 1994).

THE POTTER'S CRAFT AT GORDION

In the first half of the 1st millennium BC, distinct combinations of forming, finishing, and firing methods specific to individual shapes and sizes of vessels define Gordion's potter's craft — a culturally distinctive complex of material, technology, and behaviors. The potters were specialists, flexible and pragmatic, working in a limited number of workshops and producing a large number and range of vessels. Given that some non-local clay sources were used, not all workshops may have been at Gordion. In the early 1st millennium BC, Gordion already drew on a wider area for basic commodities like pottery. Later, as foreign hegemony had increasing impact on the local society and culture, including the ceramic industry, the technological core of the craft persisted and influenced how local potters adapted alien ceramics for local production, especially among the utilitarian wares.

III Gordion in Its Regional Context

11

THE GORDION REGIONAL SURVEY

Settlement and Land Use

LISA KEALHOFER

The nature of the relationship between political and economic change has been the subject of long and extensive debate (e.g., Hirth 1996; Marx [1887] 1992). The long-term history of the Gordion region includes the expansion and contraction of several states and empires (Hittites, Phrygians, Romans), and it provides an excellent opportunity to study how economic strategies changed with political transformations (see Table 3-1).

This chapter presents the preliminary results of the Gordion Regional Survey (GRS)(1996–2002)[1], which collected information on both settlement patterns (settlement distribution over time) and ancient environments (soils, hydrology, erosion). Environmental data include a palimpsest of land use and climate change that are often difficult to untangle. Evidence from settlements provides one means to interpret environmental palimpsests.

The goal of the survey was to understand how social and political changes related to major changes in land use, as a proxy for economic change. Pre-industrial societies were dominantly agricultural economies, so major shifts in agricultural strategies can be used as a measure of overall economic transformation.

PREVIOUS SURVEYS AT GORDION

The best known and most visible archaeological sites in the Middle East are large mounds (tepes or höyüks). These sites represent long-term accumulation of architectural and domestic debris often over thousands of years. Less visible in the landscape are surface scatters of artifacts representing short occupations, from decades to a few centuries. In regions where systematic surface surveys have been completed, however, surface sites are often more abundant than mounded sites. Systematic and intensive survey is therefore necessary to gain a more representative understanding of regional population dynamics.

The first settlement survey at Gordion began with the most recent phase of archaeological research in 1987. In 1987–1988 Sumner identified settlement sites in a broad region surrounding Gordion (a 40 km x 40 km square area). Sumner worked by himself, locating mounds and sites with architecture within the region. In 1987, he surveyed the immediate area around Gordion (8 km radius) on foot, and in 1988 he visited sites in the larger region by motorbike. While identifying mounded sites was relatively easy, he estimated that his discovery rate for unmounded surface sites was about 20%. Sumner's (1992) survey identified 39 sites (including the excavated sites of Gordion and Polatı). Periods of occupation (components) were preliminarily defined from grab samples of diagnostic ceramics at each site.

Sumner's settlement data also reveal some of the geomorphological issues that affect site recovery during survey. For example, no surface sites date to the Early Bronze Age (EBA), only two to the Middle Bronze Age (MBA), with a steady increase over time. After the MBA the number of mounded sites decreases. It is most likely that early surface sites are either buried or eroded, while later sites have had less time to accrete multiple phases of debris—factors that have little to do with settlement pattern.

In the early 1990s, focus shifted to the immediate area surrounding Gordion. Wilkinson (1992) provided a preliminary assessment of site survey potential. Dickey and Goldman then intensively surveyed the immediate environs north and west of Gordion—an area identified as the Outer Town. In 1995, Goldman revisited sites discovered by Sumner within a 5 km radius of Gordion in order to distinguish the distribution of Roman occupation (Goldman 2000). Goldman joined the GRS crew for the 1996 pilot season, providing useful local knowledge. The surveys of 1987–1995 contributed important context for interpreting Gordion and demonstrated the presence of long-term settlement in the region, beginning by the EBA (Fig. 11-1). GRS began systematic regional and environmental survey in 1996.

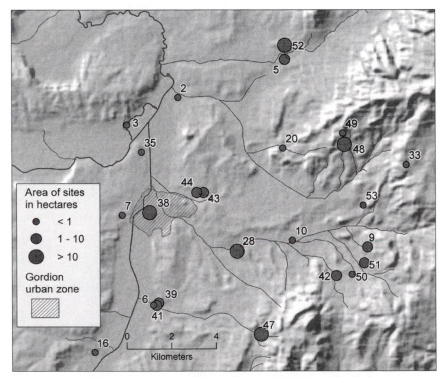

Figure 11-1 Sites in the Gordion Regional Survey area identified by Sumner, Goldman, and GRS surveys.

Plate 1 Old Citadel, Megaron 2 at time of excavation, with its patterned, pebble-mosaic floor, the earliest of its kind known.

Plate 2 Two the extant fragments of a Phrygian painted vessel (P 3396a–d), part of which is from below the lowest floor of the South Cellar.

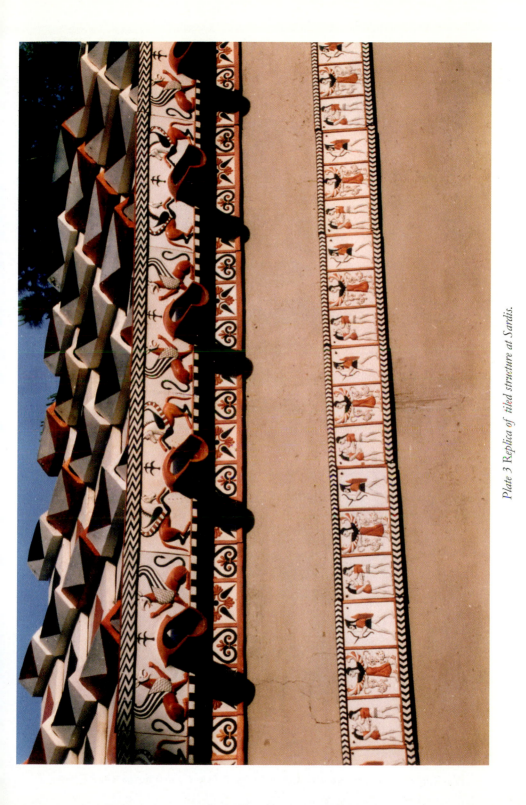

Plate 3 Replica of tiled structure at Sardis.

Plate 4 Wide-bodied core-formed alabastron. Height 7.5 cm. Gordion inv. no. 6462 G261.

Plate 5 Dümrek looking north with inset of stepped altar.

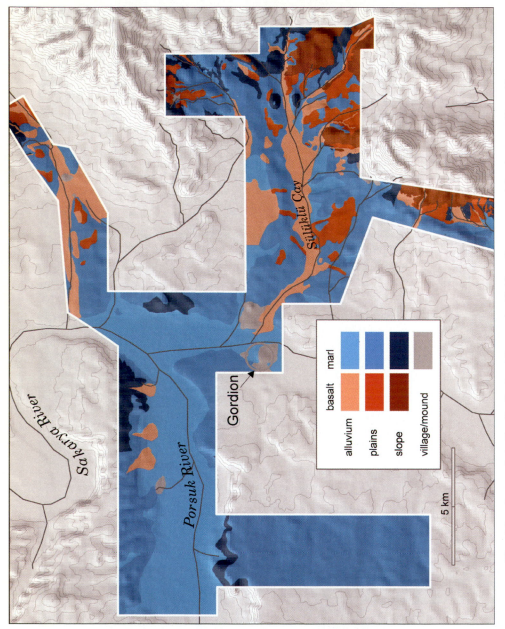

Plate 6 Landscapes of the Gordion Regional Survey, classified by soil parent material and topographic position.

Legend:

alluvium	basalt	marl
plains		
slope		
village/mound		

5 km

Sakarya River

Porsuk River

Sülüklü Çay

Gordion

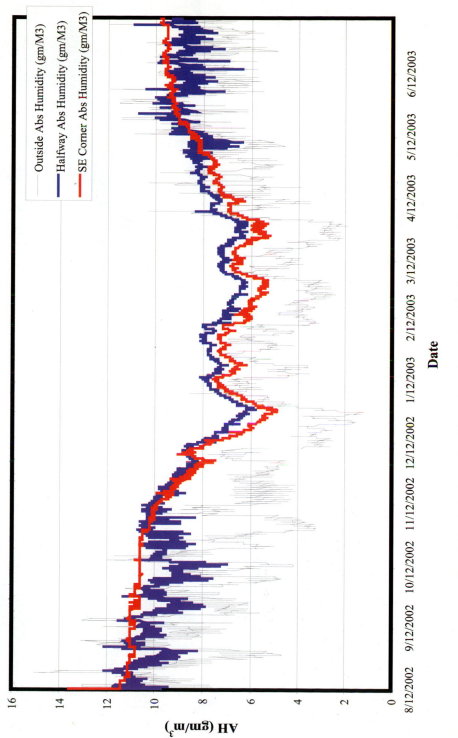

Plate 7 Graph of absolute humidity in the tomb, tunnel, and outside, August 2002–June 2003.

Plate 8 Documenting cleared wall before buttressing and capping; applying sand buffer layer prior to capping wall, July 2000.

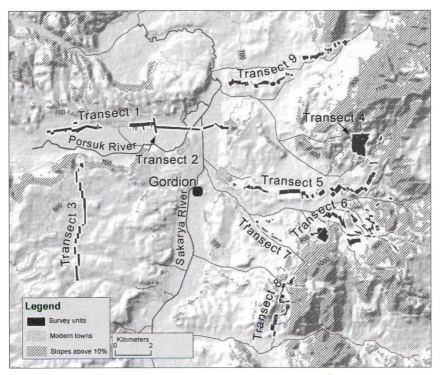

Figure 11-2 GRS survey region (geographic subregions and transects).

GORDION REGIONAL SURVEY METHODOLOGIES

The specific goal of the GRS was to investigate how land use changed during periods of political transformation. To achieve this goal two types of data were collected: archaeological data (ceramic and lithic concentrations) to determine the location of human activities over time, and environmental (land use) data to address how agricultural patterns changed over time relative to settlement organization.

Archaeological Methods

Archaeological data were collected from a 20 km x 18 km region centered near Yassıhöyük. Within this region five geographical subregions were defined based on topography and streams (hydrology): the Porsuk Valley (NW), southwestern uplands (SW), Gordion catchment (E, Sülüklü Basin), Ezineli Valley (S), and the Şabanözü Valley (N) (Fig. 11-2). Every subregion was sampled with at least one transect, as a continuous series of collection units. Transect areas varied from ca. 0.5–1.0 km², depending on the size of the subregion. In terms of the overall survey area, ca. 1–2% of the 360 km² region was surveyed; in terms of the stable landscape within the survey area, ca. 5% of the region was surveyed (see discussion below); while ca. 50% of the land within 500 m of water was surveyed (excluding river floodplain).

Within each transect, units varied in size based on sherd density and field sizes. Crews of 5 to 15 walked 5 m apart, collecting all visible artifacts for each unit. The Gordion catchment was sampled more intensively (four transects of different shapes, 2.6 km^2), to gain a more comprehensive understanding of the immediate region around the site (Transects 4 to 7; see Fig. 11-2).

The ceramics collected during the survey were analyzed in two ways. Those clearly stylistically diagnostic were identified and recorded as such (e.g., Hellenistic amphora, Roman cups). The majority of the collected sherds, however, were not (chronologically) diagnostic. Grave developed a new methodology to match the clay fabric characteristics of survey ceramics to the clay fabric characteristics of sherds from well-dated excavation contexts. All sherds from the survey, including diagnostics, were fabric matched. All fabric types are being analyzed geochemically to identify period-and/or location-specific fabrics, matching unknown types with known types from excavated contexts (see Chapter 12, this volume). Until these results are finalized, the patterns discussed here rely on the fabric matches with excavated diagnostics (Table 11-1).

Environmental Research

Environmental research for the survey was undertaken to address several issues. First, over the course of the last 10,000 years (i.e., the Holocene), the environment in Turkey has changed, both in terms of climate (rainfall, temperature, wind) and vegetation. One basic research question was the nature of environmental change during the periods of occupation in the Gordion region.

Second, as human impact on the environment has increased over time, landscape change has accelerated. Evidence from both Wilkinson's (1992) and Marsh's (1999) work in the early 1990s suggests that 3 to 5 m of sediments had been deposited in the Sakarya floodplain near Gordion, and thus large areas of the adjacent hills were eroded. Due to these changes, largely over the last 2,000–4,000 years, archaeological sites of earlier periods have been eroded, redeposited, or buried. Choices about where to survey needed to be informed by which landscape surfaces have remained relatively stable over the last 4,000–6,000 years, and which had been either eroded away or buried (and would therefore be unproductive for archaeological survey). Environmental, specifically geomorphological, research was necessary to define the geologically stable areas within the larger survey area.

Environmental research included mapping the distribution of current soils, sediments, hydrological patterns, erosional features, and so forth (Chapter 13 this volume). Both coring and augering were used in each subregion to define the rate and timing of erosional and depositional processes in relation to each transect. Soils were dated from each sequence to understand the timing of erosional events and the rate of landscape change.

Settlement Patterns

Since 1996, GRS has conducted three seasons of settlement survey in addition to three seasons of environmental sampling. Ceramic distribution varies by subregion (transect)(Figs. 11-3 and Fig. 11-4). The majority of the transects

Table 11-1 Diagnostic Ceramic Fabric Matches by Period and Transect (raw counts)

Transect	Other	EBA*	MBA	LBA	EIA	EP	MP	LP	Hell	Roman	Medieval	Transect Totals
1	254	16	44	13		1	2	1	35	52	13	431
2	209	30	19	4					25	82	3	372
3	2		1								1	4
4	2637	48	104	92		15	25	7	44	135	59	3166
5	316	12	29	14	4	5	11	4	4	48	3	449
6	2627	76	121	34	13	86	111	28	28	105	22	3251
7	646	2	25	4	2	15	18	5	4	17	1	737(3918)
8	761	5	19	17	3	4	13	7	6	22	12	869(3154)
9	1089	3	18	13	10	50	74	14	10	10	7	1298(8804)
Period Totals	8541	182	318	157	17	107	149	40	137	422	101	10577
												analyzed (collected)

* EBA= Early Bronze Age, MBA= Middle Bronze Age, LBA= Late Bronze Age, EIA= Early Iron Age, EP= Early Phrygian, MP= Middle Phrygian, LP= Late Phrygian, Hell= Hellenistic.

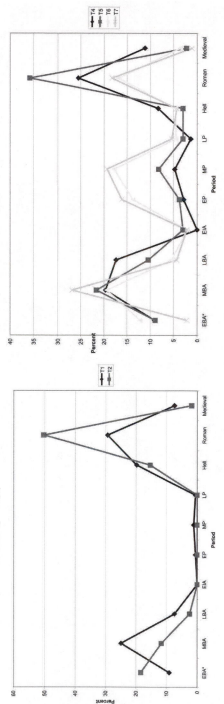

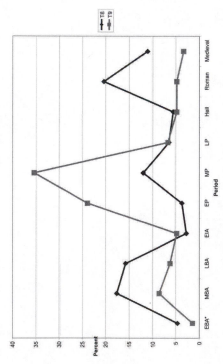

Figure 11-3 Graphs of site components and diagnostic sherds by period.

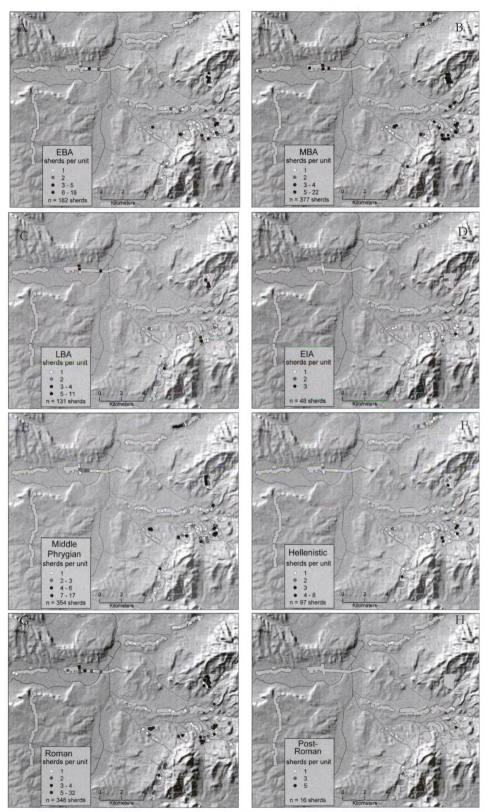

Figure 11-4 GIS map of diagnostic ceramic fabric matches by period (a-h).

reveal two major periods of settlement intensification: MBA(/LBA) and Roman. This includes all the transects in the Gordion catchment (T4 to T7), T1 along the Porsuk to the northwest, and T8 south of the Gordion catchment. T9 is the one exception, with Early and Middle Phrygian ceramics dominating (although GS-5, an adjacent mound, has a much longer sequence). In the transects closest to both Gordion and the springs to the east (T6 and T7), Phrygian components dominate.

Beyond these periods of expansion, EBA sites are best represented along T6, near springs in the foothills east of Gordion. Early Iron Age sites are relatively rare and occur only in the Gordion catchment and just to the north on T9. The same pattern is seen in the Late Phrygian period. Hellenistic ceramics are somewhat more common, but they are more widely distributed through all the transects (except T3). Medieval ceramics are rare, but occupation clearly centered on two springs (T4 and T8), suggesting a heavy pastoral focus.

In addition to the chronological patterning of settlement change, site patterns are also affected by the distribution of agricultural soils and water. For example, overall sherd density is about twice as great in areas with fertile basalt soils.

Proximity to water, and specifically springs, was a very strong determinant of settlement location ($r^2=45\%$). About 75% of the sherds occur with in 250 m of a spring or water source. Several transects cut through areas where springs were few or nonexistent (more than 500 m from water). For example, Transect 3, to the southwest, has no springs, and only four sherds were collected. Currently this area is used for dry farming of wheat and barley, as tractors and mechanized equipment have made the subregion more accessible.

Transect 1, along the Porsuk footslope, while close to water (the river), showed limited evidence of human activities. Dates from the river alluvium indicate that over 5 m of sediments have been deposited in the Porsuk floodplain over the last 2,700 years (AA33551). The combination of poor marl soils on the footslope and a narrow steeper floodplain may have made settlement much less attractive here. However, the current village of Sazilar may cover an earlier site.

The archaeologically ephemeral character of pastoralism undoubtedly means that this component of the economy is under-represented. While occupation sites demonstrate population concentration, the lack of occupation sites may also mean a more dispersed population, in pastoral camps or small villages.

The Ancient Landscape

Until very recently, regionally specific environmental histories have been rare in Anatolia. Across the broader region, the environment and climate changed significantly during the Holocene (Bar-Yosef and Kra 1999; Bottema and Woldring 1990). A warming trend that began ca. 16,000 years ago continued until ca. 5,000–6,000 years ago (mid-Holocene), with a short but significant interruption around 11,000-10,000 years ago, known as the Younger Dryas. This warming trend included an increase in rainfall, as well as a shift toward more seasonal patterns of rainfall and temperature.

For central Anatolia, forest and scrub forest expanded during the period from 10,000 to 5,000 years ago. Increased vegetation and rainfall created a relatively stable environment, with little erosion of soils and a relatively high water table. Between 4,000 and 5,000 years ago, the environment shifted toward a cooler and drier regime, which affected EBA settlements across the region (Rosen 1997; Weiss et al. 1993).

In this same period, increasing agricultural colonization of new econiches with innovations in agricultural strategies and technologies escalated human impact on the environment—often exacerbating the effects of climate changes. As Marsh notes (Chapter 13 this volume), forest clearance and plowing commonly lead to recession of the water table, the retreat of stream flow upslope, and loss of perennial stream flows. While these generalized patterns are known, specific changes within central Western Anatolia have not been investigated.

The settlement pattern provides indirect, or proxy, information about environmental and land use changes, particularly when used in combination with geomorphological data. For the Chalcolithic Period (5500–2300 BC) we currently have only one site in the survey area (Fig. 11-2, Table 11-2). The site is located relatively high in the catchment (ca 850 m), near the base of a basalt ridge. Like an EBA (and Chalcolithic?) site downslope, it is no longer immediately adjacent to a spring. Soil evidence suggests a spring that existed adjacent to the site when it was occupied has since retreated as the water table dropped (Chapter 13 this volume). The lower elevation EBA site is currently buried in 5–7 m of alluvium, making it difficult to discern its relationship to ancient springs (modern springs are ca. 500 m south).

The isolation of these sites suggests that from the Chalcolithic through the EBA the upland areas were more vegetated and had more active, perennial streams and springs. Later sites are located on springs that are still active today. Sometime between the EBA and the Iron Age changes on the environment and use affected the location of reliable springs, leading to shifts in settlement location.

Comparison of the upland and river valley geomorphological landscapes demonstrates the complex problems associated with understanding the dynamics of human impact on the environment (Chapter 13 this volume). The deposition of 3.5–5 m of sediment in the Sakarya River valley after the Phrygian period at first appears to suggest that the most significant human impact in the landscape occurred during and after the Roman period.

More recent work in the upland areas, however, indicates that the deposition of sediments in the Sakarya Valley adjacent to Gordion is not clearly linked to erosion and aggradation in the adjacent uplands. The uplands also show dramatic patterns of erosion and aggradation, but these occur both earlier and later than in the Sakarya floodplain (Chapter 13 this volume).

In the uplands, the early period of landscape stability ends during the EBA or early MBA; apparent not only in dated sediment profiles but also supported by MBA increases in site frequency and size. Substantial increases in erosion and instability occur again in the post-Roman period, with remnants of the Roman road on the hillslope cut by 4–5 m deep erosion gullies. In the valley, on the other hand, evidence of landscape instability (major increases in sediment deposition

Table 11-2 Archaeological Sites in the Gordion Region and Ceramic Periods Identified at Each. Sites Identified during Surveys by Sumner, Goldman, and GRS (1987-2002).

Site #	Name	Type of site	Diameter	Paleolithic	Chalcolithic	EBA	MBA	LBA	EIA	Phrygian	Hellenistic	Roman	Byzantine	Ottoman
49	Kara Tepe Quarry	Quarry/surface	ca. 300 m x 25 m	X?	X?	X								
10	Cekirdeksiz	*Mound, oval*	small? [buried at least 5-6 m]		X?	X								X
50	Dedeler Dere	Surface/slope	100 m x 100 m											
38	Gordion Citadel Mound & adjacent Lower Town and cemeteries	*Mound*	13 ha				X	X						
6	Beylikopru East A	*Mound*	d=90 m; h=3 m			X	X	X			X	X		
9	Topsogutler/Hamam Bogaz	*Mound*	d=120 m for mound, scatter much larger			X	X	X	X	X	X	X	X	X
16	Beylikopru	*Mound? ridge*	d= 50 m			X	X	X		X	X	X		
48	Kara Pinar	Surface/slope	500 m x 500 m			X	X?	X		X	X	X		
5	Killik Tepe (Sabanozu)	*Mound*	2.5 ha? 10 m tall			X	X	X		X	X	X		
7	Bebi West & Bebi	Surface (mainly), small mounds	?				X	X				X		
3	Kollar Tepe, Kiranharman	surface/ridge	1 ha				X	X		X		X		
2	Kizilarini Tepe	*Mound* (4 small)	2= 100 m diam; 2= 50 m diam				X	X		X				
43	Kayran Dere A	Surface/slope	100 x 300 m				X	X					X	
47	Ezineli Ciftlik spring	Surface/slope/terrace	ca. 300 m x 400 m				x?			X	X	X		
39	Beylikopru East B1	Surface	200 m x 100 m							X	X	X	X	
28	Cekirdeksiz B	Surface/slope	300 m x 450 m							X	X	X		
42	Hasansih Pinar	Surface/slope	ca. 150 m x 500 m							X	x	X		
51	Kizilcapinar North	Surface/slope	200 m x 100 m							X	X	X		
44	Kayran Dere B	Surface/slope	ca. d=130 m							X		X		
35	Kiranharman	Surface/ridge	ca d=100 m							X		X		
20	Kisakli	Surface	?							X			X	X
52	Sabanozu	Surface/slope	>200 x 1000 m							X			X	
53	T5/T6	Surface	ca. 100 x 100 m									X	X	X
41	Beylikopru East B2	Surface	ca. 150 m x 350 m										X	
33	Kale	Tumulus & hillfort	ca. d=50 m										X	X
	TOTAL # of sites	(7 mounded sites)		1	2	7	11	10	1	15	10	15	8	5

in the floodplain) begins after the foundation of the Phrygian city and increases rapidly after the Roman period. Studies of the floodplain, therefore, do not provide a good basis for understanding early land use in the adjacent hilly areas.

If we compare this geomorphological data with the settlement distribution, the number of sites increases steadily from one in the Chalcolithic to twelve by the Middle Bronze Age (Table 11-2). Subsequent Early Iron Age (late 2nd millennium BC) settlement in the region is ephemeral (although it may just be unrecognized). During the Phrygian period (16 sites) some of the previous Bronze Age site locations were reoccupied, mainly those closest to the floodplain. Nearly 70% of the Phrygian sites were founded in new locations, with no evidence of prior occupation. This lends some support to Voigt's suggestion that new groups settled the site (and region) in the Early Iron Age (Chapter 3 this volume).

On the other hand, sites occupied by the Phrygians often were used by later Hellenistic and Roman populations. This suggests that land-use strategies from the mid-1st millennium BC until the early centuries AD were relatively stable and successful, and landscape change was slow. Occupation sites rapidly decline after the Roman period. This seems to corroborate the upland geomorphological data and to suggest a shift toward a more pastoral (upland?) economy.

In sum, using settlements as a proxy for landscape change, apparently stable EBA landscapes were increasingly degraded through the Middle Bronze Age as population and agriculture intensified. Occupation began declining in the LBA. While little can be said about the ephemeral Early Iron Age, it is followed by a period of rapid Phrygian expansion. Phrygian Gordion was affected by a slow increase in sediment deposition in the floodplain, likely expanding the marshy habitat around the city. After the Roman period settlement disruption again occurred—whether driven by soil and vegetation loss or other cultural factors is unclear, although there is evidence for both.

THE DYNAMICS OF LAND USE AND SETTLEMENT

Returning to the goal of the project, to investigate how land use changed during periods of political transformation, several tentative conclusions are possible. Chronological patterning is currently based only on a small percentage of diagnostic fabric matches, so the data are preliminary until the geochemical analyses are complete.

Settlement and land use expanded substantially during the Middle Bronze Age, as new sites were established and expanded, often closer to the floodplain. Sites near the floodplain today, and historically, correlate with irrigation, and the MBA may in fact be the period in which irrigation becomes a significant component of the agricultural regime. Sediments begin infilling the middle regions of the Gordion catchment by the LBA, suggesting that agricultural strategies (including pastoralism?) were already impacting the upper hillslopes.

Settlement drops off substantially during the LBA (sherd density declines ca. 50%). This suggests that the economic stimulation of Hittite power, while strongly apparent at Gordion itself (Henrickson 1995b), corresponds to a depopulation of the smaller towns and villages. The subsequent Early Iron Age is thin on the ground and relatively high in the catchment. At least two interpretations for this can be suggested: either the landscape was depopulated, or Early Iron Age ceramics are indistinguishable from LBA or Early Phrygian wares.

The Phrygian ceramic distribution suggests a relatively rapid expansion of Phrygian occupation, reaching a maximum during the Middle Phrygian period (as at Gordion itself), and declining relatively quickly during the Late Phrygian period. Some expansion occurs during the Hellenistic period, with the greatest extent (but not intensity) of land use and settlement during the Roman period. Given earlier patterns of erosion, the stability of occupation from the Hellenistic through the Roman period, and density of the Roman sites in the region, it seems likely that agricultural strategies by the Roman period had changed considerably. Some type of soil conservation, fallowing, and herd management strategies must have been developed to limit erosion. While land degradation accelerates after the Roman period, the evidence for population and settlement declines. Several factors might account for this: increasing pastoralism across the region, unsustainable intensification after the 2nd century BC, or shifts in the climatic regime (increasing seasonality and changes in rainfall that maximize erosion).

In general, land use for farming increased during periods of political integration: Hittite, Phrygian, and Roman. However, the Persian and Greek empires appear to have fostered less agricultural intensification. Settlements changed rapidly as people responded to short-term extra-regional political and economic shifts. If we can interpret lower elevation settlement as more intensive farming, based on ethnoarchaeological data (see Chapter 14 this volume), then the most intensive farming clearly occurs in the Phrygian period. Upland springs were important, likely for both farming and pastoralism, throughout the occupational sequence. Transects 4 and 6, adjacent to springs, show a series of nearly continuous occupations since the Bronze Age.

The answer to the fundamental question, whether we can archaeologically link economic and political change across a region, would seem to be "yes." However, political expansion in the region had very different repercussions in the Hittite period than in the Roman period. Maximum Hittite period (LBA) expansion effectively reduced the number of villages and towns, Phrygian occupation introduced a major shift in settlement distribution and land use, while integration of the region into the Roman Empire led to the widest distribution of settlement and land use in Gordion's history.

12

CERAMIC COMPOSITIONAL ANALYSIS AND THE PHRYGIAN SANCTUARY AT DÜMREK

PETER GRAVE, LISA KEALHOFER, AND BEN MARSH

Phrygian (or stylistically similar) ceramics are a common component of Iron Age sites in central Anatolia, but much of Phrygian culture remains obscure. In this chapter we use a combination of systematic survey and archaeological science at the ritual site of Dümrek to help us understand the extent of Early and Middle Phrygian cultural interaction in central Anatolia.

Only two major Phrygian sites have been excavated—Yassıhöyük and Midas City. Yassıhöyük, identified as ancient Gordion, is the most comprehensively studied of these and represents the Phrygian type site for Anatolia. Our knowledge of the Phrygian occupation of Gordion is largely based on excavations of its monumental urban center (DeVries 1980b; Sams 1995). While current survey work in the surrounding landscape is helping to establish a broader context for Gordion (Chapter 11 this volume), the nature and extent of its political and cultural influence, particularly during the Phrygian period, is unknown.

Dümrek, 40 km northwest of Gordion (Fig. 12-1), one of the few "high place" sanctuaries in central Anatolia, provides a unique view of Phrygian culture and the role of ritual in integrating Phrygian centers across Anatolia (Mellink 1981). Dümrek never appears to have functioned as an occupation site. The crude stepped altars carved out of local boulders (Pl. 5), known from other Phrygian sanctuaries, traditionally have been the basis for defining it as a Phrygian sanctuary (e.g., Haspels 1971). The large quantities of ceramics covering much of its surface are presumed to relate to its ritual function. The lack of excavations, however, means we know little about how long the site was occupied or how it was used.

In 1996 GRS surveyed the site as the first attempt to address these general issues. Two critical issues are discussed here: the duration and patterning of site use at Dümrek, and how much of central Anatolia used Dümrek as a ritual/sanctuary site. Analysis of the ceramic assemblage at Dümrek provides a systematic means to address these issues.

WHY CERAMIC ANALYSIS?

Classification of ceramics in any context aims to reduce the variation in an assemblage to a set of representative types (Rice 1987; Sinopoli 1991). Most classification procedures rely on the preservation of a large body of "diagnostic" ceramics to build interpretations (e.g., Wilkinson and Tucker 1997). Sherds

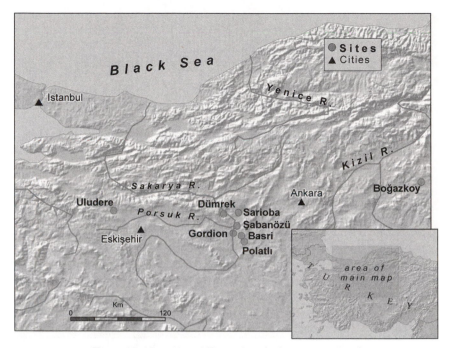

Figure 12-1 Location of Dümrek and other sites mentioned.

collected during survey are commonly cleaned and stored for further study. From this point on, specialist knowledge of styles, technologies, and forms is required in order to advance analysis and interpretation. Diagnostic characteristics of ceramic lots are described and recorded. Diagnostic identification is based on comparison with known, dated ceramics from excavations and published fragmentary or reconstructed ceramics. Subsequently, a large proportion of survey sherds are discarded or set aside as unidentifiable. After field analysis, further specialist studies may be undertaken on technology (e.g., Henrickson 1994; Kingery and Smith 1990), characterization (e.g., Vitali and Franklin 1986), comparisons of trade wares (Dickinson et al. 1996), and so forth (e.g., Glascock 2002; Grave et al. 1996; Griffiths 1978; Knapp et al. 1988; Neff et al. 1989).

Two problems limit the use of diagnostics for interpreting the Dümrek survey assemblage. First, a large proportion of the survey ceramics are nondiagnostic, undecorated body sherds. Second, regional archaeological sequences in Anatolia are still not sufficiently developed to identify production centers on the basis of style alone.

Alternatively, we can use the geochemical and mineral characteristics of ceramics to gain both chronological and provenience information from otherwise nondiagnostic sherds. For Dümrek, with few diagnostics, geochemical and mineralogical classification provides a means to organize ceramic fabrics into compositional groups that tell us something about where and how the ceramics

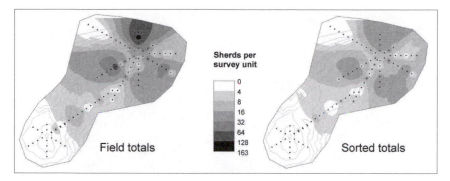

Figure 12-2 GIS of surveyed area and transect collection unit locations, comparing frequency of sherds from field totals with number analyzed from each unit (sorted totals.)

were made. Comparisons of Dümrek ceramic geochemistry with similar analyses from other sites across central Anatolia make it possible to assess which ceramics were imported and which were locally made. From these groups we can discern the range of ceramic types represented at Dümrek and the extent of interaction between central Anatolian centers.

THE METHOD

To implement this analysis, which encompasses the entire assemblage of survey ceramics, we developed a three-stage approach: (1) field fabric matching, (2) sherd refiring and regrouping, and (3) physical analytic (geochemical and mineralogical) grouping. These stages represent a strategy of nested classification with each stage targeting a more exacting measurement of the characteristics of the assemblage. Typically each step substantially reduces the number of types. These data, including location and fabric type, are integrated with the survey database using Geographic Information System (GIS) software (ArcGIS). ArcGIS allows us to map and analyze the spatial distribution of the chronologically diagnostic ceramic classes over time. The immediate object of the ceramic analysis is to understand changes in the distribution of ceramics, when the site was occupied and abandoned, and which parts of the site were used by which groups over time. This in turn provides the material basis for developing an interpretation of wider cultural dynamics.

Field Methods

Dümrek's position at the top and end of a steep ridge precipitously overlooking the Sakarya River made survey difficult (Pl. 5). Traditionally survey includes walking linear transects systematically across a site and identifying and/or collecting the artifacts encountered. At Dümrek we used a modified strategy that involved defining two radial transect zones, each one centered on a high point on the ridge. Transects radiated out and down the hill from this central point in 40

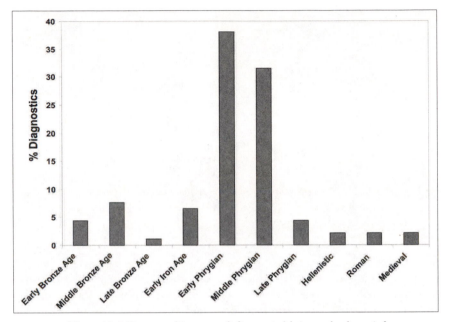

Figure 12-3 Frequency histogram of diagnostic fabric matches by period.

to 60° intervals (i.e., 6-8 per point; Fig. 12-2); the direction of the transect was shifted when the slope was too steep. Ceramics were collected every 25 m, in "dog-leash" units with a radius of 5 m. The length of each line was constrained by the steepness of the hill or other features (roads). A total of 92 units were collected, creating a ceramic assemblage of 1,413 sherds.

Field Fabric Sorting

All of the ceramics collected in 1996 were processed in 1999. Due to time constraints, half of every collection unit was processed at the dig house, except where there were very few sherds, and then all the unit's sherds were processed (804 of the original 1413 sherds). Diagnostic forms were described when present.

Processing involved reducing the sample by using a matching procedure. The fabric of fresh breaks on survey sherds was compared and matched with sherd fabrics of known period from excavated contexts at Gordion, ranging from the Early Bronze Age to Medieval period. Matches had to agree closely in fabric color and appearance (e.g., reduction/oxidation banding), size and color of inclusions, size and orientation of pores, and fracture pattern of the break (a measure of hardness and coherence of the matrix). If any of these criteria could not be met the sherd was treated as a new fabric type, added to a reference sheet, and used to compare with the remaining sample.

With this process, the initial classification of the Dümrek assemblage created a large number of new fabric types. Ninety-two samples could be matched with the excavated reference sherds from Gordion, but most could only be matched against new unknown fabric types created from the Dümrek sample itself. At the end of this procedure 804 individual sherds had been grouped into 413 classes (dighouse types).

Laboratory Procedures

Laboratory analysis employed a three-stage procedure. In the first stage, we visually analysed the 413 dighouse types to remove redundancy, creating 257 laboratory groups. We then refired all the samples to eliminate variability due to color effects introduced during firing. By refiring the samples to 1000°C (a temperature likely to be beyond the range originally achieved) fabrics were saturated with an oxidizing atmosphere to normalize fabric color. The refired fabrics could then be grouped on the basis of their more uniform oxidized color as well as the particle, pore, and fracture criteria to develop a sense of the range of fabric types (rather than technological practices) represented. This stage reduced the number of groups to 20.

In the second stage, a sub-sample of 123 samples from these 20 new classes was selected for geochemical analysis. Multiple samples from each class were analysed to assess the internal geochemical homogeneity of each class. We used both the refired classes and the original (varied) appearance of these sherds to develop this representative group of samples for analysis.

For the elemental composition of the ceramic fabrics Proton-Induced X-ray and Gamma Ray Emission spectrometry (PIXE-PIGE) was used. This ion beam technique is well suited to measuring X-ray and gamma-ray emissions from the cut and cleaned sample surface. Compared to other elemental techniques such as Atomic Absorption and X-ray Fluorescence Spectrometry, PIXE-PIGE analysis is relatively rapid and does not require samples to be elaborately pre-treated. However, sherds with very different mineralogy, and hence different geological sources, can have a similar elemental composition (Hein et al. 2002). Therefore, thin sections of the same samples analyzed by PIXE-PIGE were also assessed for the variety, size, and density of minerals present. The final sample was classified into eleven compositional groups.

Comparing proportional representation of groups at each stage of the analysis provides a confirmation of sampling accuracy. The final eleven groups are composed of representatives in proportion to classes from each preceding stage of the sampling procedure (Fig. 12-3) and can be used to reclassify the original survey ceramic database by tracing the sampling procedure backwards. By reclassifying the initial population of 804 sherds, we can study the variability in fabric types across the site of Dümrek as well as the extent to which fabrics from other sites are represented.

RESULTS

The results of the ceramic analyses can be divided into four sections which provide different types of information: the fabric matches made at the

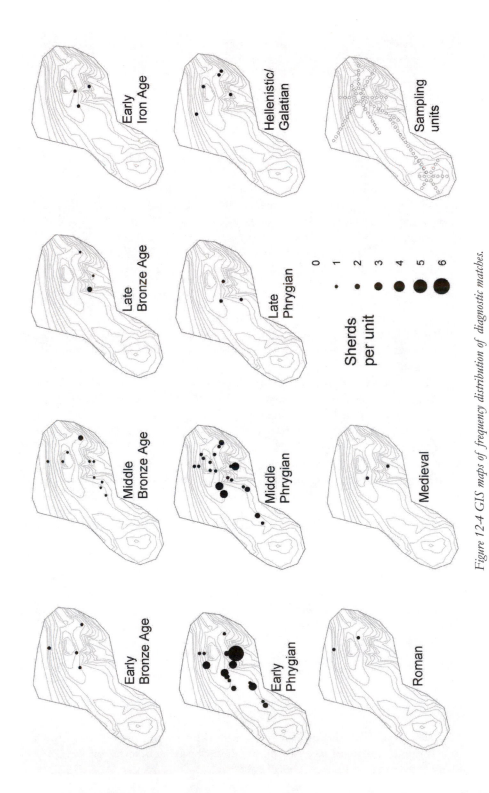

Figure 12.4 GIS maps of frequency distribution of diagnostic matches.

dig house with the reference sherds from excavated contexts, the geochemical groups defined by statistical analyses, the comparisons of Dümrek and Gordion geochemical groups with groups from other sites around central Anatolia, and the spatial analysis of both of these groups.

Fabric matches with excavated reference ceramics (YHS series)

While diagnostic forms were not common in the Dümrek assemblage, 92 of the Dümrek samples (about 10% of the processed sample) could be matched with reference ceramics from Gordion. The relatively large size of this component is important as it provide us with a preliminary framework for interpreting the Dümrek assemblage both in time and across the site. Of these matches 70% were Early and Middle Phrygian types, with the remainder (EBA–Medieval) accounting for between 2% and 7% each (Fig. 12-3). While well represented in the reference ceramics, the virtual absence of Late Phrygian diagnostics was surprising.

Identification of which survey lots produced diagnostic material indicates that the Phrygian types are distributed differently than other diagnostics. However, to assess whether these patterns represent broader, spatially discrete areas across the site, the diagnostic matches and their locations were integrated spatially through the GIS database (Fig. 12-4). The resulting GIS maps indicate that the Early and Middle Phrygian types are concentrated around the south and eastern sides of the Kale, with a significant group in the Middle Phrygian period just downslope to the north. Based on the topography, most of the sherd concentrations appear to occur on terraces or saddles below the Kale (as do the altars), except in what appears to be the slope accumulation to the north. Sherds from other periods appear to be more randomly located (e.g., EBA and Hellenistic).

Geochemical Analyses and Groups

The PIXE-PIGE results for the 123 samples examined, representing 12% of the survey sample, were statistically analyzed to identify elementally similar groups (the procedure, employing a combination of Principal Components and Canonical Variates Analysis is detailed in Grave et al. 2000). The analysis isolated the eleven elementally discrete groups, mentioned earlier (Fig. 12-5). These compositional and visually similar groups formed the basis for matching the remaining (refired but not analyzed) 134 laboratory samples to geochemical groups. Recombining the total refired samples associated with the eleven geochemical groups enables an assessment of the overall frequencies for the total ceramic sample. Making use of the diagnostic matches in these groups, and assuming proportional representation, the most heavily represented groups in this sample (in decreasing order Dümrek Groups 4, 6, 9, and 3) should correspond to the most abundant diagnostic Early and Middle Phrygian groups (Fig. 12-6).

Comparison of the spatial distribution of these groups with the spatial distribution of the diagnostic ceramics suggests that Groups 1, 3, 4, 6, 7, 9, 10, and 11 are most similar to the Early and Middle Phrygian diagnostic distributions (Fig. 12-7). The proportional matches (cf. Fig. 12-3) generally support this similarity.

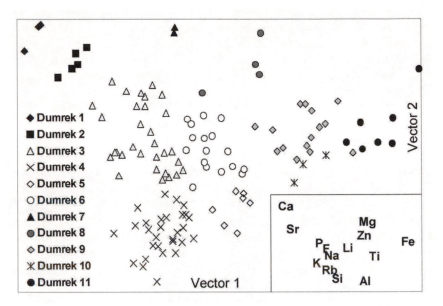

Figure 12-5 Canonical Variates Analysis: scatterplot of Variates 1 and 2 for elemental data with 11 compositional groups identified.

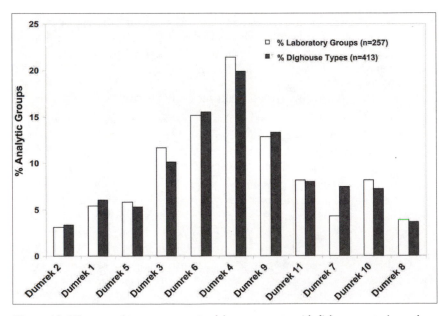

Figure 12-6 Frequency histogram comparing laboratory groups with dighouse groups by geochemical group. The graph demonstrates that the groups created in the laboratory (257 groups) are closely representative of the dighouse fabric types, thus validating the reassignment of dighouse types to geochemical groups. The sequence of geochemical groups was determined by matches with chronologically diagnostic fabrics and the shape of the diagnostic distribution by period.

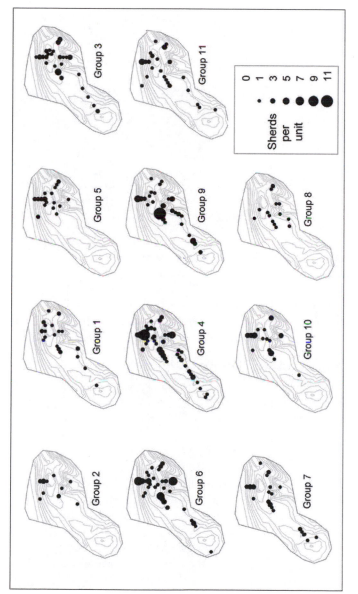

Figure 12-7 GIS maps of the frequency distribution of reclassified dighouse groups.

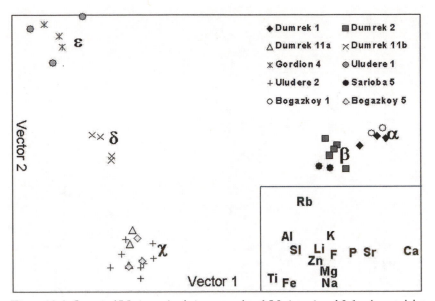

Figure 12-8 Canonical Variates Analysis: scatterplot of Variates 1 and 2 for elemental data showing relationship between Dümrek and non-local samples.

However, perhaps more interestingly, the number of groups and their distinctiveness suggests that potentially eleven different sites (or ceramic technologies) across central Anatolia provided the offering vessels recovered from Dümrek.

Comparisons: Dümrek and Other Sites

As part of the larger GRS project, ceramics from sites in the Gordion region as well as more distant centers (Fig. 12-1) were analyzed by the same set of procedures. This sample was obtained from the British Institute's surface collection of ceramics from sites across Turkey (courtesy of the 1995-2001 Director, Roger Mathews). These analyses provide a larger geochemical context for assessing the variability in the Dümrek assemblage. The results provide a measure of the compositional variability for locally produced fabrics as well as a basis for identifying the presence of wares from more distant centers.

The majority of the Dümrek compositional groups matched the elemental signature of wares from Gordion and surrounding sites. These results indicate that Dümrek was primarily used by the Early and Middle Phrygian occupants of the Gordion region. However three of the eleven Dümrek groups, representing a relatively small component of the overall sample, do not match this regional signature.

Thus far, three locales provide geochemical matches with these Dümrek exotic ceramics. The first is Uludere, 25 km NW of Eskişehir; the second is Sarıoba, 50 km north of Gordion. The third match comes from a subset of excavated Iron Age samples from the Hittite capital at Boğazköy (modern Boğazkale) (courtesy of Herman Genz).

Prior to this comparison, the fabrics from each of these sites were analyzed separately in order to identify the range of elemental compositions present. A Canonical Variates Analysis (CVA) was used to map within-group and between-group elemental differences (Fig. 12-8; groups defined by Greek letters). The results can be summarized as follows:

- Group α, distinguished by relatively high calcium, includes Dümrek and Boğazköy Groups 1, the latter decorated bichrome ware. Mineralogically, this group consist of fine grains of quartz and feldspars in a light brown fabric.
- Group β, distinguished by a small but systematic elemental separation from group α (lower calcium and phosphorus), includes Dümrek Group 2 and Group 5 from Sarıoba. The two Sarıoba samples are a small part of the overall sample from this site, and further work would be required to establish whether Sarıoba was a production center.
- Group χ, distinguished by relatively high concentrations of titanium and iron, is composed of eight samples from Uludere (Uludere Group 2), three Boğazköy samples (Boğazköy Group 4), and a subset of Dümrek Group 11. Unlike the calcareous fabrics of Groups α and β, Group χ mineralogy features abundant fragments of a type of titanium-iron rich volcanic mineral (titanium augite?). The Uludere area is proposed as the most likely origin for these wares for several reasons: because the site is located in the center of a Miocene (?) volcanic intrusion distinct from the Pleistocene vulcanism of regions farther east including Gordion (Bingol 1989); and for Uludere, unlike the Boğazköy or Dümrek samples, several different ceramic types from widely differing periods belong to the high iron-titanium elemental group. If further analysis confirms this, then it raises an intriguing question as to the character of a Phrygian presence in the Uludere region and its role in ceramic production for long-distance exchange or ritual.

Not all known Early and Middle Phrygian wares were used at Dümrek. For example, we find no evidence of the fine decorated Middle Phrygian buff wares common at Gordion. Dümrek is dominated by large coarse jar sherds suggesting domestic use (storage). The distinctive composition of group ε with high rubidium (see Fig. 12-8) typifies a fabric common to both Uludere and Gordion but not found at Dümrek. Conversely, Group δ, only found at Dümrek, appears to be a local product.

DISCUSSION & CONCLUSIONS

Two specific questions were raised at the beginning of this chapter: what was the duration of site use at Dümrek, and what was the extent to which other sites/groups in central Anatolia used the ritual site? The results strongly suggest that use of this sanctuary was almost exclusively limited to the Early and Middle Phrygian periods. Sherds from other periods are comparatively rare.

The identification of fabric types through geochemical analysis has made it possible both to identify ceramics made within the local region and to distinguish those made in other regions. The ceramics at Dümrek are strongly dominated (85%) by local fabric types. This suggests that the main users of the sanctuary were the inhabitants of Gordion and its nearby settlements. However, several fabric types are clearly identifiable as exotic. By comparing these types with fabrics from more distant sites we can suggest that at least two other remote sites match these exotic fabrics in the assemblage at Dümrek: Uludere, ca. 150 km to the west, and Boğazköy, ca. 300 km to the east. The number of groups present (11) indicates that minimally within these 3 areas multiple sites (and/or types) were brought to Dümrek, most likely as offering vessels.

The data raise additional questions about the significance of Dümrek's use. The simple stepped altars (Pl. 5), the high-elevation location with dramatic views, and the lack of architecture suggest the ritual was in some way related to nature or to links between nature and the gods. The utilitarian nature of the vessels suggests these relationships were domestic rather than public. Certainly, the contemporary urban center of Gordion had a much more architecturally and symbolically complex monumental organization and construction. While Gordion continues to function uninterrupted through the Late Phrygian period, Dümrek appears to have been abandoned.

This seems to suggest a strong ideological change in Phrygian society. Two major outside influences might be responsible for this shift: (1) the Persian/ Achaemenid conquest and (2) the incorporation or the increasing influence of Hellenistic societies (and exchange). At Gordion, the strongest influences appear to be the longer-term Hellenistic interactions. Greek ceramic imports increase dramatically in the Late Phrygian period (Chapter 4 this volume). Given the strong link between Gordion and Dümrek, it might be that this interaction affected the use of older Phrygian ritual sites.

An ideological shift in Phrygian society is also supported at Gordion. While the site remains a major center, tumuli construction virtually ceases in the Late Phrygian period (DeVries 1980b; Sams 1995). At Midas City, religious architecture also assumes a much more formal and Hellenized form in the Late Phrygian period (Haspels 1971).

When viewed together, economic and religious spheres appear to converge in the Late Phrygian period. The evidence for abandonment of the sanctuary site of Dümrek provides a new line of support for what seems to be a major ideological shift.

13

Physical Geography, Land Use, and Human Impact at Gordion

Ben Marsh

The aspects of the physical landscape that are most relevant to ancient occupation are bedrock, topography, soil, and streams and springs. Topography guides the important human activities of transportation, agriculture, settlement, and defense. Soil supports agriculture and natural vegetation and is thus the foundation of subsistence systems. Streams and springs provide water for domestic uses and for irrigation. Beneath all of this, bedrock is the primary influence on the other aspects of the physical landscape—it erodes into topography, it is the parent material of the soil, it channels groundwater to the springs and streams. And bedrock provides raw material for human industry: for lithics, for buildings, for ceramics, and potentially for metallurgy.

This chapter focuses on the region within 10 km of Gordion, an area encompassing the Gordion Regional Survey described in Chapter 11 this volume, and it includes three parts: first, the physical geography at Gordion, second, human land-use patterns, and third, human impact on the landscape.

Physical Geography of Gordion

The mound at Gordion is situated on the west edge of the floodplain of the Sakarya River. To the west is a broad, arid plateau rising to 100 m above river level; to the east is a 15 km long valley system rising 600 m to a ridge complex (Fig. 13-1). Gordion experiences a moderately dry Mediterranean climate.

Bedrock and Landscape Evolution

The landscapes of the Gordion region closely reflect the two major rocks upon which the topography developed—a thick section of silty marl and a later intrusion of basalt. Marl is a light, weak, lime-rich sedimentary rock laid by rapidly evaporating lakes; it dominates the areas of low-relief in the western two-thirds of the Gordion region. Basalt, which is black and dense, is the most common product of volcanic action. The mountains in the eastern third of the study area are basaltic (Plate. 6).

Human environments of the Gordion environs, listed as "landscape types" on Table 13-1, can best be differentiated by their underlying bedrock and their slope. Each landscape type has a distinct geomorphic history, each bears a characteristic soil, and each responds characteristically to the human factors that accelerate soil erosion.

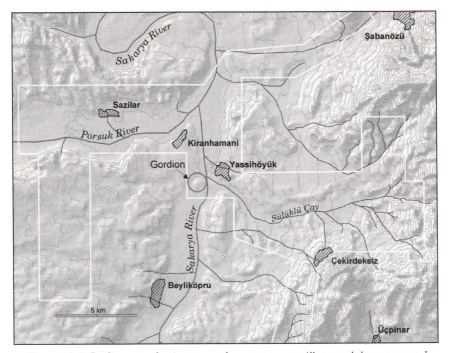

Figure 13-1 Gordion area, showing topography, contemporary villages, and the reconstructed pre-human pattern of perennial streams. The Gordion Regional Survey lies within the polygon shown in white. Topography from the Shuttle Radar Topography Mission; contour interval 20 m.

The sedimentary bedrock near Gordion is a section of lake deposits several hundred meters thick—marly siltstone with gypsum evaporite and gravel. The timing for this depositional series was late Tertiary, ca. 1.0–2.5 mya (Bingol 1989).

Basaltic rocks were subsequently erupted over and into the eastern third of the study region after most of the marls had been deposited. As the basalt was injected into the marls, the marls were uplifted, folded, and deformed.

The basaltic intrusions created the eastern mountains (Çile Dağ, Dua Dağ, etc.). Deformation of the adjacent marls was great near the mountains, raising a series of linear marl ridges that parallel the face of the uplands. Between episodes of uplift, erosional surfaces developed, creating a flight of pediments stepping down from the uplands. Deformation decreases away from the mountains, ultimately yielding undisturbed marls beneath the broad plateau west of the Sakarya River.

Neither the brittle, light marly siltstone nor the vesicular, fractured basalt is good building stone—neither can be polished or finely carved and neither will bear heavy loads. Some of the siltstone even dissolves slowly in rain water. This fact helps account for why the Gordion citadel mound shows a paucity of fine stonework structures.

These two rocks created significantly different soils. It is because of this strong contrast that soil type is an effective way to organize the study of this landscape (Table 13-1). Marl-derived soils are pale and alkaline and low in nutrients

Table 13-1 Landscape/Soil Typology of the Gordion Region as Mapped in Plate 6

Landscape Type	Subtype	Geomorphic stability	Environmental qualities	Typical land use
Alluvial surface types	Holocene tan clay and silt floodplain from marl	Generally stable or aggrading	Fine grain soils; groundwater at 2-7 m	Plowed and irrigated
	Holocene red floodplain silt and clay from basalt	Generally stable or aggrading	Heavy soils; expansion damages roots	Grazed, not farmed
	High Quaternary gravel fans	Stable	Silt and coarser soils	Wheat and barley
Uplands plains types	Residual soil from marl/silty bedrock	Slow erosion	Pale, light, sterile soils; dry farming area	Wheat and Barley
	Residual soil from basaltic bedrock	More erodible than above	Holds moisture well	High value crops
	Plains capped by basalt gravels	Prone to erosion	Good soil, but rocky	Mixed crops
	Broad regions of fractured basalts	Erodes readily	Locally rich soils	Too rocky to farm
	Conglomerate and karstic gypsum (west of Gordion)	Slight wind erosion	Light, silty soils; very dry areas	Wheat and barley
Hillslope types	Marl/siltsone slopes	Eroding	Light, medium soil depth	Plowed or grazed
	Gypsum cliffs	Rapid erosion	Shallow, loose alkaline soil	Grazed
	Basaltic mountainsides	Very rapid erosion	Fractured red rock and soil	Steep grazing land
	Eroded geothermally baked marl siltstone	Very rapid erosion	Loose, rough, 'porcelain' chips	Dry and sterile
	Folded ridges of basalt near uplands	Finer material eroding	Closely associated with springs	Steep and rocky

and moisture capacity. They support only sparse agriculture without irrigation. The red basalt-derived soils are far better at holding nutrients and water.

These two rocks also conduct groundwater differently. The foamy or fractured basalt is highly porous and permeable, holding and releasing groundwater throughout the year. Most of the marl is nearly impermeable, permitting neither rain water to percolate into an underlying aquifer nor groundwater to rise up as a spring. Most of the good springs are where water is forced to the surface as it tries to pass down through the contact between basalt ridges and marl lowlands.

Water

Most springs now closely cluster around basalt ridges to the east (note stream sources in Plate 6). The pattern of modern villages east of Gordion is substantially responsive to spring locations—Çekirdeksiz, Şabanözü, and Üçpinar are each in the midst of multiple springs below basalt uplands. The other spring location—typified by Yassıhöyük, Kıranhamanı, and Beyliköpru—is where low-slope landscape features are truncated by major river valleys. Post–Bronze Age silting-in of streams would have buried many earlier springs in this situation.

A few streams in the region are now perennial or nearly so, although no perennial tributaries reach the rivers. Most dry-season streams head in basalt and flow only a short distance over alluvial portions of their channels before sinking entirely into the sediment. Perennial streams were far more common in antiquity because dry season spring flow was higher prior to loss of upland vegetation and soil. (A now-dry spring area is visible on the landscape east of Çekerdeksiz: a hollow of dark, hydric soils that is drained by an abandoned channel. Chalcolithic stone tools and flakes were found nearby.) Streams would have had more bedrock at the surface to flow across before the massive post–Bronze Age alluviation choked the valleys. Some springs also may now be buried if they were in those valleys. Presently irrigation pumps are lowering the water table significantly in the upper valley floodplains, which has caused even more streams to migrate below ground for much of the year.

AGRICULTURAL LAND

Three major classes of arable soil occur near Gordion in patterns closely controlled by bedrock. First, tan alluvial soils on stream floodplains below marl slopes are usually productive and easily irrigable. Significantly less of this soil was present before the post–Bronze Age period of upland erosion and valley alluviation. Floodplain agriculture is suppressed where heavy, heaving, basalt-derived soils are present.

Second, pale fan soils, pediment soils, and related residual soils derived from marl and siltstone cover the largest amount of land of any type. These soils are loose and drought-prone and are now almost exclusively in wheat and barley. In their thin phases these soils are left fallow during alternate years to permit soil moisture to build up through two rainy seasons for each season of growth. More area of this soil type existed in earlier times, before extensive erosion in the uplands.

Third, basaltic pediment and gently sloping upland regions bear dark-colored, light-textured basalt-derived soils with high nutrient and moisture capacity. These high-quality soils are discontinuous on the landscape, but are readily located because they are planted in crops that remain green after wheat harvest—typically melon and sunflower. These soils are highly prone to erosion and are much less extensive now than in antiquity.

Human Impact

It is readily apparent that massive soil erosion has been a major influence on the geomorphology, hydrology, and soils of the Gordion region. Evidence for this influence is both depositional, in the river valleys, and erosional, in the uplands. The floodplain of Sakarya River at Gordion is about 4 m higher than it was at the time of earliest-known human activity at the mound. In cases of rapid historic sedimentation like this, a ready presumption is that accelerated soil erosion in the watershed has choked the streams with sediment and caused them to aggrade (Goudie 1993). The primary initiating cause of such accelerated soil erosion in human-influenced contexts is the removal of vegetation, with plowing creating the most erosion. Overgrazing is also very damaging, especially on steeper slopes, and wood cutting for timber or fuel may cause local erosion and can also open land for subsequent farming and grazing.

River History

The earliest settlement at Gordion was built upon floodplain alluvium of the Sakarya River. Previous research has shown that 3.5–5.2 m of sediment has accumulated since the establishment of the Bronze Age settlement (Marsh 1999). A generalized stratigraphic section taken from floodplain cores and river banks within 1 km of the mound shows the stages described in Table 13-2: The upward progression in this section—from bedded and coarse to massive and fine—reflects major changes in the form and behavior of the Sakarya River as it deposited its excess sediment materials. In general terms, a clean, straight, stable mid-Holocene river evolved into a silty, meandering, aggrading post-Roman river.

Stage I: A large Pleistocene river laid coarse gravels in a low river channel. The sandy "Ib" deposit suggests that by the mid-Holocene, the Sakarya was an energetic stream with little suspended load sweeping repeatedly across a 700 m wide valley.

Stage II: The paleosol deposit is a widespread layer upon which the Iron Age city was built—and into which its wall foundations were cut. The paleosol itself is directly dated to 2140–1920 BC (Table 13-3). Bronze Age cultural material in the lowest excavated levels of the mound is at roughly the level of the paleosol. The top of the paleosol is dated to 770 to 410 BC by radiocarbon analysis of a stump which grew upon it.

This layer was a flood deposit around the early mound and into the growing city. Its existence implies early increases in Bronze Age soil erosion, which is exactly the type of impact a growing settlement would have on its hinterland. But sedimentation rate was slow and this surface was almost stable for many

Table 13-2 Stratigraphic Section of the Sakarya River Plain near Gordion, with Landscape Evolution Stage Designations

Stage	Depth (cm)	Name	Description
IV	0–10	'Red Fan' clay	Red-brown (10YR 4/4) expansive clay at distal end of the Sülüklü Çay fan
IIIb	10–400	Post-Iron Age floodplain silt-loam	Weakly bedded tan (10YR5/3) silt-loam overbank sediment from Sakarya River
Approximate base of Roman Occupation			
IIIa	400–520	Pre-Roman floodplain silt	Massive tan (10YR6/3) silty sediment
Approximate base of Iron Age Occupation			
II	520–540	Paleosol deposit overbank silt	Coherent, pedogenically altered, gleyed silt
Approximate base of material evidence of Bronze Age Occupation			
Ib	540–1000	Pre-Bronze Age (?EBA) sand	Fining upwards cycles of caliche sand
Ia	1000–	Pleistocene gravel	Coarse quartzite gravels

Table 13-3 Radiocarbon and Archaeological Dates in Sakarya Section

Sample	Depth (cm)	Material	RC years BP (2σ calendric conversion)	Archaeological Date
Tx8533	170	Wood, log	1010 ± 40 (AD 890-920, 950-1160)	
Roman level	420	Rock structures		AD 0-300
Tx8532	520	Wood, stump	2460 ± 50 (770-410 BC)	
Phrygian city	520	Rock structures		Ca. 800-400 BC
Bronze Age town?	Ca. 500	Excavated horizons		Ca. 1500-1200 BC
Beta 149217	530	AMS date on paleosol	3660 ± 40 (2140-1920 BC)	

Archaeological dates from Voigt 1994; Beta 149217 courtesy of Gordion Regional Survey

centuries, accumulating only a thin layer. This thin layer was altered by soil-forming processes into a thin soil with a dark surface (A) horizon and distinctive plate-like soil aggregations.

Stage IIIa: Between the development of the Phrygian city on the paleosol and the time of greatest Roman influence, about 1 m of quartz-rich, light-colored, and poorly bedded silt was laid on the floodplain at the city. It is best dated by the large stonework atop it at a Roman settlement north of the mound. This layer buried the lower parts of the city.

Taking the pre-Roman and paleosol deposits together, the lower silty layers suggest, in nature and the timing, an affinity to the Beyşehir Occupation phase described from SW Turkey (Bottema and Woldring 1990), although sedimentation started somewhat later at Gordion. This occupation phase is apparent as a widespread increase in fine-grain sedimentation observed in the Konya region, presumed to be indicative of an early human landscape disturbance between 3000 and 1300 BC. The difference between the record at Gordion and at Beyşehir may show timing or land-use differences between Gordion and the Beyşehir site, 220 km to the southeast, or it may reflect the finer resolution of a lake sediment record.

Stage IIIb: The thickest post-Pleistocene deposit comprises up to 4 m of massive silt-loam with inter-bedded sands. This layer created the first significant accumulation of clayey alluvium. The sediment closely matches, in color and texture, the material now in suspension in the Sakarya River. A log in this deposit is dated to AD 975–1035. When this layer was laid down the river had changed from a straight, sandy-bedded stream, to a meandering stream that deposited fine-grained sediment onto its floodplain. During this time, the meandering Sakarya eroded out significant sections of the city and its walls.

Stage IV: A local deposit at Gordion is a fan of basalt-derived reddish clay from a stream that enters the floodplain within the urban limits of Gordion, which eventually forced the Sakarya to shift to the west side of the mound.

Figure 13-2 graphs the sedimentary chronology (from Table 13-3). The sedimentation model on the graph shows a low rate of deposition prior to the Early Iron Age (ca. 0.2 mm/yr), then a consistent rate of deposition at ca. 2 mm/yr for 26 centuries.

Erosion

This sedimentation sequence is related to the erosional history of the source regions of the sediment, of course. The watersheds of the streams entering the Sakarya from the east within the study region (see Fig. 13-1) are used here as a model of the larger Sakarya basin upland source areas. The bedrock types are typical of the upper Sakarya watershed, and the climate of the whole region is fairly uniform, though one can only posit whether occupation history in the wider Sakarya basin was comparable at the important periods. The local watershed bears a rich record of geologically recent erosion and redeposition. Sharp gullies are cut into the rounded landscape, typical grassland soils lie buried in footslopes, and fans of fresh alluvium overlie Bronze Age sites and well-developed paleosols.

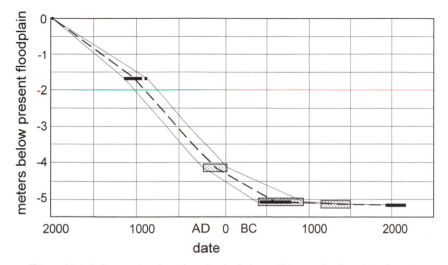

Figure 13-2 Sedimentation chronology for the Sakarya River at Gordion, from dates in Table 13-2. Horizontal bars show calendric conversions of two-sigma radiocarbon date ranges; shaded boxes show archaeological dates; dashed line (drawn within confidence envelope) presents simple model of alluviation.

Archaeobotanical evidence at Gordion supports a model of ongoing loss of complex vegetative cover between the Bronze Age and Medieval times (Miller 1993), loss that would account for accelerated erosion in the watersheds. Specific transitions are weakly dated, but the general picture shows loss of tree species and an increase in scrub. Concurrent decreases in the quality of timber in archaeological contexts—in burial mounds, for example (Young 1981)—support a model of ongoing deforestation.

Erosion is harder to date than deposition since the premier data are absences and inherently undateable. However, a fortuitous landscape marker, a Roman road, crosses the study region, offering an unusual dating opportunity. This road can be followed eastward from the floodplain edge at the mound to the upland crests 14 km away. Where preserved, the road is 6 m wide and bounded by curbs. The road may have had pre-Roman precursors, but its last form was built during the Roman occupation of central Anatolia, which began in earnest in the 1st century AD (Chapter 5 this volume). Maintenance of the road probably ended when Ancyra (modern Ankara) fell in AD 622 (Mitchell 1993).

In several places it is clear that dissection of the surrounding landscape postdated the abandonment of the road. Constituent blocks of the road have been rolled by energetic surface flow that had to have crossed places that are now deep gullies; thus gullies to 8 m deep must postdate the road. Numerous other deep gullies intersect the road in similar cross-cutting relationships. Generally these gullies, and many more across the landscape, have developed along beds of volcanically baked marl perpendicular to the direction of the larger, long-term local dissection of these pediments.

Small-stream Deposition

Depositional features made from recently eroded material encroach upon most of the smaller streams in this area. Valley fill has accumulated to a depth of 6 m in many places. Close to the edge of the uplands the stratigraphy of this alluvium is "coarse-over-fine" in texture, showing a long-term increase in local stream energy. This change probably correlates with a transition from early, slow sheet erosion of plowed soil to the later energetic gully cutting described above.

By the time these streams travel 2 or 3 km from the edge of the uplands, all coarse material has been removed from the alluvial system except within the actual stream channel. Floodplain material is nearly as fine here as when the streams reach the Sakarya plain, 6 km farther along.

Presently most streams are downcutting, and some streams have cut entirely new courses through nearby bedrock ridges. This downcutting and other related evidence indicate that sediment supplies have been decreasing in the recent past. In some higher basins, very little transportable soil remains after centuries of erosion, and relatively clean runoff is yielded quickly over bare rock. The walls of these valleys frequently show sherd-bearing, fine-grained floodplain fragments abandoned several meters above present stream level, documenting an entire historic episode of floodplain growth and decay.

Other factors besides depleted sediment supply may be at work in the present downcutting. Villagers report a recent decline in the intensity of sheep grazing. Non-linear stream reactions to climatic influences or other changes are also possible.

Decoupling of Deposition and Erosion

Comparing the evidence of these tributaries with the alluvial deposit of the river, one sees that erosion and deposition within the Sakarya basin seem to be poorly linked in time and in material form. The evidence of Figure 13-2 shows that the depositional rate has been roughly constant since the Iron Age, while local upland erosion probably increased significantly after AD 600. Also, the alluvial section of the Sakarya River shows a progressive fining of material since the Iron Age at the same time that the vigorous downcutting of later upland erosion mobilized increasingly large sized sediments. This disjunction is illustrated by the small-stream fans which show coarse material overlying fine—the reverse of the upwardly fining river stratigraphy.

This poor match between erosion and deposition may have two explanations. First, only a fraction of the sediment removed from the uplands is delivered to the river. The fans and floodplains near the uplands hold a sizable reservoir of sediment. The volume of sediment per km of channel in certain small tributaries may be as much as one quarter the volume of sediment stored along the very much larger Sakarya River. These smaller stream systems are also very effective at sorting out coarse sediment long before it reaches the river.

The second part of accounting for the decoupling between erosion and deposition is the depositional behavior of the Sakarya. An increasing amount of fine grain material in suspension in a river need not have a direct impact on the rate of aggradation (Schumm 1985). For example, the paleosol was formed by the Sakarya after it had a significant increase in its silt load ca. the Early Bronze Age. Yet the floodplain aggraded barely 10 cm over a thousand years and the river channel remained straight.

Later the river began to lay silt rapidly on the plain and to meander so vigorously that kilometers of city walls were completely removed, at a time when no obvious external change in erosion is observable. And thereafter the rate of aggradation remained roughly constant in spite of large increases in upland erosion after AD 600.

The overall picture shows the river had a straight course and was vertically stable through the early Holocene and into the early Iron Age, in spite of increasing sediment content. Then, after crossing some threshold, the river began to meander and aggrade. The river was then consistent again in spite of increasing sediment supply—aggrading at a near-constant rate.

The general point, that streams and the upland system may be poorly coupled, is an increasingly familiar theme in the study of removal efficiency of anthropogenic soil erosion, for example, in the U.S. interior after European agriculture arrived (Knox 1999). The present study extends that observation to a very different landscape and to a much longer time period.

HUMANS AND THE PHYSICAL LANDSCAPE

As in all cultural landscapes, human land use at Gordion was conditioned by differences in water, soil, and rock resources in different places and by the shape of the topography. The human impact on that land and those resources can be clearly documented at Gordion to reveal a progressive degradation of the land and an ongoing sedimentation of the streams and rivers.

The Gordion research shows two apparent occupation phases in the local upland erosion record that are not obvious in the river. The first is a Bronze Age silt increase that is barely apparent in the sedimentary column as the paleosol; the second is the large post-Roman erosion increase that is obvious from the erosion of the Roman road, but is hidden in the aggradation rate curve of Figure 13-2. At Gordion the changes in river level obviously affect the interpretation of the archaeology of the mound. Within the larger GRS study area, this geomorphic evidence helps to narrow the regions of interest for archaeological analysis to those upland surfaces that have not been eroded or buried since the time that archaeological material was laid on them. Within wider Anatolian archaeology, this study is cautionary against seeking to read upland events too closely from lowland data.

14

ETHNOGRAPHIC LESSONS FOR PAST AGRO-PASTORAL SYSTEMS IN THE SAKARYA-PORSUK VALLEYS

AYŞE GÜRSAN-SALZMANN

Were the farmer not to plant, the builder would not build and the weaver would not weave.
—Ibn Wahsiya, *The Nabatean Book of Agriculture* (in Watson 1983)

Research on living pastoralists in southwest Asia has proliferated in the last two decades. Using ethnographic and historical sources to supplement archaeological surveys of campsites we have gained insights into the pastoral component of ancient economies. Hole's (1979) pioneering work in Luristan, Iran, documented Tepe Tula'i as a prehistoric pastoral campsite and demonstrated the need to design guidelines derived in part from ethnographic observations to locate early pastoral sites. Although much has been learned since then about the archaeological correlates of pastoral behavior, especially the material indicators of pastoral sites and settlement patterns, more research lies ahead, particularly on the dynamics of pastoralists' interactions with the agricultural sector.

This chapter examines the process of transformation from a primarily pastoral to an agro-pastoral economy in the Sakarya-Porsuk River region of north-central Turkey over more than half a century. The ancient Phrygian capital of Gordion, Yassıhöyük, and other nearby villages provide the ethnographic context (Fig. 14-1). Contemporary economic strategies in the Gordion region vary significantly, reflecting, in part, responses to social and economic forces, primarily the availability of resources such as water and labor and the political decisions of local and state governments.

Our surveys, conducted in the region from 1995 to 2000, point to striking changes in the overall land-use patterns from 1925 to 2000, with a dramatic increase in agriculture and the shrinking amount of pastoral land. Despite the reduced numbers of animals, the present pastoral sector appears economically viable when examined by total yield per animal per household. This discussion links economic strategies to changes in the agro-pastoral landscape. We shall then present some implications from the ethnographic data in order to aid archaeologists in interpreting the dynamics of socioeconomic behaviors of the ancient peoples at Gordion.

The study examines a set of interlocking environmental and cultural parameters on a regional scale. The empirical data for this study include interactive

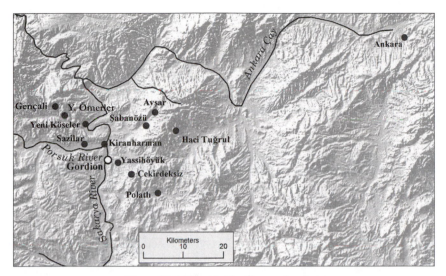

Figure 14-1 Yassıhöyük village and environs.

interviews with individuals and groups from 14 villages, in their native Turkish, land-use surveys, and historical records. The information should provide rich cultural insights that would not be directly observable in the archaeological record or clearly etched on the landscape, and it is therefore of value in building an ethnoarchaeological model of pastoralism.

ETHNOGRAPHIC CONTEXT

History of Settlement and Land Tenure

Pastoralism has long been a major component of the local economy in the Yassıhöyük region. Ottoman tax records from the 16th to 18th centuries, along with 19th century travelers' accounts, indicate large shipments of Angora wool textiles to France, Britain, and Holland. The wool was obtained from local village herders and manufactured in Ankara (Ergenç 1988:514–18; Hamilton 1842:418, 434; Leiser 1994:5–23).

The settlements in these valleys were sparse; at the turn of the 20th century a few families of Turkoman pastoralist ancestry (*Türkmen Yörügü*) settled at Yassıhöyük, and over time they became powerful feudal landlords [*aghas*]. As the land near the Sakarya River, teeming with wild boars, was cleared of thick stands of reeds for agricultural plots, herding was the major component of the economy. The Sakarya River's frequent flooding, which destroyed fields and caused malaria, forced the village to move to its present location (Fig. 14-2). Following World War I and the Turkish War of Independence (1919–21), new settlements formed in the region, carved from state-owned grazing territories, and settled by the ethnic Turkish populations arriving from the Balkans. By the 1920s, the population of

Figure 14-2 Views of (a) the Yassıhöyük-Ankara road, the main artery of the village. To the right is a partly finished extension of the coffeehouse (brick construction), and to the left is a demolished courtyard being restored.(b) An overview of the village from the minaret, looking west.

Yassıhöyük had grown to 12 households, largely from the immigration of shepherds from the northern province of Bolu, who worked as hired laborers for the *aghas*. The dramatic turning point, however, in the demise of herding came in late 1950s and early 1960s when American-made tractors became available as part of the Marshall Plan Aid. This prompted the Turkish government to initiate land reform, distributing arable and grazing lands to landless farmers in the low plain villages. In contrast to the low plain villages, land distribution in upland villages, where herding is more viable, proceeded at a slower pace. Today, the majority of upland village land is still State property, rented out to individual households.

Study Area: Landscape and Environmental Zones

The explicit aim of our survey (an area of ca. 600 km²) was to document changes in land use and to establish the distribution of contemporary farmland

*Figure 14-3 The volcanic hill Keçi Kalesi (goat fortress) west of the Sakarya River. Farmland
is at about 850 m, irrigated by the Porsuk River.*

and pastoral sites in the Gordion region in order to understand the changing
dynamics of farming and herding over the last half-century (Fig. 14-1).

The two rivers in the region, the Sakarya and the Porsuk, give life to the
valleys. The Porsuk joins the Sakarya a few km north of Gordion, continuing
northward to the Black Sea (for geological context see Chapter 13 this volume).

On the plateau east of the Sakarya are wide, flat upland valleys, rich with farmland
and encircled by majestic mountains. The terrain slopes gently with rolling hills and
is blessed with a few springs. In late spring and summer, shepherds take their herds
of sheep and goats onto high plateaus at 900–1400 m for grazing. Farmers practice
dry farming of cereals, legumes, sunflowers, and fruit trees. The western landscape
of the Porsuk-Sakarya presents a sharp contrast in its broken relief, denuded mesas,
and peaks of marl, except for the rejuvenated oak-juniper forest (Fig. 14-3). In the
foothills, caves provide shelter for the flocks year round (Fig. 14-4).

There are two broad environmental zones, the floodplain of Sakarya-Porsuk,
where Yassıhöyük—Gordion—is located, at 600–700 m, and the uplands, hilly
slopes/foothills at 900–1400 meters. The overall region is characterized by semi-arid
climate, hot and dry summers (18–25°C), and rainy, cold winters (-5 to 8°C). The annual
average rainfall in the region is 386 mm, variable annually and by elevation, falling
mainly in the winter and spring months, based on a 60-year average, 1931–91, at the
Polatlı District Meteorological Station. The amount of rainfall and its distribution
through the winter and spring months are critical to agricultural productivity. Some
villagers recalled cycles of droughts since the 1940s when they were forced to eat
dark barley bread and wild plants to supplement their diet.

Figure 14-4 Flock of sheep resting outside the cave shelter near the upland village of Ömerler, about 22 km northwest of Yassıhöyük village.

In the floodplain, earlier vegetation would have been a mix of juniper, pine, and oak (Miller 1999). Under current land use, trees and shrubs have receded above hilltops a distance of 20–50 km (Miller 1992). Except for the willows lining the springs and thick stands of reeds that grow by the rivers, herds of sheep and goats quickly eat a small shrub, *Artemisia* sp. (*yavsan otu*) and wild rue, *Peganum harmala* (*üzerlik otu*) in late spring and early summer. In upland areas, the vegetation shows gradual changes, from spiny legumes (varieties of *Astragalus*) to a more varied plant cover of fragrant wild oregano (much favored by the herds), oak, almond, walnut, wild pear, and rosehips.

Current Agriculture and Herding Strategies

Modern herders believe that herding provides a safety net against unpredictable crop disasters, that a pastoral economy can be profitable if "intelligently" combined with agriculture. Herds also provide ready cash needed for such important social and religious events as weddings, circumcisions, and children's education. One strategy is trade between the upland and lowland villages. In the rugged upland terrain, rain-fed barley grows well, carries little risk, and is harvested earlier than wheat. Surplus barley is thus produced for barter or cash exchange with lowland villages. The shortage of pasture in the lowlands encourages farmers to exchange their wheat for feed (barley). In the past, but less so today, this mechanism worked well among kin-related groups.

At present, the proportion of farmland to grazing land varies significantly between plain and upland villages (Table 14-1). At Yassıhöyük, a medium-sized

Table 14-1 Village Land and Proportions of Farmland
to Pasture Land (in hectares)

Location	Plain	Upland	
Village	Yassıhöyük	Şabanözü	Avsar
Land area	1,600	5,000	300
Number of households	82	350	9
Agriculture:grazing	4:1	1:2	1:2

village in the Polatlı province, all crops—including cereals, sugar beets, and onions—are irrigated, which cannot be done in the uplands.

Upland farming is labor intensive; it includes strict two-year fallowing of 50% of the arable land, multi-cropping, and partial use of animal manure in place of chemical fertilizers. Crops include sesame, cumin, and some legumes (lentil, chickpea, bean), which are well adapted to the cooler zones and alternately grown with cereals. Despite its hard labor and higher cost, upland farming helps to maintain the soil's fertility and moisture retention.

The use of irrigation and intensive mechanization, which replaced human and animal labor in the low plains in the 1950s, is not widespread in upland zones. To understand the emphasis on the pastoral economy in the upland zone, we need to consider such environmental and cultural factors as the inability to expand farmland due to rough topography, shortage of water, better herd management, and trade networks among villages. The last three factors are especially critical to the survival of a strong pastoral base. We may add to the list shepherds' pride in the herding tradition.

In upland villages animal husbandry is nearly 40% of the economy; households own an average of 50–75 animals, a higher number than in the plains. Herd management involves year-round grazing near mountain pastures at a distance of 3–13 km from the village. Although arduous, trekking enables the shepherd to exploit various grazing niches between 900 and 1,200 m. Each day, before sunset, the milking ewes are brought back to the village where they stay until the next morning's milking. The flock stays outdoors from mid-April to mid-December, when it is taken to enclosed winter sheepfolds (ağıls), near or in the village. In addition to Merino sheep, upland herders breed a fat-tailed, wooly sheep (Karaman), well adapted to colder climates and the rugged terrain. This pastoral rhythm is economical only if family members provide labor.

In Table 14-2, if we compare the low plain with upland villages in the proportion of grazing land to farmland, and grazing land to herd population, we see a wide gap that illustrates the importance of pastoral economy in upland villages. This is further corroborated by larger herd population per household. Data from the two upland villages suggest that they may closely approximate earlier stages of the Sakarya-Porsuk Valleys' pastoral landscape. A larger proportion of

Table 14-2 Comparisons of Low Plain with Upland Villages: Land Available for Agriculture and Grazing Activities, by Village and by Household (in hectares)

	Low plain Villages		Upland Villages	
	Yassıhöyük	Kıranharman	Hacı Tugrul	Yeni Köseler
Grazing:Agriculture (ha)	1:4	1:3	2.5:1	2:1
* Grazing:herd pop.	1:3.5	1:1	1.6:1	15:1
Herd population /HH	3.3	8.4	30	8.3
Arable land /HH	20	23	20	10.9

* amount of land available per head of sheep/goat

grazing land means lower food cost to maintain herds. Considering the yield in dairy products, herding appears to be more lucrative than agriculture in upland villages, if the cost of labor is overlooked.

According to villagers' accounts, in general, a family of five needs two hectares of land and 30 sheep plus a "modest surplus" for subsistence. Based on that, in upland villages, barley production, under reasonably good climatic conditions, would exceed the amount needed to sustain a household herd, so the sale or trade of the surplus could pay for part of essential needs such as industrial feed, salt, medicine, extra labor. Successful herd management in the upland villages lies in doubling the herd size annually and selling 70–80% of the male lambs/kids, old and sick animals.

In the pre-tractor period before 1950, inter-regional trade or exchange in crops and animal products was one of the ways in which balance in a regional economy could be attained. As one villager commented:

> in the 1930s and 1940s, farmers from Çalcı, Aydın [a town on the Aegean coast 350 km to the west], brought *kilim*, grapes, figs, and olives to exchange for cheese from Yassıhöyük. They produced and ate a lot of molasses [*pekmez*], and they had to balance their diet by eating salty cheese which they bought from us. (Gürsan-Salzmann 1996 field notes)

Pride in the pastoral tradition is one of the driving forces behind its endurance. In the words of an elderly shepherd, Hacı Ismail:

> it comes from the family—if your great-grandfather and grandfather were big herd owners, in other words a pastoral *Agha*, it becomes part of your identity, almost a family symbol. Even if it is an unprofitable preoccupation, just having herds around provides emotional satisfaction. There have been herd owners who died after selling their herds. The combination of sheepdogs, sheep and goats, and shepherd is a whole culture. Shepherding is a total way of life. (Gürsan-Salzmann 1995 field notes; see Fig.14-5)

Figure 14-5 Hacı Ismail, an 89-year-old shepherd, still supervises the family herds, which now belong to his three sons, during the 2½ months of high plateau (yayla) grazing, at Köroglu Yaylası, near Bolu province.

To Hacı Ismail, animal husbandry represented power, good judgment, and thrift.

Changing Land Use and Spatial Organization of Herding Sites

The shift from a primarily pastoral economy to one based on mixed agro-pastoral farming at Yassıhöyük in the late '50s and early '60s serves as a useful model for understanding the process of transition in the economy of ancient Gordion. Currently agriculture is expanding into areas of gentle slopes and rolling hills (Figs. 14-6a and 14-7a). Areas targeted for farming are alongside perennial

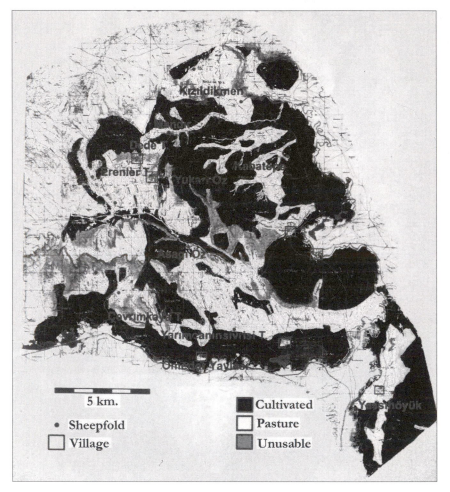

*Figure 14-6a Western portion of surveyed area and modern period distribution
of agricultural and grazing lands.*

sources of water and valleys that connect those sources, formerly used exclusively
for pasture (Figs. 14-6b and 14-7b). Pastureland is currently limited to narrow
cliff slopes and pockets of upland plains. In the surveyed area, the present ratio
of farming to grazing is ca. 2:1. Pre-1950, this ratio may have been reversed, when
regional herd size was nearly 15 times that of today.

Pastoral Sites

We mapped and documented 85 sheep/goat folds, corrals, and herd
catchments in the Sakarya-Porsuk Valleys. The distribution of the abandoned and
living pastoral sites across the landscape and their structural features provide insight

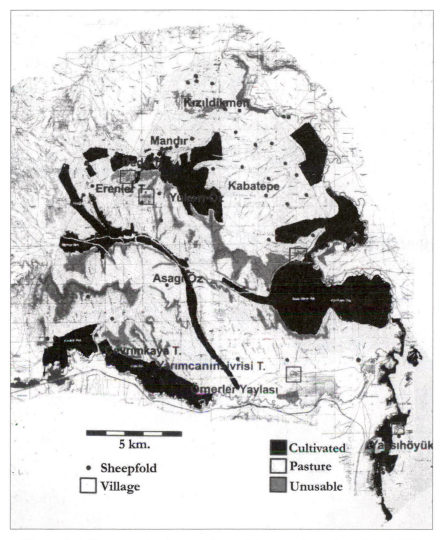

Figure 14-6b Western portion of surveyed area of the pre-mechanized period (pre-1950s) distribution of agricultural and grazing lands.

into the dynamics of changing land use in the region and help us recognize the material traces of the "ephemeral" pastoral economy in the archaeological record. Both survey evidence and historical records indicate the rich pastoral potential of the larger region. Until the 1940s, in an area of 100,000 hectares, a conservative estimate of 500,000 sheep and goats could be sustained (Archives of Village Affairs, Polatlı District). This population of animals would fit within the enclosures identified and measured in our survey. Over the last 60 years, the sheep/goat population has decreased by 50%.

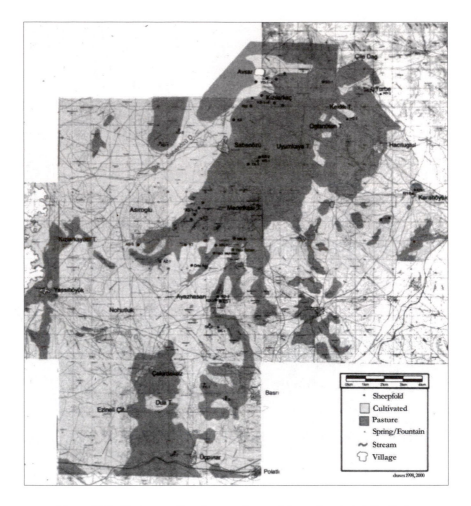

Figure 14-7a Eastern portion of surveyed area of the modern period distribution of agricultural and grazing lands.

Several types of pastoral sites were recorded:

Sheepfold (ağıl) complex, consisting of a roofed structure adjacent to an unroofed enclosure, a shepherd's hut which sometimes doubles as a feed storage space, used year round (Fig. 14-8);

Corral (yatak yeri), an open enclosure often on a raised earth platform, sometimes surrounded by stones, used summer and fall;

Windbreak (rüzgarlık), an open stone enclosure, 50–75 cm high, to protect young ewes and lambs from cold winds on summer nights;

Milking station (mandıra), an open enclosure for milking, like a corral; generally

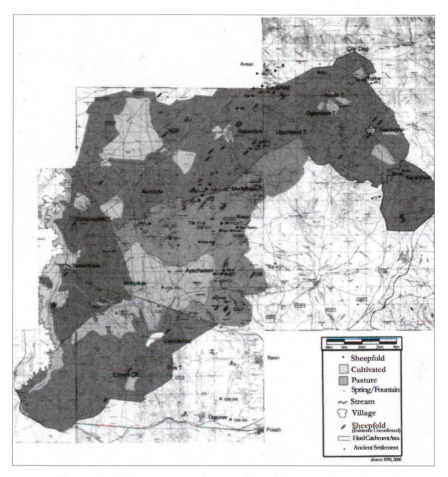

Figure 14-7b Eastern portion of surveyed area. The pre-mechanized period (pre-1950s) distribution of agricultural and grazing lands.

close to villages, used in summer (Fig. 14-9);

Herd Catchment locations (Çoban Tepeleri), a water hole or a shaded area where several flocks are gathered before they set out for daily grazing, a rest stop, shearing place, yearly use.

Folds, Locations, and Land Use

According to the elderly shepherds, a minimum of four variables are necessary for choosing a fold location: (1) animals' nutritional needs, (2) protection from natural disasters (snow, wolves, floods); (3) protection from thieves; and (4) the distance from village/farmland. Sheepfolds are generally built on an incline to

Figure 14-8 Fold (ağıl), *near Gençali village, west of Sakarya, at 900 m. Typically built on a hillside, protected from strong winds, this* ağıl *is near another (Fig. 14-11) which belongs to the same extended kin group. The fold is semi-abandoned with weeds already spreading over the ground. The roofed area has many divisions: two unroofed sections, one for goats, another for sheep.*

Figure 14-9 *Milking station located in the unroofed area of a fold. While women do the milking twice a day, men do the tying of the sheep, with each head opposite the other, so they will stay still.*

Figure 14-10 A fold abandoned c. 1995 near the highland village of Ömerler. The surrounding fields are taking over another fold which is only 300 m from the abandoned one, the only remains of which is the stone enclosure wall.

enable rain run off, facing south, away from northerly winds. Favored locations are on high plains at 950–1,200 m where agricultural land is marginal, and preferably on the side of a steep valley, separated from other sheepfolds by a ridge barrier. Ridges form physical boundaries between folds to keep and guide each flock of sheep in a different pasture, which also minimizes conflict between shepherds and prevents overgrazing. Natural caves and steep hillsides backed by natural rock are also ideal locations, providing protection from winds and predators. The herd size in an upland village can be as large as 3,000 animals, nearly double the size of flocks on the plains, and the grazing radius can be 1–10 km from the folds (likely closer in the past). In upland villages where the terrain is more rugged, animals get exhausted quickly, and catchment locations are more common. In the low plains, agriculture has erased many of the older sheepfolds near villages, leaving behind a few stones, dung heaps, and disturbed plant growth (Fig. 14-10).

Architecture

Folds vary little in architectural features, except size and spatial organization. Construction materials include stones, mudbrick, and reeds. Reeds are used where wood is unavailable for fencing and room divisions. The roof beams are covered with straw and reeds which, in turn, are plastered with mud.

The fold typically faces south and has a uniform plan: a long, roughly rectangular/L-shaped building with roofed and unroofed sections. The roofed area, held up by wide beams of poplar, is walled on three sides (Fig. 14-11). It can be divided into individualized spaces by portable wooden dividers to accommodate

Figure 14-11 The Akça sheepfold is ca. 2 km from the village of Gençali in the western Sakarya zone, 26 km northwest of Yassıhöyük. It is 125 years old and accommodates 700 animals. The roofed part of this fold has a very thick stone wall; the original builders made small rooms, with wide interior dividing walls of wide upright blocks. The shepherd's hut is at the far end.

nursing lambs and aggressive rams. The open front faces a circular pen (*salak*) where the sheep/goats sleep at night in summertime (Fig. 14-8). A fold can shelter an average of 400 animals under roofed space and can hold 800 in the unroofed pen. (The largest fold, KB-3 measures 850 m², accommodates 1,200 animals; Fig. 14-12). The rest of the complex includes a storage room for hay and feed, a doghouse, and a shepherd's hut. The floors of the fold and pen are thick with animal dung, which the owner periodically scrapes up to use as fertilizer or fuel (dung cakes). Up until the 1970s, when the Angora goat was still popular and economically feasible to herd, goats were kept in separate folds in cave enclosures on high, rocky terrain perfectly suited to the goats' rock climbing behavior (Fig. 14-13).

The shepherd's one-room hut is a freestanding structure strategically placed to view the fold, its roof supported by a large central beam. A fireplace with a chimney is directly across from the entrance. Among the artifacts are an oil lamp, teapot, fork, and spoon on wooden shelves next to the fireplace. The shepherd's wool bedding sits on a raised platform, and his bags of food hang from the ceiling. The floor is fitted with fieldstones or packed mud. If the room is also used for storage, bales of wool, lamb feed, and barley balls (dog food) are stacked in a corner.

Outside the fold are some tractor tires, old agricultural tools, and wooden feeding troughs. The most visible organic deposits are strands of wool, dung, and heaps of hay.

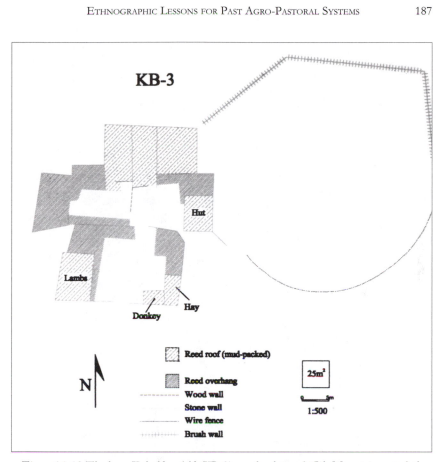

Figure 14-12 The large Kabaldere fold (KB-3), on the slopes of Çile Mountain east of the Sakarya, is located about 100 m from the streambed and covers an area of 850 m².

ARCHAEOLOGICAL IMPLICATIONS AND CONCLUSIONS

This study shows that ethnographic evidence can aid in archaeological interpretation. The modern agro-pastoral activities near Gordion may represent an integrated economic system not too dissimilar from those in the past. Using our survey evidence, we can address questions of how and why a variety of economic strategies are used in a region by farmers/herders to procure food in a rural household context.

Archaeological indicators of pastoralism can be identified in courtyards, pastoral sites, and organic deposits. The size of the folds and their material remains shed light on the size of the animal population, their productive yields, and, indirectly, the size of the human populations. The proximity of some pastoral sites to ancient settlements suggests that pastoral site locations might aid in locating other ancient settlements. And, conversely, the topographic and hydrological patterns in the landscape can be good indicators of pastoral activity areas such as folds and windbreaks.

*Figure 14-13 The famous Angora goat with its long, silken coat,
on the high plateau of Köroglu Yayla, near Bolu.*

Patterns of land use vary within the region according to both cultural and environmental variables: population size, availability of labor, regional trade, government regulation, soils, land forms, and precipitation. The variability and complexity of these patterns over the 20th century suggests that ancient populations, including the Phrygians, would also have had a rich and diverse set of economic choices.

Based on both the ethnographic evidence presented here and archaeological evidence from Gordion, pastoralism was a significant component of Phrygian society (see Chapter 6 this volume). A heavy investment in an agro-pastoral economy, with large flocks, would have put pressure on natural pastures. These pressures might have resulted in exploitation of different environmental zones by competing herders and eventually led to overgrazing. Geomorphic evidence suggests that upland erosion patterns increased significantly several times in the past (see Chapters 11 and 13 this volume), possibly related to changing investment in a pastoral economy.

If the past and the present are to shed light on the future of the agro-pastoral economy in the Sakarya-Porsuk Valleys, agricultural expansion with a concomitant loss of grazing is clearly inevitable. However, modern farmers are optimistic that the pastoral economy will become increasingly profitable as they are increasingly linked to the world market and as they acquire better entrepreneurial skills to sell their products. While today's economic conditions are very different from those of the past, extra-local interaction would, undoubtedly, have shaped pastoral economies in the past.

IV CONSERVING GORDION AND ITS ARTIFACTS

15

SUPPORT AND CONSERVE
Conservation and Environmental Monitoring of the Tomb Chamber of Tumulus MM

RICHARD F. LIEBHART AND JESSICA S. JOHNSON

The burial mound known as Tumulus MM is by far the largest of approximately 80 tumuli around Gordion marking the burials of the Phrygian elite. Excavated by Rodney Young in 1957, the tumulus has since been developed by the Turkish authorities as an archaeological attraction for some 40,000 local and foreign visitors each year. The tumulus itself currently stands about 53 m high, and it contains a wooden tomb chamber that is approximately 2,700 years old and is considered to be the oldest standing wooden building in the world (Fig. 15-1; Young 1981).

Although traditionally Tumulus MM ("Midas Mound") has been associated with the legendary King Midas, recent analysis dates it to ca. 740 BC—too early for the burial of Midas, who died near the end of the century (DeVries et al. 2003). Midas, most likely, built Tumulus MM for his father. Whoever the actual occupant, that Tumulus MM was created for a Phrygian king seems beyond dispute: it is the largest of the tomb chambers thus far excavated; it has a double pitched roof unlike the flat roofs in other tumuli; its grave goods were more numerous and expensive than those of other tombs; and finally, the tumulus that covered the tomb chamber was over twice as high as any other tumulus in the area. In recent years, archaeologists and conservators have worked on a series of projects to improve the documentation and interpretation of the tomb construction, to create an improved support structure, and to define the current environmental parameters affecting the long-term preservation of the chamber. A brief account of its unique construction and excavation provides a foundation for understanding the current project. The excavation and construction of the tomb is described in Rodney Young's (1981) posthumous volume on the *Three Great Early Tumuli*; while certain construction details there are wrong, the basic outline remains the same.

CONSTRUCTION

The Phrygians began MM tomb construction (Figs. 15-2, 15-3) by digging a roughly rectangular foundation pit about 2 m deep, which was then lined with soft limestone blocks and filled with rubble. The tomb chamber measured 5.1 m x 6.2 m and was constructed of well-finished squared pine timbers, with a

Figure 15-1 View of Tumulus MM.

double-pitched roof supported by three sets of beams stacked in pairs and trimmed to the proper angle. The pine timbers were held by a system of notched joints designed to withstand the inward pressure of the tumulus which would cover the tomb. Surrounding the pine tomb chamber was an outer casing of rough juniper logs, set about 0.5 m out from the chamber walls. Stone cobbles filled the area between the pine tomb chamber and the outer casing and between the outer casing and a stone perimeter wall (the continuation of the lining of the sides of the foundation pit). The entire structure was raised level by level, with the stone cobbles holding the juniper logs in place and the stone perimeter wall held by the surrounding fill of the tumulus which was being built at the same time.

The burial of the king took place before the placement of the pine roof timbers, which sealed the tomb. A mound of stones covered the tomb chamber complex, and the earthen tumulus was extended upward to a height even greater than its current 53 m. The tumulus sealed the wooden tomb and created a dry, cave-like environment that protected the wood from biological attack, with only a slow-acting soft rot fungus able to cause any serious damage to the wood in the next 2,700 years. Although the fungus weakened the timbers, it did not ultimately destroy them: today most feel solid to the touch, while portions of some timbers are soft and powdery.

Upon its completion, Tumulus MM contained over 3,500,000 m^3 of earth which once covered hundreds of stone blocks, millions of rough cobbles, over 180 wooden timbers, a vast array of grave goods, and the body of one man.

EXCAVATION

In 1955 and 1956, based on his experience excavating smaller tumuli, R. S. Young used a water-assisted drill to locate the stone packing the excavators expected to find over the tomb chamber in Tumulus MM. Unfortunately, as the drillers were delimiting the boundaries of the stone packing, the water that was supposed to recirculate back out through the hole was instead dumped into the stone packing, soaking the tomb and its contents.

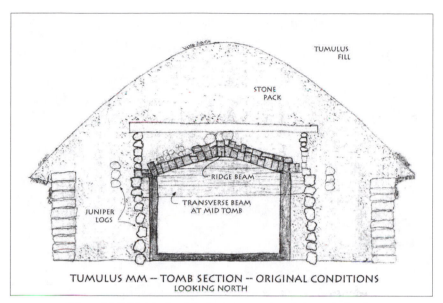

TUMULUS
FILL

STONE
PACK

RIDGE BEAM

TRANSVERSE BEAM
AT MID TOMB

JUNIPER
LOGS

*Figure 15-2 Sketch of original west-east section of the tomb chamber
and surrounding stone wall. After a drawing by Conor Power.*

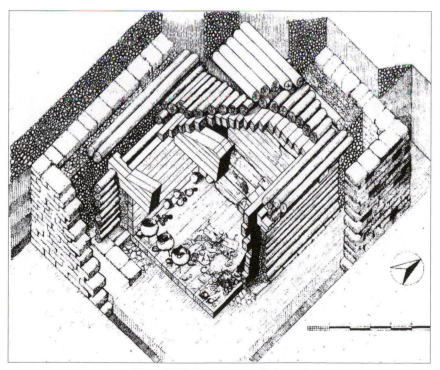

Figure 15-3 Cutaway view of the tomb.

Actual excavations of Tumulus MM took place in 1957 by means of an open trench through the erosion slump, and then through a tunnel 70 m long dug along the ancient ground level (Fig. 15-4). This opening now provides the visitors' approach to the tomb chamber. When the excavators breached the stone perimeter wall, they were greeted by a shower of stone cobbles that took seven days to remove. Above them was a clay dome formed by the great weight of the tumulus compressing the clay immediately above the stone packing (the clay dome is still intact, though the excavation team was never certain if it would collapse as they worked underneath). The excavators then cut through the outer casing of juniper logs, only to remove more cobble packing. When a hole was cut through the final wall of squared pine timbers, Young found himself literally at the feet of the dead king, whose bones stretched out before him on the remains of a hollowed-out cedar log.

Initial Efforts at Preservation

One immediate concern for the excavators was keeping the tomb chamber standing. Upon entering the tomb, Young found the central cross-beam system sagging badly, with the lower two of its four members cracked. A temporary wooden prop was added, later replaced by a series of steel I-beams and posts resting directly on the original wooden floor.

The construction of the tomb was designed to prevent the inward collapse of the roof and walls, but with the removal of the rubble packing around the tomb,

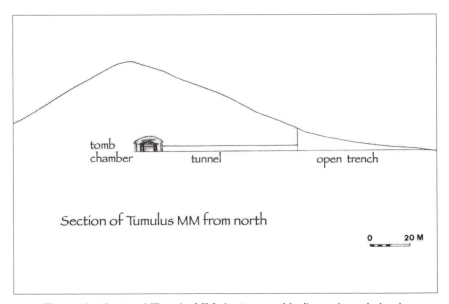

Figure 15-4 Section of Tumulus MM showing tunnel leading to the tomb chamber.

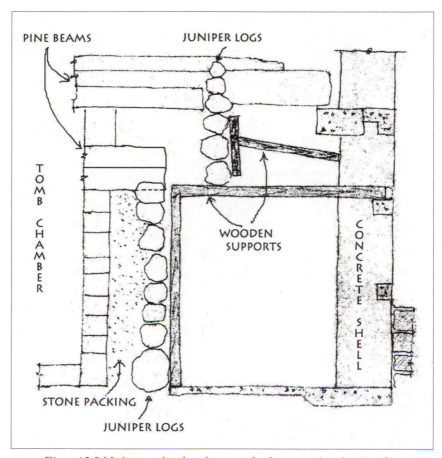

Figure 15-5 Modern wood and steel supports for the outer casing of juniper logs. After a drawing by Conor Power.

the timbers were in danger of falling outward. Wooden braces had to be added to hold them in place as the stones were removed. The upper levels of juniper logs were set out from the tomb chamber, also requiring support from below. Wooden support posts and beams were later augmented by steel I-beams, though these only supported the vertical loads of the upper juniper logs (Fig. 15-5).

The floor inside the tomb was found covered with collapsed furniture, bronze fibulae, and bronze vessels in many shapes and sizes. Young was sobered by the realization that the tomb had been soaked from the water dumped from the drilling operation and that there was even water standing in some of the bronze bowls resting on the floor. As the team documented and cleared the tomb chamber, they noticed cracks appearing in the now-drying walls. In an effort to slow the drying process and minimize damage, the archaeologists brushed boiled linseed oil onto the surface of the wood (though this primarily served to darken the wood and make its surface more difficult to inspect).

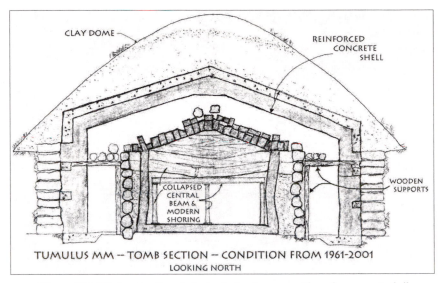

Figure 15-6 West-east section of the tomb chamber area with modern concrete shell and early supports. After a drawing by Conor Power.

In 1960, a reinforced concrete shell was built above the tomb to protect the chamber from any collapse of the clay dome. The concrete roof is supported by concrete pilasters that also buttress the perimeter stone wall and help prevent wall collapse (Fig. 15-6). The pilasters are connected by a series of concrete "shelves" poured against the faces of the stone perimeter walls. A thin concrete floor was poured between the stone perimeter wall and the outer casing of juniper logs.

While serving ultimately to protect and preserve the tomb chamber, this operation caused some immediate damage. The concrete formwork created a forest of modern timbers and caused some physical damage to the ancient wood, mostly dents and chips. Much more serious was the introduction of a white rot fungus with the modern wood. With the tremendous rise in humidity in the tomb caused by the water used in mixing the concrete, this new fungus spread rapidly over the tomb. Though now inactive, the fungus left whitish mycelium remains over much of the interior of the tomb chamber roof and upper walls.

In 1963, the trench and the tunnel leading to the tomb chamber were lined with concrete and stone. A vented stone wall with a metal door was installed at the outer end of the tunnel and a metal screen and gate were built a few meters away at the end of the trench leading up to the tunnel. Visitors are kept a little over a meter away from the outer casing of the tomb by a metal grill, with electric lights providing a view of the northwest corner of the tomb and its interior.

Excavation and subsequent efforts to preserve and protect it caused some obvious structural damage to the tomb. Most of this went largely undocumented. The actual physical condition of the tomb was never described in detail, nor was complete photographic documentation ever carried out. The tomb became a major part of every visitor's trip to Gordion, but it was not until the 1980s that the tomb chamber once again became a major concern. Recent work in the tomb chamber has resulted in both the development of a system for monitoring the building's structural stability and the design and installation of a new support system for the ancient logs.

STRUCTURAL MONITORING

With the renewal of excavations at Gordion in 1988 came a renewed interest in Tumulus MM and its wooden tomb chamber. Elizabeth Simpson, of the Bard Graduate Center for Studies in the Decorative Arts, was first to inspect the condition of the tomb in connection with her work on the wooden furniture from MM and elsewhere at Gordion. She first brought plant pathologist Robert Blanchette, of the University of Minnesota, to study fungal damage in the tomb. Later, then Director of Conservation Stephen Koob, of the Corning Museum of Glass, installed glass-and-plaster crack monitors at various locations in order to detect movement in the walls. The modern concrete shell around the tomb was professionally inspected and judged sound. In 1990, Richard Liebhart began an architectural study of the tomb chamber and quickly became aware of the precarious condition of many portions of the tomb and of the deficiencies of the support system.

In 1993, a conference on the ancient wood from Gordion—including conservators, structural engineers, architects, and archaeologists—led to pivotal efforts to preserve the tomb. One of the structural engineers, Conor Power of Structural Technologies in Boston, has remained active in developing the plans for monitoring and maintaining the structural aspects of the tomb chamber. On Power's advice, Liebhart undertook a more extensive program of photographic documentation and introduced several new methods of monitoring the structural stability.

Because of the lack of sufficient early documentation of the tomb, the only method to evaluate changes in the tomb was to study the few photographs taken in 1957 showing various portions of the tomb. This comparison suggests that the interior walls of the tomb chamber have remained stable since excavation. To monitor accurately the structural stability of the tomb chamber, plumb lines were installed along the north and south interior walls. Measurements between the plumb lines and the joints in adjacent wall beams were recorded. Similar measurements were recorded from points on the inner walls and outer casing to fixed points on the vertical steel beams and on some of the concrete pilasters. To date, none of these measurements has changed significantly, indicating that the tomb interior has remained stable at least since monitoring began.

In 1994, four calibrated telltales were installed to monitor movement in the spaces between the logs at each corner of the outer casing (Fig. 15-7). When checked during the next summer, the telltales showed no appreciable movement, so it was assumed that the outer casing was stable, just as plumb lines indicated for the interior walls. However, checking during an unplanned, off-season visit

Figure 15-7 Calibrated telltales at the northwest corner of the outer casing of the wooden tomb.

to Gordion in 1996, the two plates at the northwest corner of the tomb had moved apart approximately 1 cm. Three months later, the plates were back flush and reading the same on the graph as the summer before. A second telltale was added at this corner to measure the movement in the direction perpendicular to the movement monitored by the original telltale. All of these telltales, along with the plumb lines, selected fixed-point vertical measurements, temperature, and humidity are now checked monthly by the Gordion Museum staff.

The environmental monitoring, discussed below, shows that late summer marks the highest moisture levels in the tomb, with late March/early April marking the lowest. It appears that the ends of the 2,700-year-old juniper logs are bending outward slightly as the moisture level in the tomb declines (late winter/early spring). In contrast, the interior pine walls appear to remain stable throughout the year, possibly because of their less dense cellular structure or the fact that the construction of the tomb chamber prevents any seasonal movement. The tomb environment continues to affect the wood, making careful analysis of humidity and temperature changes essential in developing plans for long-term preservation. All of these issues were considered during the development of the new support system for the juniper logs of the outer casing that was installed in 2002.

ENVIRONMENTAL MONITORING AND STUDY

Monitoring of temperature and humidity in the tomb began in the early 1980s using mechanical hygrothermographs, installed by then director Keith DeVries in and around the tomb chamber. More recently, the use of battery-powered electronic dataloggers allows more accurate monitoring of the tomb environment. Jessica Johnson, former head of the Gordion Objects Conservation Program, has been analyzing the data from the hygrothermographs and the dataloggers. While complete documentation of this work is still in process, preliminary results show a number of trends that directly relate to the structural preservation of the tomb.

Because of logistical problems, the data from the hygrothermographs can only be used to evaluate trends in the fluctuations of temperature and relative humidity and cannot give exact environmental conditions. Despite these difficulties, the data clearly show seasonal variations in the conditions inside the tomb. Since the temperature inside the tomb chamber ranges only from about 12.5-15.5 °C throughout the year, the calculated absolute humidity levels (AH equals the weight of water in a defined space) are more useful than the relative humidity (RH) collected by the instruments. Figure 15-8 shows the average absolute humidity inside the tomb chamber from hygrothermographic data collected between 1993 and 1996 compared to the average absolute humidity in the region from 1930 to 1970. The amount of water inside the tomb chamber rises and falls in a pattern similar to that seen in

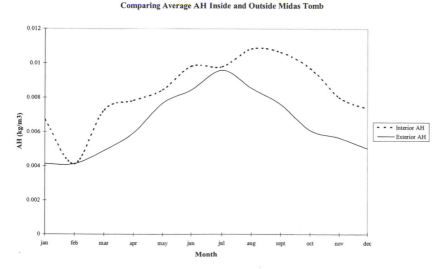

Comparing Average AH Inside and Outside Midas Tomb

Figure 15-8 Graph of absolute humidity in the tomb (1993-96) versus monthly average absolute humidity in Anatolia (1930-70). Data for exterior are taken from Ortalama ve Kıymetler Meteoroloji Bülteni, Devlet Meteoroloji Genel Müdürlüğü (1974). Data for interior is from Gordion Project hygrothermographs.

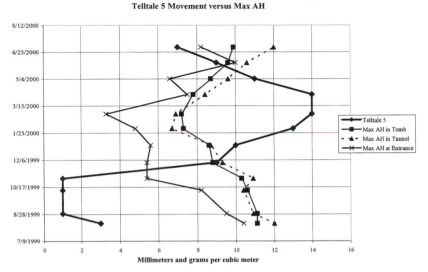

Figure 15-9 Graph of absolute humidity in the tomb versus movement of Telltale 5
at the northwest corner of the outer casing.

the outside environment. There also appears to be more moisture inside the tomb chamber than outside. The sources of this moisture are unknown, but might be due to variations in ground water levels, human activity (breath and perspiration), or even to accumulated dust on the hygrothermographs themselves. In 1997, to further investigate how the AH variation in the tomb related to the AH outside, the Gordion Objects Conservation Program placed electronic dataloggers in three positions: at the outer entrance to the tunnel, directly exposed to the outside air but protected from rain and snow; halfway down the tunnel; and near the interior gate on a log at the northwest exterior corner of the outer casing. Plate 7 shows how the wide ranges in AH outside the tomb (even buffered by the concrete roof) are minimized halfway down the tunnel to about the same level as inside the tomb chamber.

The variations in absolute humidity throughout the year appear to explain the previously documented movement of the juniper logs of the outer casing. Figure 15-9 shows the direct correlation between the AH at the northwest exterior corner of the tomb chamber and movement of the wooden timbers monitored at the same corner. As the AH decreases during the winter months the end of the beam moves out; as the AH rises in the spring and summer the end of the beam moves back to the original location.

There is no present indication that changing the environment of the tomb would be worth the risk of damage caused by the inevitable unintended consequences of such a change. Continued monitoring will show if intervention will be required. The fungus that has damaged the wood over the centuries is inactive, and while humidity levels reach higher-than-desired levels in late summer, the humidity levels during most of the year are well below that at which fungi can grow.

CURRENT RESIDENTS

During examination and documentation of the tomb chamber, beginning in 1990, a tiny insect was noticed on one of the juniper logs of the outer casing. This disturbing discovery led to a systematic investigation of the presence of any potentially harmful insect life in the chamber. Between 1993 and 1999, non-toxic insect sticky traps were installed in order to capture any insects living in the vicinity. These traps were placed inside the tomb chamber, on the juniper logs, on the concrete floor, and in the upper part of the concrete shell around the tomb. They were in place for about eleven months before replacement.

Chris Durden, entomologist from the University of Texas at Austin, identified the insects collected in 1993. Conservation staff did all subsequent identifications. A variety of individual insects was found, including a few carabid beetles which are carnivorous, tenebrionid beetles that eat seeds and fungus, various species of flies and moths, and spiders. Usually these species number fewer than ten individuals per annum and appear to be nuisance species brought in with human visitors.

In contrast, a species of psocid, which eats fungus, is common, and upwards of 100 individuals were often found in single traps. Commonly known as booklice, they are often found in libraries feeding on fungus growing on the paper in books. This discovery created some concern that the fungus was active in the wooden chamber, but it appears that many more psocids are found on the concrete floor and ledges around the chamber. These areas are dirty and dusty and may harbor mold growth that is not occurring on the wood. In addition, mold fruiting bodies have been found on the sticky traps and may be a food source for the psocids.

The annual number of trapped psocids indicates that a self-perpetuating population lives around the tomb chamber, but there is no evidence that they are feeding on wood mold. No insects that directly feed on wood were found. Insect monitoring was suspended in 2000, in part because of the mold growth found on the cardboard traps and in part because the captured insects apparently attracted mice into the area. The latter residents are trapped and removed whenever their presence is noted.

NEW STRUCTURAL SUPPORTS

By the mid 1960s, the tomb had received all the structural support and protection it would get for the next 30 years. While the project engineers have deemed replacement of the steel supports for the central cross-beam system inside the tomb chamber desirable, it is not considered to be immediately necessary. The supports outside the tomb chamber were another matter, and in 2002 an entirely new system for the outer casing was installed.

The design of this new system began in earnest with Conor Power's work after the conference in 1993. Ural Engineering of Ankara was in charge of the final engineering, designs, and installation. Liebhart, contractor Nejat Sert

Figure 15-10 New steel support system for the outer casing.

from Ankara, and a Turkish crew of four carried out the actual installation on site.

The basic concept for each new brace is the creation of a rigid frame anchored by the reinforced concrete shell that surrounds the tomb chamber. Each frame consists of a new concrete footer cast in place against the foundations of the concrete shell, a steel post bolted onto a plate cast into the new foundation, a beam bolted onto the top of the post at one end and onto the concrete shell at the other, and a series of adjustable arms with flexible heads that support each juniper log (Fig. 15-10). The heads on the adjustable arms are fitted with neoprene pads to allow for continued seasonal movement of the juniper logs. An inert membrane ("Marvelseal") provides a barrier between the neoprene and the ancient wood. Tension rods were added near the junctions of the main posts and beams to prevent lateral movement on the upper corners of the frames during a low-level earthquake.

The Future of the Tomb Chamber of Tumulus MM

The unique nature of this monument cannot be overstated. No other excavated wooden Phrygian tomb is as well preserved, nor are the remains of any other still accessible. From all the other tombs excavated, only a few fragments of wood have survived. No known comparable extant wooden monument from any other culture exists.

The oldest standing wooden building in the world implies several levels of responsibility for its preservation. We would have known nothing of its special nature had it not been excavated in 1957, yet that very excavation exposed the tomb to a whole new set of threats to its existence. For more than four decades American and Turkish archaeologists, architects, engineers, scientists, and conservators have worked to keep it standing. The recent studies discussed here have created a detailed understanding of the tomb. Nevertheless, the monitoring of the tomb is an ongoing project that should never be allowed to lapse. Any future intervention should be based on the cumulative data and the collective knowledge of those studying the tomb. As an organic structure, the tomb chamber of Tumulus MM cannot be expected to last forever, but it is our responsibility to preserve it to the best of our ability for future generations.

16

RECENT CONSERVATION RESEARCH

Soluble Salts in Gordion Ceramics

JULIE UNRUH AND JESSICA S. JOHNSON

Each time archaeologists excavate artifacts from the earth—be they ceramic sherds, bone or ivory decorations, faunal remains, copper jewelry, iron tools, burnt wooden furniture or any of a multitude of other materials—they remove them from an environment where they have lain safely for decades to millennia. The excavation process is inherently disruptive, destroying both the layers of information preserved in the soil and the environment that has preserved artifacts and structures. Archaeological methods attempt to document as much information as possible, so that materials can be interpreted now and in the future.

The objects or artifacts are another record that remains, and in order to clean and preserve them for analysis, as well as to make them available for exhibit and other more general public educational programs, archaeological conservators work on-site alongside the archaeologists at Gordion.

If not monitored and minimized, agents of deterioration (such as temperature and humidity variation and poor-quality storage) can lead to the loss of artifacts either soon after excavation or over decades in storage. A number of textbooks have been written about archaeological conservation (Cronyn 1990, Payton 1992, Sease 1988), and the organization and techniques of the Gordion Objects Conservation Program have been described previously (Johnson et al. 1996). This chapter focuses on research being conducted at Gordion that combines the practicalities of field conservation with a scientific approach to identifying better methods for preserving one major type of material excavated worldwide—ceramics.

Excavations at Gordion over more than 50 years have recovered massive amounts of ceramics, both as whole pots and as individual sherds. Numerous researchers have used these abundant collections to investigate such topics as technology, trade, economics, ethnicity, and artistic tradition (e.g., DeVries 1993; Henrickson 1993; Chapters 4 and 10 this volume). Since 1988, in addition to improving basic storage and treatment, conservators have been investigating sources of one agent of deterioration known as "soluble salts."

All groundwater contains hydrous or soluble salts. Soluble salts are chemical compounds, such as sodium chloride (table salt), that dissociate in water. When they dry, soluble salts become crystalline solids. However, with the addition of water or water vapor, they become liquid salt solutions again. Soluble salt levels in groundwater are generally higher in arid regions as well as in areas where agricultural fertilizer and irrigation are used, such as the environment around Gordion (Dregne 1976).

Figure 16-1 Salts efflorescence on ceramics and spalling slip.

If soluble salts remained in their solid state, they would not cause damage, but, when dissolved in groundwater, soluble salts flow into any porous material that is buried. In this way, archaeological structures and artifacts become salt contaminated. Once the salts have entered artifacts, they migrate within the artifact while dissolved, and become crystallized again when dry. Some salts expand up to 300% during crystallization; the pressures generated by these growing and shrinking salts can be up to 2,000 times normal atmospheric pressure. This pressure can cause substantial damage to ceramics.

Soluble salts are one of the worst agents of destruction of excavated archaeological ceramics. They dissolve at different relative humidities, depending on the exact chemical composition of the salts. If the relative humidity in a storage area fluctuates above and below the humidities at which the salts in the ceramics dissolve, the cycle of crystallization and decrystallization will continue. If this happens, eventually the ceramic will disintegrate. Certain physical characteristics of ceramics—including surface finish and small variations in rim, handle, and foot shapes—are diagnostic features that aid in identification of the date and provenience of the ceramic that can be lost due to soluble salts damage. Warning signs of a soluble salt problem include a white haze or crystals forming on the surface (salt efflorescence), lifting and dissociating slips or glazes, and powdery, fragile ceramic surfaces (Fig. 16-1).

A conservation treatment called desalination removes soluble salts from ceramics. While no "best" method has been determined, over time a standard conservation treatment procedure has evolved. The ceramic is immersed in a bath of clean water. The soluble salts in the ceramic dissolve and migrate out of the ceramic into the clean water. The salinity of the bath water is usually monitored using a conductivity meter, which measures to what degree the water conducts an electrical current. The more dissolved salts in the water, the higher the reading. After waiting a period of time, the bath water is replaced with clean water, and the emerging salts are again monitored. The procedure is repeated until the conductivity of the bath water measures a standard level, typically a measurement of 100 microSiemens/centimeter ($\mu S/cm$). At that point, the treatment is terminated and the ceramic is air-dried.

The standard 100 $\mu S/cm$ endpoint seems to have evolved anecdotally. Endpoints of 150 and 100 $\mu S/cm$ were suggested, though neither publication investigated these endpoints (Olive and Pearson 1975; Paterakis 1987). More recent studies have questioned the standard endpoint for ceramics desalination (Beaubien 1999; Holbrow et al. 1995).

Desalination may be destructive to ceramic fabrics. Shipp and Lippert (1997) found that two hours of soaking in water softened the surface of low-fired ceramics to the point that they could be abraded by a soft brush, and Willey (1995) found that the ceramic surfaces reflected less light after desalination, indicating a surface change. Willey (1995) and Tsu (1997) found minerals in desalination bath water that implied that the ceramic fabric had begun to disintegrate due to prolonged soaking. Based on Tsu's investigation, Beaubien (1999) proposed that this damage began at day four or five of the desalination treatment.

Desalination may also affect an object's analytical potential. Willey (1995) has demonstrated that desalination will remove residues of the vessel's original contents. Ling and Smith (1996) note that salts may be evidence of manufacturing processes or use rather than intrusive burial salts, in which case removing them will eradicate valuable information about production techniques and original source locations. Tsu (1996) identified uncarbonized plant temper in low-fired ceramics, likely to be removed at least partially during desalination.

In the past many ceramics were automatically desalinated with the idea that to desalinate was "better safe than sorry." It is becoming clear that it is safer not to desalinate unless necessary. If the salt content of the soil is high enough to warrant desalination, then the options must be weighed. Leaving ceramics undesalinated may allow the loss of diagnostic features due to salts activity, but desalinating them may compromise their potential for other analytical techniques. The best solution is a climate-controlled storage area that maintains a stable relative humidity. A stable environment prevents salt crystallization cycles and the resulting damage.

Unfortunately, this is not an option at Gordion or at many archaeological sites. If climate control is not possible, ceramics that are candidates for organic residue analysis ideally should be identified and excluded from desalination treatment, with the understanding that this may be at the expense of their physical morphology. However, ceramics of interest are frequently identified after they have undergone conservation. Therefore, if desalination is to be performed, the shortest desalination treatment that leaves the ceramic in stable condition is the

1.	Weigh out 20 gms of soil sample (removing larger contaminants such as rocks and roots)
2.	Place the sample in a clear glass jar
3.	Add 100 ml of deionized (or distilled) water with a conductivity of 0 μS/cm
4.	Stir the sample for 20 seconds every 5 minutes for an hour.
5.	Allow the solution to settle for 30 seconds
6.	Take the Conductivity keeping the probe in the clearer, upper part of the solution

Figure 16-2 Methodology for identifying salinity of soil samples.

most preferable. The shorter the desalination treatment, the more likely it is that the ceramic fabric will not be weakened and that enough organic residues will remain to allow analysis.

The Gordion Objects Conservation Program is pursuing two areas of research. First, the standard desalination technique has been reevaluated in order to develop an improved method and to identify an appropriate desalination endpoint (Unruh 2001). We are also attempting to develop simple methods conservators can use to gain a clearer understanding of the variation of soil salt levels across the archaeological site and how these levels compare to variability in salt levels of recovered ceramics. This work is at an earlier stage. With a better understanding of soluble salts contaminating ceramics from Gordion we hope to limit the need for spending resources (time, water, funds) on the treatment of ceramics and, more importantly, to protect and maintain the research potential of the collections.

UNDERSTANDING SOURCES OF SOLUBLE SALTS AT GORDION

Excavated ceramics often contain high levels of soluble salts. While some ceramics show evidence of soluble salt damage, comparable ceramics of the same age exhibit no damage, despite storage in similar conditions for 40–50 years.

Several explanations for this variability can be suggested:
- variable clay sources and production practices including firing temperature and additives;
- variable water sources during post-excavation washing;
- previous treatments including acid cleaning or cleaning with chelating agents (EDTA, Calgon);
- depth at which the item was buried;
- slight variations in salinity due to the soil context; and
- variation in soil salinity across and through the site

A pilot project was carried out to examine the vertical distribution of soluble salts in the profile of a single trench and to define a working methodology for further studies. This project was carried out in collaboration with conservators from the site of Kaman Kalehöyük and Troy who carried out similar examinations of profiles at their sites (Johnson et al. 1997). The goal was to develop a method accessible to all conservators by using simple and familiar techniques. A basic extraction methodology was adapted (Bower and Wilcox 1965:935), and conductivity was recorded for each sample (see Fig. 16-2).

Samples were collected each 10 cm from the surface to the bottom of a 2.5-m vertical profile in the main excavation area of the Citadel mound. Salt levels are quite low near the surface but rise to as much as 14,000 μS/cm at a depth of 1 m below the surface. This rise in conductivity probably reflects the maximum depth to which surface water rinses soluble salts downward.

This pilot project confirmed that there is vertical variability in salinity of a profile. However, horizontal variability of salinity across a single level and variability across the site is yet to be examined in detail. Other preliminary work has shown that soil salinity is related to the salinity of the ceramic matrix (Kariya 1997), but this needs to be tested systematically.

DESALINATION OF CERAMICS AT GORDION

Burial salts have caused severe damage to some ceramics in on-site storage at Gordion (Fig. 16-3). Desalination of registered ceramics began with the addition of a staff conservator in 1988, using the standard conservation procedure described above. This treatment necessitated the prolonged soaking of dozens of ceramics

Figure 16-3 Salts damage to ceramics at Gordion.

every excavation season. The possible damage being done to the ceramics by this treatment was a concern. Additionally, at Gordion—as at many archaeological sites—both clean water and staff time are in limited supply.

It has been observed that ceramics not "completely" desalinated nonetheless appear stable over the long term. Because of this observation it is generally agreed that not all soluble salts need to be removed for a desalination treatment in order to be successful, but the question remained as to how much desalination was sufficient. Previous studies have focused on identifying the most thorough method of salt removal possible. In contrast, the Gordion experiments attempted to identify the minimal degree of desalination that is effective.

Standardization of Conductivity Measurements

The first problem with the standard desalination procedure is that the way the treatment is monitored is not very meaningful, failing to take into account the volume of water in which the conductivity reading is being taken. The overall salinity of a solution depends not only on the amount of salt present, but also on the volume of water in which the salts are dissolved. Therefore, desalinating ceramics to "100 μS/cm" in an unknown volume of water means that in the end, different ceramics are desalinated to different, and unknown, degrees.

Moreover, the mass of ceramic is not taken into account. A large storage amphora might contain 10 mg of salts without being in danger, but 10 mg of salts within a small spindle whorl could be damaging. It is not enough to know only the amount of salts released during desalination: the amount of ceramic material from which it came must also be known in order to evaluate the severity of the problem. A measurement of the mass of ceramic material has never been a part of the conservation desalination procedure.

In short, the traditional desalination endpoint of 100 μS/cm is a meaningless measurement because it does not take into account the mass of the ceramic or volume of the desalination bath. To correct this problem, Unruh devised a simple equation that includes the water volume and the ceramic mass and allows all conductivity measurements to be evaluated against a universal scale. The volume of bath water and the weight of the ceramic must be measured prior to desalination.

If k = conductivity in μS/cm, L = volume of the bath water in liters, and gm = weight of the ceramic in grams, then: $k(L)/gm = k_{adj}$

A new term, "adjusted conductivity," or "k_{adj}" was introduced to represent the conductivity reading adjusted for the volume of water and the amount of ceramic involved. "k_{adj}" can be used in the same way many conservators currently use a conductivity reading alone. Using this equation, conductivity measurements are standardized with respect to each other, allowing any desalination treatment to be directly compared to another.

The application of the new calculations to desalination treatment measurements made desalination trends visible for the first time and allowed accurate evaluation and comparison. Methodically tracking desalination trends allowed the development of a new desalination treatment, resulting in less damage to the pot and to the data it contains. The new method has also resulted in reduced water usage and treatment time.

Revised Desalination Procedure

Experiments were performed at Gordion to clarify the salt removal pattern during the desalination process and to investigate two variables directly affecting the amount of water needed: the frequency of water bath changes and the ratio of the ceramic mass to the amount of water used (the gm:ml ratio).

The experimental procedures are published in Unruh (2001). The test ceramics used in the study were non-diagnostic body sherds selected in order to represent a characteristic cross section of ceramics found at Gordion.

"Equilibrium" Desalination vs. Daily Changes of Water

One common desalination theory holds that the bath water should not be changed before the conductivity reaches "equilibrium" or a maximum reading. Proponents of this theory believe that the treatment cannot be adequately monitored without waiting for the conductivity to stabilize (MacLeod and Davies 1987). Opponents of this theory argue that desalination is expedited by frequent water changing (Koob and Ng 2000). Published studies comparing the two methods are flawed by non-standardized data or by invalid comparisons of the total time needed to attain target conductivities rather than comparisons of the amount of salts extracted per unit time by each method.

The Gordion experiments found that both theories are wrong. In the water volumes tested, the salts emerged into bath water on the same schedule for both methods. Changing the water daily (more water intensive) was not necessary. However, the experiments also demonstrated that if equilibrium does not occur in fewer than five days, no significant amount of additional salts will be recovered no matter how long the ceramic is soaked—making the achievement of equilibrium a potentially damaging goal.

In short, in spite of long-held assumptions to the contrary, the frequency of water change is not an important factor in ceramic desalination. Changing the water occasionally has one advantage: Braun (1998) reports that the rate of biological growth is noticeably greater in water that is never changed.

Volume of Water and Salt Removal

It is generally held that desalination will be quicker and more thorough in larger water volumes. This assumption had not been adequately tested. At Gordion, a larger volume of water did correspond to a slightly larger amount of salts extracted for some of the test ceramics. However, for others, there was no correspondence at all. In an attempt to settle the issue, one additional test was run for five days with daily changes of water at five water volumes (gm:ml ratios): 1:5, 1:10, 1:15, 1:20, and 1:25 gm:ml. For these parameters, extracted salts did not increase with increasing water volume (Fig. 16-4). In all experiments, the removal *time* did not change, and desalination followed the same pattern regardless of the amount of water used.

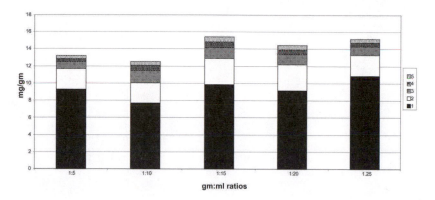

Figure 16-4 Amount of salt removal per day for experimental sherd group H.

Therefore, greater volumes of water provide little advantage, despite an assumption to the contrary in the conservation field. The amount of extra salts potentially recovered with what would have to be drastically larger volumes of water does not appear to be worth the extra water at Gordion.

Ceramic Desalination Patterns

The Gordion tests indicated that every ceramic displays the same pattern: regardless of fabric and thickness, initial degree of salts contamination, water volume used, and whether or not the water was changed daily, an identical pattern of salt extraction occurred. When the results are graphed, the rate of salt removal graphs as a steep slope for a maximum of 4–5 days, after which the slope levels out at a k_{adj} of 2 or below, and never again changes significantly (Fig. 16-5). This means that after the fourth or fifth day desalination has become unproductive.

Figure 16-6 shows the same data expressed as daily percentages of the total salts recovered during treatment. For sherd groups A–E, 50% or more of all salts emerge in the first 24 hours; an additional 20–25% are removed the second day; and after 4 days, between 80–90% of all salts that will be recovered in a 12-day period have been removed. Group F, a group of pithos sherds 2 cm thick was anomalous in that only approximately 35% of all recovered salts were removed on the first day, though by the fourth day approximately 80% were removed.

Ceramic desalination patterns at Gordion have been tracked on site since 1998. In real-life desalination at Gordion, the salt removal patterns match those seen experimentally. Regardless of where the ceramics were found on site, porosities, thicknesses, ceramic fabrics, firing temperatures, surface finishes, or other variables, the characteristic pattern occurs: removal of 80–90% of all recovered salts occurs in four days and is followed by an indefinite period of removal of much smaller amounts of salts.

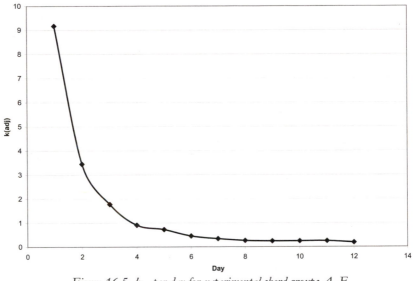

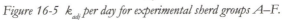

Figure 16-5 k_{adj} per day for experimental sherd groups A–F.

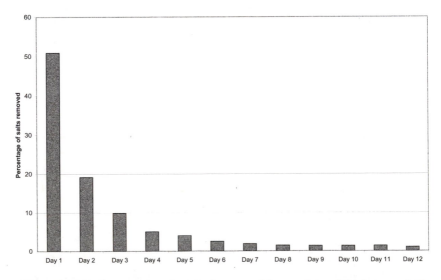

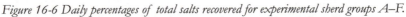

Figure 16-6 Daily percentages of total salts recovered for experimental sherd groups A–F.

CONCLUSION: THE CHANGE OF SLOPE AS AN ENDPOINT FOR DESALINATION

Desalination occurs on a consistent and predictable schedule across a range of Gordion ceramic types. For all ceramics monitored, both experimentally and on site, 80–90% of salts removed were recovered in the first four days. By graphing each ceramic's desalination treatment data as adjusted conductivity (k_{adj}) per day, a new endpoint for ceramic desalination was identified. The graphed data indicated that desalination treatment becomes unproductive at a maximum of five days and prolonged soaking produced no appreciable increase in the amount of salts removed. For Gordion ceramics, across a range of ceramic types, desalinating past that point is unproductive and potentially deleterious. Therefore, the point at which the slope of the "k_{adj} per day" graph changes and levels out is proposed as an appropriate endpoint for desalination.

It is useful to have a numerical endpoint as well, to know immediately when a satisfactory end to the treatment has been reached. At Gordion, the change of slope consistently occurs at adjusted conductivities of 2 or below. Therefore it appears that at Gordion, the target "change in slope" endpoint corresponds to a

---

1. Record the gram weight of each ceramic in the test group, and record the volume of water in liters used for each desalination.
2. In many situations there may be no advantage to changing the water during desalination. At Gordion, an advantage to changing water regularly is to impede biological growth. If the water is to be changed during the desalination, it is helpful to mark the water level on the side of the desalination container to avoid having to re-measure the bath.
3. Every 24 hours, monitor the conductivity of each desalination bath in $\mu S/cm$.
4. Using the equation $k_{adj} = k\,(L)/gm$, convert each conductivity measurement to k_{adj} in order to standardize all measurements across the group of ceramics. (If water is not changed after each measurement, compute the Δk_{adj} each 24 hours using the equation $\Delta k_{adj} = \Delta k\,(L)/gm$.)
5. Graph k_{adj} (or Δk_{adj}) vs. time for each ceramic.
6. Continue desalinating until the k_{adj} vs. time curve has become roughly horizontal.
7. For each ceramic, identify the point at which the slope of the k_{adj} vs. time curve began to level out. This is the endpoint for desalination of that ceramic. If the endpoints consistently occur at the same k_{adj} point across the group of test ceramics, it is reasonable to establish that k_{adj} as the endpoint for the assemblage.

Figure 16-7 Methodology for defining an endpoint for desalination.

numerical endoint, $k_{adj}=2$. Most of the ceramics monitored reached $k_{adj}=2$ after only two or three days. This degree of desalination may be adequate. As of the 2000 excavation season, ceramics desalinated on site were removed at $k_{adj}=2$ or below. They are undergoing long-term monitoring for stability.

The procedure used to establish a numerical endpoint at Gordion may be used to determine an endpoint for ceramic assemblages at other sites. By tracking desalination data for a test group of ceramics, a consistent pattern and an endpoint for any assemblage may be identified (Fig. 16-7).

FUTURE INVESTIGATIONS

The continuous and long-term nature of the conservation program at Gordion has allowed in-depth research of conservation methods that is not possible at most sites that focus on the more immediate concerns of retrieval and restoration for publication. Future investigations at Gordion will continue to clarify the salinity levels in soils and their relation to the salts removed from ceramics during treatment. Another aspect of the desalination process not yet investigated is how to better identify when desalination is necessary. It is puzzling that extremely high salinity ceramics at Gordion do not always exhibit salt activity. In fact, the majority of the thousands of ceramics excavated since 1956 have not experienced salt damage. A productive course of future investigation would be to identify the circumstances that have allowed salt activity in some pots, while similar salty pots in the same situation remain stable.

17

ARCHITECTURAL CONSERVATION AT GORDION

MARK GOODMAN

After a catastrophic fire destroyed much of the Old Phrygian Citadel in the late 9th century BC, the Phrygians buried the ruins under 3–5 m of clay soil. The architectural plan of this Citadel, protected from subsequent stone robbing and reuse, was found to be largely intact. Excavations of this Destruction Layer in the 1950s and 1960s unearthed some of the best examples of monumental Phrygian architecture in Iron Age Anatolia.

Preserving and presenting these architectural ruins has been the focus of site conservation at Gordion. The development of new techniques of on-site conservation will have a favorable impact on other sites in Anatolia.

THE SITE

The exposed Old Citadel, located within an excavated area of approximately 2.5 hectares (Fig. 17-1) includes the Citadel Gate (A), outer and inner Palace Courtyards flanked by freestanding megaron structures (larger main room entered through smaller anteroom or porch) (B), and the Terrace Building Complex on a raised terrace southwest of the Palace Quarter (C). Ramps and securable passageways controlled movement within the city, with at least two staircases linking the Palace Complex with the terrace above.

Although following the basic megaron plan, each building is unique in dimension and detail of construction. Megarons 1 (M1) and 4 (M4) were constructed of mud brick. Megarons 2 (M2) and 3 (M3) were constructed of a combination of mud brick and stone masonry. Close analysis of the Palace Complex indicates a cumulative plan that resulted from at least two major building campaigns (Sams 1994b). The Palace Quarter, including the Citadel Gate, M1-3, and the surrounding courtyards, was constructed first. Megarons 2 and 3 were later incorporated into the retaining structure of the massive platform upon which the Terrace Buildings and Megaron 4 were built.

SITE CONSERVATION: BACKGROUND

Site conservation is not a new concept at Gordion. Excavation in the 1950s and 1960s exposed many walls that required structural support. Excavators used rubble debris to buttress the walls. Rubble was also packed into voids remaining from the disintegration of timber stringcourses. These measures addressed safety

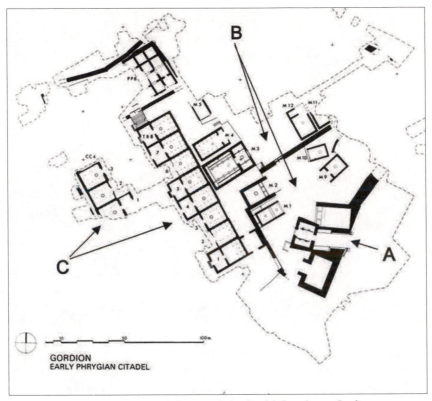

Figure 17-1 Exposed elements of the Citadel Complex at Gordion.
Courtesy of Gordion Excavations.

and stability during excavation, but they were neither adequately documented nor systematically applied.

By the early 1960s, deterioration of exposed megarons prompted the reburial (backfilling) of M1-3 using several different techniques with varying degrees of success, all of which resulted in a negative visual impact. This is particularly true of the Palace Megarons, which played a major role in defining the city plan by retaining the Upper Terrace (Fig. 17-2). The erosion and reburial of Megarons 2 and 3, and the modern projection of that Terrace into the backfilled room of Megaron 1, have distorted a key topographical and social boundary of the city.

CONSERVATION STRATEGY

For more than a decade the conservation team at Gordion has been evaluating the effectiveness of previous efforts in order to develop a strategy appropriate for the site (Koob et al. 1990). It was recognized that the exposed architecture was

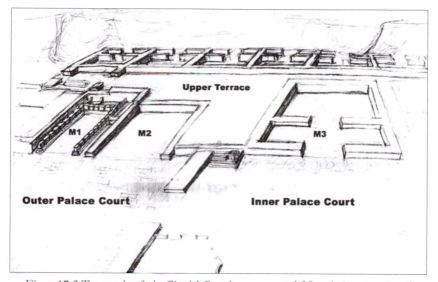

Figure 17-2 Topography of the Citadel Complex as excavated. Note the incorporation of Megarons 2 and 3 within the retaining wall of the Upper Terrace. Drawing courtesy of Banu Bedel.

deteriorating at an accelerating rate that could not be controlled by consolidation or sheltering alone, given current budget constraints. Conventional techniques of reburial protected the ruins but distorted the topography and legibility of the archaeological site.

To reverse this trend, it was necessary to develop a conservation program that would engage the entire site as an archaeological landscape, preserving the fabric and legibility of the Citadel Complex. It also had to be economical in order to be implemented and maintained on a wide scale using available resources and skills.

As a preliminary step, principles of conservation and a site risk assessment were drafted to establish the conservation philosophy at Gordion. Highest priority was given to protecting significant features threatened by structural collapse, such as the Citadel Gate, Terrace Building Complex, and exposed portions of the Megaron Buildings (see Tables 17-1 and 17-2).

The Citadel Gate

The Citadel Gate, built in the 9th century BC, is the best-preserved architectural monument exposed at the site (Fig. 17-3). Over 10 m high, it guarded a major entrance into the Palace Complex and defined the perimeter of the Citadel.

The gate is built of roughly squared and chinked limestone with earth mortar filling gaps between the stones. Walls were plastered with mud, and possibly lime washed, to minimize footfalls and provide a protective and aesthetic skin (Young 1956). For enhanced stability, the walls were battered inward at the entrance approximately 5 cm for every 1 m in height.

Table 17-1 Site Conservation Guidelines

I.   All conservation and restoration work should follow the principles codified by international charters (e.g., Venice 1964, Lausanne 1990), stressing minimal intervention and maximum retention of historic fabric. As the bulk of exposed architectural remains date from the Early Phrygian Period, it is natural to emphasize this period as the main theme of the site. However, it is important to represent the scope and configuration of all occupational phases, using graphics and text to present the state of knowledge regarding the entire occupational history of Gordion.

II. Topography played a major role in defining the different urban components of Phrygian Gordion. Topographical features of the site, including terraces, ramps, access routes, etc., should be preserved to illustrate the plan and functions of the ancient city.

III. Each structure should be fully documented before, during, and after intervention.

IV. All materials introduced into the site should be structurally and chemically compatible with historic building fabric and free of cultural material (such as pottery), which could contaminate the archaeological record.

V.   The intent of conservation should be to present and preserve the form and fabric of the architectural features of the site for future analysis. Thus, any intervention should follow the original technique and character as accurately as possible, while remaining distinguishable from original fabric in a subtle, aesthetically acceptable, and consistent manner. The scope of architectural restoration should be limited to reintegrating the configuration of structures as excavated.

Table 17-2 Site Risk Assessment

Priority I (*integrity of structure*): Significant monuments in imminent danger of structural collapse. These include the Citadel Gate and sections of the Terrace Building Complex.

Priority II (*integrity of structural components*): Structural fabric in danger of erosion or collapse. These include upper courses of walls, steps, and paving which are directly exposed to weather erosion (especially freeze/thaw cycling)

Priority III (*integrity of site aesthetic*): Restoration and re-integration of missing features considered critical to interpreting the site. These include collapsed walls, eroded terraces, etc. which are documented but have disappeared through erosion or post excavation activities.

Excavation photographs taken in 1955 reveal relatively tight and flat walls retaining plaster in areas protected from the weather. To prevent water penetration over the exposed top of the gate, a cement capping was applied in 1956. This capping soon developed cracks, allowing water to erode and weaken the bond between the masonry core and the veneer (Rogers 1989). Although replaced in 1989 by an improved capping/drainage system, exposure to weather and seismic activity accelerated the deterioration and detachment of load-bearing veneer stones. This became particularly evident in the south chamber, where an ominous bulge developed.

In 1999, structural engineer Conor Power developed a simple method using a plumb bob to measure structural movement at critical points along the bulge (Fig. 17-3). As displacement continued, particularly during seismic activity, remedial work was deferred for safety reasons pending construction of supportive bracing. By 2001 sufficient funding enabled the installation of supportive scaffolding and trials of a specialized consolidation technique known as "gravity grouting" to stabilize the gate in its original configuration. As the name implies, the method uses gravitational pressure to inject a hydraulic lime consolidant into the wall, restoring the bond between veneer and core. Properly done, grouting can effectively preserve the structural and aesthetic integrity of a monument without having to dismantle and rebuild its components.

The grouting system was tested on a relatively stable section of fortification wall south of the Citadel Gate (Fig. 17-4). The apparatus uses standard PVC pipe, firehose, and a specially constructed 70 liter grout bucket raised by a compound pulley to a height at least 2 m over the injection point. The mortar injected into the core is pumped upwards in grout "lifts" to ensure effective filling of interior voids.

Following successful trials, the system was adapted in 2002 to begin grouting the south court of the Citadel Gate. The wall face of the structure was digitally photographed and rectified to document pre-consolidation conditions and provide a visual reference for recording the amount of mortar injected into the walls. Additional scaffolding was used to construct an expanded work platform, paying particular attention to creating a safe and efficient setup to mix, move, and inject the large quantities of grout needed for this massive structure. The mining railroad originally used to excavate the site was reassembled to transport materials to the mortar mixer. A second railroad was constructed on the scaffold using a specially modified "grout wagon" to transport mortar to pumping stations at intervals along the wall (Fig. 17-5). Complete stabilization of the southern court is projected to take three more seasons, after which work will begin on the north court building.

THE TERRACE BUILDING COMPLEX

The size (over 100 m long) and plan of the Terrace Building (TB) Complex embody the urban character of Iron Age Gordion, presenting a vivid picture of food and textile production on a grand scale (Sams 1995; Chapters 2 and 6 this volume)

*Figure 17-3 Monitoring structural displacement of the Citadel Gate
using plumb lines, August 1999.*

The interlocked walls of the TB Complex indicate construction within a single phase (mid to late 9th century BC). Various types of ashlar limestone were used, with wooden timbers serving as leveling courses and to provide vertical supports for the roof and inner galleries.

The timber-laced masonry construction of the TB was particularly vulnerable to fire. Combustion of the timber stringcourses within the masonry caused the walls to splay outward and collapse. Both Terrace Buildings were destroyed and abandoned following the 9th century BC catastrophic fire marking the end of the Early Phrygian Period.

Although rubble buttresses built during excavation helped to support the unstable walls, they were aesthetically incompatible with the original ashlar walls. Because the buttresses were not applied systematically, many walls continued to deteriorate. In some instances, the buttresses themselves had eroded and were no longer effective.

The walls were also exposed to severe weather conditions, including significant winter freeze/thaw cycling. Comparisons of excavation photographs reveal that

Figure 17-4 Grouting system being applied to the Citadel Gate.

significant deterioration occurred after excavation (Fig. 17-6). The outward splay of walls increased due to seismic activity and "frost wedging." Numerous fire-damaged stones disintegrated. Entire features of buildings, such as doorjambs, had completely disappeared in some places.

Interpretive Stabilization of the Terrace Building Complex

The most pressing need was to arrest the collapse of unstable walls by employing a more effective method of supportive buttressing and to protect exposed walls from freeze/thaw cycling. Evaluation of previous buttressing suggested the need to incorporate additional features such as wall plasters and ovens, and include an effective method of capping protection. It was necessary that the buttressing and capping be distinguishable from the original building fabric and also be economical and versatile enough to allow for systematic implementation on the entire range of site architecture (See Table 17-3).

*Figure 17-5 "Railroad" constructed on scaffolding to transport mortar
to pumping stations for grouting the walls.*

Supportive Buttressing

In 1999, a pilot program of supportive buttressing was applied to several endangered walls of TB1, using burlap sandbags, which allowed the buttressed walls to breathe. Burlap offered a superior substrate for the application of protective dressing. It was locally available and inexpensive (ca. 30 cents/bag).

The area adjacent to the wall was documented, cleared, and graded to facilitate drainage (Pl. 8). Sections of extant wall plaster were photographed and covered with fine landscaping fabric (G2). Although geotextile was originally procured for this purpose, the unwoven material tended to adhere to and to remove friable wall plasters.

A bedding of coarse, clean sand (graded <3 mm) was spread in a 3-5 cm thick layer extending 1 meter from the wall base. The first course of sandbags was laid over this bedding layer, leaving a gap of approximately 30 cm from the wall. This gap was packed with sand, becoming progressively narrower as the buttresses were built up and battered inward approximately 60° for stability. The top course of sandbags, packed directly against the wall, was contoured to facilitate drainage.

Sandbag Protection

To prevent ultraviolet degradation it was necessary to protect the burlap from direct sun exposure using inconspicuous fabric protection less vulnerable to

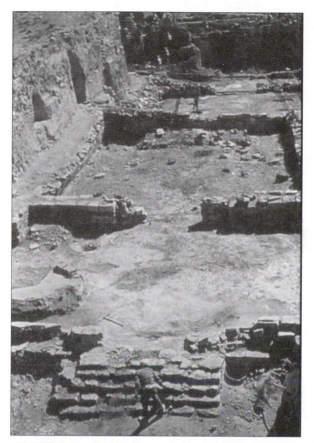

Figure 17-6 TB-5 immediately after excavation, 1961, illustrates the condition as excavated. Courtesy of Gordion Archives.

theft. It was discovered that the unwoven polyester of geotextile adheres naturally to burlap sandbags, creating a form-fitting cover. As clean white geotextile is both conspicuous and degradable by ultraviolet radiation, the geotextile was saturated in a slurry mixture of lime-stabilized clay (Table 17-4). The resulting wet geotextile dressing was then molded to the contour of the sandbags. After drying, the geotextile was painted with two coats of clay/lime slurry. The technique was further refined to minimize water penetration into the buttress by covering exposed seams with expansive clay, burlap and saturated geotextile (Fig. 17-7). The finished product is asthetically pleasing, with light brown buttresses contrasting with dark brown capping.

The exposed staircase attached to TB8 was treated in a similar manner, with missing stones visually reintegrated using sandbags molded to fit step dimensions.

Table 17-3 Criteria for Interpretive Stabilization System

1. *Protective*: should stabilize structural remains in their existing configuration and protect from weather erosion, particularly freeze–thaw cycling
2. *Compatible*: should be physically, mechanically, and chemically compatible with historic building materials of the site
3. *Reversible*: should be easily reversible and re-workable, reusing the bulk of material to maintain and upgrade the system
4. *Economical/Sustainable*: should benefit the local economy by employing local materials and labor, and remain inexpensive enough to be implemented and maintained on a wide scale
5. *Flexible*: should incorporate architectural elements (wall plasters, ovens, etc) and be applicable to features such as staircases, restored structures, etc.
6. *Aesthetic*: should be easily distinguishable from the original fabric, while remaining visually compatible with the site
7. *Interpretive*: should preserve and if possible enhance visitor interpretation of the site. Missing or incomplete features (properly documented) can be schematically represented to preserve clarity of form. The system should also differentiate restored features while integrating them in the general scheme

Table 17-4 Conservation & Restoration Formulae

Application	Constituents & Bulk Proportions					
	Soaked Hydrated lime	Local clay	Acrylic Co-polymer emulsion	Sand ≤ 3mm	Ceramic ≤ 4mm	Binder/ Aggregate Ratio
Buttress protective slurry (2000)	20 liters	400 Kg	—	—	—	- - - -
Protective slurry (2001)	20 liters	400 Kg	5 liters			
Restoration mortar	3 liters (27%)	—	—	7 liters (64%)	1 liter (9%)	1-2.6

Figure 17-7 Applying protective Geotextile dressing over sandbag buttresses, August 2000.

Capping

In 1988, additional sections of the Terrace Building were exposed during excavation. As long-term exposure was clearly damaging, the excavators capped the newly exposed walls with earth-covered polyethylene sheeting anchored by small stones. This provided effective protection against freeze/thaw damage. However, since the earth was obtained from excavation dump, it contained cultural material that could eventually contaminate the archaeological record. Various alternatives, such as textured concrete, were rejected as obtrusive and inappropriate for archaeological sites.

The search for an appropriate capping material ended in 2000 when a large amount of clay was discovered along the road leading to the site. This local clay had been used in ancient earthwork projects—including tumuli, fortifications, and terraces—and for flood protection. Geomorphologic research at Gordion has characterized this soil deposit as red fan clay, a highly expansive mixture of illite and montmorillonite (Marsh 1999). The Phrygians buried their destroyed citadel using this clay, creating a protective seal until excavation nearly three thousand years later. It is an early example of a protective material used (albeit unwittingly) to preserve the ruins of an ancient site.

The potential for a plentiful and culturally clean material for capping the walls was quickly recognized at the Gordion site. By expanding when saturated with water, such clay provides an efficient moisture barrier, restricting water penetration into the walls. Upon drying the shrinkage and cracking of the clay allows for the release of moisture that had penetrated into the wall and imparts a rustic aesthetic appropriate for an archaeological site.

*Figure 17-8 Tamping clay capping over buffered polyethylene,
anchored at margins by rubble "capstones," July 2000.*

The 1989 technique was implemented in the 2000 season, using clay as the
capping material, with the following modifications. Following documentation, the
wall tops were cleaned and a layer of sand contoured for drainage was applied
to absorb condensation. The sand was covered with a double layer of 0.2 mm
UV-resistant polyethylene sheeting later changed to geotextile for enhanced
permeability, secured by "cappingstones" of similar color to the original wall. A
deep layer of clay was mounded and tamped over the polyethylene (Fig. 17-8). To
cover walls preserved to different heights, larger clods of clay were used to retain
the finer material.

SITE INTERPRETATION

As work progressed, the potential to facilitate visitor interpretation was
recognized and exploited, by schematic representation of the entire building

Figure 17-9 Terrace Building after interpretive stabilization. Supportive buttressing and capping protects eroded structure while providing a schematic and reversible restoration of the building plan. Pending evaluation of the stairway protection, the cinderblock encasement can be removed and the geotextile treatment extended along the steps to recover original site topography.

plan. Where local collapses created gaps in the walls, the caps provide visual linkage between surviving wall sections (Fig. 17-9). Protective buttressing of eroded doorjambs schematically restores features while preserving the original material underneath. As the Terrace Building was built of stones obtained from different sources, this was conveyed by using compatible rubble to retain the clay cappings. The contrast between the dark clay and the lighter earth shades of the site makes it possible to represent portions of the TB Complex that are obscured by eroded baulks (such as the cross walls of Terrace Building 3) by superimposed cappings.

DISCUSSION

The Interpretive Stabilization System implemented at Gordion follows the conservation guidelines (see Table 17-3) while protecting the archaeological remains. Environmental protection is provided by reducing the two main causes of freeze/thaw cycling: (1) water saturation of the masonry pores to 91%, and (2) exposure of water-saturated masonry to temperatures fluctuating above and below freezing.

The expansive clay, the mildly hydrophobic geotextile dressing, the coarse sand within the buttresses, and the configuration of the buttresses themselves are all designed to direct water away from the walls, minimizing water absorption while providing a permeable, expanded area to facilitate evaporation and drainage (Fig. 17-10). The structural mass of the buttresses counterbalances the unstable configuration of the walls and provides insulation from surface temperature fluctuations.

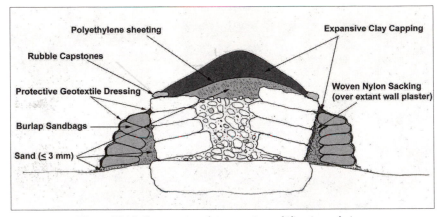

Figure 17-10 Cross-section of interpretive stabilization technique.

Cost and Maintenance

Interpretive stabilization of the Terrace Building took five months to complete, at a total cost (including materials and labor) of approximately $40,000, averaging about $140/m² of protected wall. Maintenance is projected to be ca. $400 annually, using local materials and labor to reapply the slurry and clay as needed.

Assuming the fabric form retains its integrity, the sand buttresses are expected to harden naturally through periodic wet/dry cycling. If the buttresses deteriorate through lack of maintenance, both sand and clay should still function as a protective berm. This system is both reversible and reworkable, using bulk materials that can easily be incorporated into more durable protective systems if necessary.

Monitoring

Monitoring at Gordion has two aspects—efficacy of protection and durability/*maintainability* of the protective system itself.

In 2000, field trials involving inundation of buttressed walls were carried out to evaluate water saturation adjacent to the original wall surfaces. While moisture did penetrate into the buttresses, at no point was saturation reached within the buttress core. The 2001 season commenced with inspection of buttresses and cappings (Fig. 17-11). As expected, a percentage of mud slurry applied onto the buttress had washed away, and several cappings required minor refittings and replenishment of clay. For improved durability, the slurry was amended with 2% acrylic emulsion of Volkan co-polymer binder for exterior paints.

A section of buttressed capping was dismantled, revealing no signs of frost damage within the protected walls. Since frost can be an insidious process manifesting itself only after several years, a simple monitoring method was

Figure 17-11 Restored Terrace Building unit 4 and stabilized complex after one year. Section of mortared wall capping (left of lower crosswall) is exposed to compare with protected section, June 2001. Courtesy of Richard Liebhart.

implemented in 2002: the insertion of a sacrificial material within the buttresses and capping, with control samples exposed for comparative analysis. This material consists of cast slabs of ash-modified lime mortar, a material particularly susceptible to frost damage (Goodman 1998).

Pending evaluation and possible modification, the system can be expanded to preserve all features of the site. The interpretive stabilization of palace megarons could restore the eroded boundary between the Palace and upper Terrace, recovering the original topography of the site.

Future work at Gordion includes ongoing stabilization of the Citadel Gate and updating the program of site presentation, using non-intrusive viewing stations and brochures to provide an interpretive map of the site. This includes developing a site conservation/presentation website and using digitized images and three-dimensional visualization for an exciting and informative experience of ancient Gordion.

BIBLIOGRAPHY

Åkerström, Å.

1966   *Die Architektonischen Terrakotten Kleinasiens, Skrifter utgivna av Svenska institutet i Athen*, series prima in 4°, 11 Lund, Sweden.

Akurgal, E.

1955   *Phrygische Kunst*. Ankara: Archaeological Institute of the University of Ankara.

Amyx, D. A.

1988   *Corinthian Vase-Painting of the Archaic Period*. Berkeley, CA: University of California Press.

Anderson, G. E.

1980   The Common Cemetery at Gordion. Ph.D. dissertation, Bryn Mawr College.

Angel, J. L.

1951   *Troy, the Human Remains*. Princeton, NJ: Princeton University Press.

Arnold, D.

1985   *Ceramic Theory and Culture Process*. Cambridge: Cambridge University Press.

Barag, D.

1968   An Unpublished Achemenid Cut Glass Bowl from Nippur. *Journal of Glass Studies* 10:17–20.

1985   *Catalogue of Western Asiatic Glass in the British Museum 1*. London: British Museum Publications.

Barber, E.

1991   *Prehistoric Textiles: the Development of Cloth in the Neolithic and Bronze Ages, with Special Reference to the Aegean*. Princeton, NJ: Princeton University Press.

Barnett, R. D.

1975   Phrygia and the Peoples of Anatolia in the Iron Age, *Cambridge Ancient History*, 3rd ed., part 2, ed. I. E. S. Edwards, C. J. Gadd, and N. G. L. Hammond, pp. 417–42. Cambridge: Cambridge University Press.

Bar-Yosef, O., and R. S. Kra, eds.
1994   *Late Quaternary Chronology and Paleoclimates of the Eastern Mediterranean.* Tucson, AZ: Radiocarbon.

Bass, W. M.
1995   *Human Osteology: A Laboratory and Field Manual.* Columbia, MO: Missouri Archaeological Society.

Beaubien, H. F.
1999   Desalination Parameters for Harappan Ceramics, Part 2. In *Objects Specialty Group Postprints* 6, pp. 77–93. Washington, DC: American Institute for Conservation.

Bellinger, L.
1962   Textiles from Gordion. *Bulletin of the Needle and Bobbin Club* 46,1:5–34.

Bingol, E.
1989   *Turkiye Jeoloji Haritası* (map 1:2,000,000). Ankara: Maden Tetkik ve Arama Genel Müdürlüğü.

Blackman, M. J., G. J. Stein, and P. B. Vandiver.
1993   The Standardization Hypothesis and Ceramic Mass Production: Technological, Compositional, and Metric Indices of Craft Specialization at Tell Leilan, Syria. *American Antiquity* 58:60–79.

Blitzer, H.
1990   Koroneika: Storage-Jar Production and Trade in the Traditional Aegean. *Hesperia* 59:675–711.

Boardman, J.
1974   *Athenian Black-Figure Vases.* London: Thames and Hudson.
1990   The Lyre Player Group of Seals. An Encore. *Archäologische Anzeiger.* 1-17.

Böhmer, R.
1973   Phrygische Prunkgewänder des 8. Jahrhunderts v. Chr. Herkunft und Export. *Archäologischer Anzeiger* 11,2:149–72.

Böhmer, H., and J. Thompson
1991   The Pazyryk Carpet: A Technical Discussion. *Source: Notes in the History of Art* 10,4.

Bostancı, E. Y.
1962   *A Biometrical and Morphological Study of the Astragalus and Calcaneus of the Roman People of Gordium in Anatolia.* Ankara: Türk Tarih Kurumu.

Bottema, S., and H. Woldring
1990   Anthropogenic Indicators in the Pollen Record of the Eastern Mediterranean. In *Man's Role in the Shaping of the Eastern Mediterranean Landscape*, ed. S. Bottema, G. Entjes-Neiborg, and W. van Zeist, pp. 231–61. Rotterdam: A. A. Balkema.

Bower, C. A., and L. V. Wilcox
1965   Soluble Salts. In *Methods of Soil Analysis: Part 2, Chemical and Microbiological Properties*, ed. C. A. Black, p. 935. Madison, WI: American Society of Agronomy.

Braun, T. J.
1998   Desalination of Archaeological Ceramics: Daily Water Changes vs. Soaking to Equilibrium: Which is More Efficient? Gordion Project report, Yassıhöyük, Turkey.

Brijder, H. A. G.
1996   *Corpus Vasorum Antiquorum.* Netherlands 8, Amsterdam 2. Amsterdam: Allard Pierson Museum.
2000   *Siana Cups 111.* Amsterdam: Allard Pierson Museum.

Brooks, S. T., and J. M. Suchey
1990   Skeletal Age Determination Based on the Os Pubis: A Comparison of the Ascádi-Nemeskéri and Suchey-Brooks Methods. *Human Evolution* 5:227–38.

Brothwell, D. R.
1989   The Relationship of Tooth Wear to Aging. In *Age Markers in the Human Skeleton*, ed. M. Y. Iscan, pp. 303–18. Springfield, IL: Charles C Thomas.

Broughton, T. R. S.
1938   Roman Asia Minor. In *An Economic Survey of Ancient Rome IV*, ed. T. Frank, pp. 499–918. Baltimore, MD: Johns Hopkins University Press.

Brunaux, J. L.
1988   *The Celtic Gauls: Gods, Rites, and Sanctuaries*, trans. D. Nash. London: Seaby.

Buikstra, J. E., and D. H. Ubelaker
1994   *Standards for Data Collection From Human Skeletal Remains*. Fayetteville, AR: Arkansas Archeological Survey.

Burke, B.
1998   From Minos to Midas: The Organization of Textile Production in the Aegean and in Anatolia. Ph.D. dissertation, UCLA.

Callipolitis-Feytmans, D.
1970   "Dinos corinthien de Vari." *Archaiologike Ephemeris*: 86–113.

Caner, E.
1983   *Fibeln in Anatolien I*. Prähistorische Bronzefunde 14, 8. Munich: C. H. Beck.

Çiner, R.
1971   *Gordion Roma Halki Femur ve Tibia'larinin Tetkiki*. Ankara: Ankara Üniversitesi Dil ve Tarih-Coğrafya Fakültesi Yayınları.

Coldstream, J. N.
1968   *Greek Geometric Pottery*. London: Methuen.
1971   Review of R. Walter, *Samos V*, *Journal of Hellenic Studies* 91:201–204.

Costin, C. L.
1990   Craft Specialization: Issues in Defining, Documenting, and Explaining the Organization of Production. In *Archaeological Method and Theory 3*, ed. M. B. Schiffer, pp. 1–56. Tucson, AZ: University of Arizona Press.

Cronyn, J. M.
1990   *The Elements of Archaeological Conservation*. London: Routledge.

Cunliffe, B.
1997   *The Ancient Celts*. New York: Oxford University Press.

Dandoy, J. R., P. Selinsky, and M. M. Voigt.
2002   Celtic Sacrifice. *Archaeology* 55,1: 44–49.

DeVries, K.
1977   Attic Pottery in the Achaemenid Empire. *American Journal of Archaeology* 81:544–48.
1980a   *From Athens to Gordion. The Papers of a Memorial Symposium for Rodney S. Young*. Philadelphia, PA: University of Pennsylvania Museum.
1980b   Greeks and Phrygians in the Early Iron Age. In *From Athens to Gordion: The Papers of a Memorial Symposium for Rodney S. Young*, ed. K. DeVries, pp. 33–49. Philadelphia, PA: University of Pennsylvania Museum of Archaeology and Anthropology.
1988   Gordion and Phrygia in the Sixth Century B.C. *Source* 7,3–4 :51–59
1990   The Gordion Excavation Seasons of 1969–1973 and Subsequent Research. *American Journal of Archaeology* 94:371–406.
1993   Greek Pottery from Gordion in Light of the New Excavations. *American Journal of Archaeology* 97:303.
1996   The Attic Pottery from Gordion. In *Athenian Potters and Painters*, ed. J. H. Oakley, W. D. Coulson, and O. Palagia, pp. 447–45. Oxford: Oxbow.
1997   Greek Fine Wares. In M. M. Voigt, K. DeVries, R. C. Henrickson, M.

Lawall, B. Marsh, A. Gürsan-Salzmann, T. C. Young, Fieldwork at Gordion: 1993–1995. *Anatolica* 23:1-59.

DeVries, B. Kromer, P. I. Kuniholm, S. W. Manning, M. W. Newton, G. K. Sams, and M. M. Voigt
Forthcoming *The Chronology of Early Iron Age Gordion.*

DeVries, K., P. I. Kuniholm, G. K. Sams, and M. M. Voigt
2003 New Dates for Iron Age Gordion. *Antiquity* 77, 296: *http://antiquity. ac.uk/ProjGall/devries/devries.html.*

Dickinson, W. R., J. R. Shutler, R. Shortland, D. Burley, and T. S. Dye.
1996 Sand Tempers in Indigenous Lapita and Lapitoid Polynesian Plainware and Imported Fijian Pottery of Ha'apai (Tonga) and the Question of Lapita Tradeware. *Archaeology in Oceania* 31:87–98.

Dinsmoor, W. B.
1975 *The Architecture of Ancient Greece.* New York: Norton.

Dregne, H. E.
1976 *Soils of Arid Regions.* Amsterdam: Elsevier.

Dusinberre, Elspeth R. M.
1999 Satrapal Sardis: Achaemenid Bowls in an Achaemenid Capital. *American Journal of Archaeology* 103:73–102.

Edwards, G. R.
1959 The Gordion Campaign of 1958: Preliminary Report. *American Journal of Archaeology* 63:263–68.

Eilmann, R.
1933 Frühe griechische Keramik im samischen Heraion. *Mitteilungen des deutschen archäologischen Instituts, Athenische Abteilung* 58:47–145.

Ellis, R.
1981 The Textile Remains. In *The Gordion Excavations Final Reports, Vol. I: Three Great Early Tumuli* Appendix V: Textiles, 294-310. Philadelphia, PA: University of Pennsylvania Museum of Archaeology and Anthropology.

Ergenç, O.
1988 XVIII Yuzyilda Osmanli Sanayi ve Ticaret Hayatina Iliskin Bazi Bilgiler. [Some notes on 18th century Ottoman Industrial Production and Trade.] *Belleten* (Ankara) 152:501–33.

French, D. H.
1978   Roman Roads in Central Anatolia. In *Proceedings of the Xth International Congress of Classical Archaeology, Ankara and Izmir, 1973*. Ankara: Türk Tarih Kurumu Basımevi.

Glascock, M., ed.
2002   *Geochemical Evidence for Long Distance Exchange*. Westport, CT: Bergin and Garvey.

Glendinning, M. R.
1996a   A Mid-sixth-century Tile Roof System at Gordion. *Hesperia* 59, 1:99–119.
1996b   Building Tile. In *The Oxford Encyclopedia of Archaeology in the Near East*, ed. E. M. Meyers, pp. 210–12. Oxford: Oxford University Press.
1996c   Phrygian Architectural Terracottas at Gordion. Ph.D. dissertation, University of North Carolina, Chapel Hill.
2002   Recovering the Lost Art of Phrygian Roof Tiling. *Expedition* 44,2:28–35.

Goldman, A. L.
2000   The Roman-Period Settlement at Gordion, Turkey. Ph.D. dissertation, University of North Carolina at Chapel Hill.

Goldman, A. L., and P. R. Grave.
In prep.   Characterizing the Roman-period Ceramics at Gordion.

Goodman, M.
1998   The Effects of Wood Ash on the Structural Properties of Lime Plaster. Master's thesis, University of Pennsylvania.

Goudie, A.
1993   Human influence in geomorphology. In *Geomorphology; The Research Frontier and Beyond*. ed. J. D. Vitek, and J. R. Giardino, pp. 37–59. Stillwater, OK: Oklahoma State University.

Grave, P., M. Barbetti, M. Hotchkis, and R. Bird
2000   The Stoneware Kilns of Sisatchanalai and the Early Modern Period. *Journal of Field Archaeology* 27:169–82.

Grave, P., D. T. Potts, N. Yassi, W. Reade, and G. Bailey
1996   Elemental Characterisation of Barbar Ceramics from Tell Abraq. *Arabian Archaeology and Epigraphy* 7: 177-187.

Greenewalt, C. H. Jr., C. Ratté, and M. L. Rautman
1995   The Sardis Campaigns of 1992 and 1993. *Annual of the American Schools of Oriental Research* 53:1–36.

Greenewalt, C. H. Jr., and M. L. Rautman
1998   The Sardis Campaigns of 1994 and 1995. *American Journal of Archaeology* 102:469–505.

Griffiths, D. M.
1978   Use-marks on Historic Ceramics: A Preliminary Study. *Historical Archaeology* 12:68–81.

Grose, D. F.
1989   *The Toledo Museum of Art. Early Ancient Glass: Core-Formed, Rod-Formed, and Cast Vessels and Objects from the Late Bronze Age to the Early Roman Empire, 1600 B.C. to A.D. 50*. New York: Hudson Hills Press.

Gunter, A. C.
1991   *Gordion Excavations Final Reports III, The Bronze Age*. Philadelphia, PA: University of Pennsylvania Museum of Archaeology and Anthropology.

Guy, H., C. Masset, and C. Baud
1997   Infant Taphonomy. *International Journal of Osteoarchaeology* 7:221–29.

Güner, G.
1988   *Anadolu'da Yaşamakta Olan Ilkel Çömlekçilik*. Istanbul: Akbank'n Bir Kultur Hizmeti.

Gürsan-Salzmann, A.
1995–96 Field notes.

Hamilton, W. J.
1842   *Research in Asia Minor, Pontus and Armenia. With Some Account of Their Antiquities and Geology*. London: J. Murray.

Hampe, R., and A. Winter
1962   *Bei Töpfern und Töpferinnen in Kreta, Messenien, und Zypern*. Mainz: Römisch-Germanisches Zentralmuseum zu Mainz.
1965   *Bei Töpfern und Zieglern in Süditalien Sizilien und Griechenland*. Bonn: Rudolf Habelt.

Haspels, C. H. E.
1971   *The Highlands of Phrygia, Volume I, The Text*. Princeton, NJ: Princeton University Press.

Hayes, J. W.
1997   *Handbook of Mediterranean Roman Pottery*. Norman, OK: University of Oklahoma Press.

Hein, A., A. Tsolakidou, and H. Mommsen

2002   Mycenaean Pottery from the Argolid and Achaia: A Mineralogical Approach where Chemistry Leaves Unanswered Questions. *Archaeometry* 44,2:177–86.

Henrickson, R. C.

1991   Wheelmade or Wheel-Finished? Interpretation of "Wheelmarks" on Pottery. In *Materials Issues in Art and Archaeology II*, ed. P. B. Vandiver, J. R. Druzik, and G. Wheeler, pp. 523–41. Pittsburgh, PA: Materials Research Society.

1993   Politics, Economics, and Ceramic Continuity at Gordion in the Late Second and First Millennia B.C. In *Social and Cultural Contexts of New Ceramic Technologies*, ed. W. D. Kingery, pp. 89–176. Westerville, OH: American Ceramic Society.

1994   Continuity and Discontinuity in the Ceramic Tradition at Gordion during the Iron Age. In *Anatolian Iron Ages 3: Proceedings of the Third Anatolian Iron Ages Colloquium Held at Van, 6–12 August 1990*, ed. D. French and A. Çilingiroğlu, pp. 95–129. Ankara: British Institute of Archaeology at Ankara.

1995a   A Comparison of Production of Large Storage Vessels in Two Ancient Ceramic Traditions. In *Materials Issues in Art and Archaeology* 4, ed. P. B. Vandiver, J. Druzik, J. L. Galvan, I. A. Freestone, and G. S. Wheeler, pp. 553–72. Pittsburgh, PA: Materials Research Society.

1995b   Hittite Potters and Pottery: The View from Late Bronze Age Gordion. *Biblical Archaeology* 58,2:82–90.

In prep.   "The Middle Phrygian Pottery Industry at Gordion" In *Anatolian Iron Ages 6: The Proceedings of the Sixth Anatolian Iron Ages Symposium*, Eskişehir-Turkey, 16-19 August 2004, edited by A. and A. Çilingiroğlu. Supplement Series of Ancient Near Eastern Studies. Louvain, Belgium: Peeters.

Henrickson, R. C., and M. J. Blackman

1996   Large-Scale Production of Pottery at Gordion: A Comparison of the Late Bronze and Early Phrygian Industries. *Paleorient* 22,1:67–87.

In prep.   Pottery Production during the Early-Middle Phrygian Periods at Gordion.

Henrickson, R. C., P. B. Vandiver, and M. J. Blackman

2002   Lustrous Black Fine Ware at Gordion, Turkey: A Distinctive Sintered Slip Technology. In *Materials Issues in Art and Archaeology* 4, ed. P. B. Vandiver, M. Goodway, and J. L. Mass, pp. 391–400. Pittsburgh, PA: Materials Research Society.

Hirth, K.

1996   Political Economy and Archaeology: Perspectives on Exchange and Production. *Journal of Archaeological Research* 4,3:203–39.

Holbrow, K. A., E. Kaplan, and H. F. Beaubien
1995   Desalination Parameters for Harappan Ceramics. In *Objects Specialty Group Postprints*, pp. 70–76. Washington, DC: American Institute for Conservation.

Hole, F.
1979   Rediscovering the past in the present: Ethnoarchaeology in Luristan, Iran. In *Ethnoarchaeology: Implications of Ethnography for Archaeology*, ed. C. Kramer, pp. 192–218. New York: Columbia University Press.

Hostetter, I.
1994   *Lydian Architectural Terracottas: A Study in Tile Replication, Display and Technique*. Atlanta, GA: Scholars Press.

Ibn Wahsiya
1983   Al-filaha al-nabatiya {The Nabatean Book of Agriculture. Agricultural Ms. 490, Dar al-Kutub, 1983(Cairo, 903/4). In *Agricultural Innovation in the Early Islamic World*. ed. Andrew M. Watson, Cambridge: Cambridge University Press.

Ignatiadou, D.
1997   Two Cast Glass Vessels from Derveni. In *Memory of Manolis Andronikis*. Thessaloniki, 105 114 (in Greek).
2004   Glass Vessels. In The *Maussolleion at Halikarmassos 6, Subterrean and Pre-Maussolleion Structures on the Site of the Maussolleion: The Finds from the Tomb Chamber of Maussollos*. Zahle and Kjeldsen, pp. 181–207. Jutland Archaeological Publications 15:6.

Isık, F.
1991   Zür Entstehung der töneren Verkleidungsplatten in Anatolien. *Anatolian Studies* 41:63–86.

Johnson, J. S., E. Salzman, and J. Unruh
1996   Unraveling the Gordion Knot: The History of Conservation at the "City of Midas." In Preprints of the IIC 16th International Congress, Archaeological Conservation and its Consequences, London: International Institute for Conservation.

Johnson, J. S., S. Carroll, and D. Strahan
1997   Evaluation of Soluble Salt Content in Soils: Preliminary Results from Three Archeological Sites in Turkey. Paper presented at Western Association for Art Conservation, Phoenix, AZ.

Johnston, R. H.
1970   Pottery Practices During the 6th–8th Centuries B.C. at Gordion in Central

Anatolia: An Analytical and Synthesizing Study. Ph.D. dissertation, Pennsylvania State University.

Jones, J. D.
1995   Classical and Hellenistic Core-Formed Vessels from Gordion. *Journal of Glass Studies* 37:21–33.

Kariya, H.
1997   Ceramic and Soil Research. Kaman Kalehöyük Excavations report, Kaman, Turkey.

Khlopin, I.
1982   The Manufacture of Pile Carpets in Bronze Age Central Asia. *Hali* 5,2: 116-8.

Kingery, W. D., and D. Smith
1990   The Development of European Soft-paste (Frit) Porcelain. In *Ceramics and civilisation: ancient technology to modern science 1.* ed. W. D. Kingery, pp. 235–56. Westerville, OH: American Ceramic Society.

Knapp, A. B., P. Duerden, R. V. S. Wright, and P. Grave
1988   Ceramic Production and Social Change: Archaeometric Analysis of Bronze Age Pottery from Jordan. *Journal of Mediterranean Archaeology* 2,1:57–113.

Knox, J.
1999   Long-term Episodic Changes in Magnitudes and Frequencies of Floods in the Upper Mississippi River Valley. In *Fluvial Processes and Environmental Change,* ed. A. G. Brown, and T. A. Quine, pp. 255–82. Chichester: Wiley.

Kohler, E. L.
1980   Cremations of the Middle Phrygian Period from Gordion. In *From Athens to Gordion,* ed. K. DeVries, pp. 65-89. Philadelphia, PA: University of Pennsylvania Museum of Archaeology and Anthropology.
1995   *The Gordion Excavations (1950–1973) Final Reports Volume II. The Lesser Phrygian Tumuli, Part 1: The Inhumations.* Philadelphia, PA: University of Pennsylvania Museum of Archeaology and Anthropology.

Koob, S., and W. Y. Ng
2000   The Desalination of Ceramics Using a Semi-Automated Continuous Washing Station. *Studies in Conservation* 45, 4:265–73.

Koob, S. P., G. K. Sams, and M. Rogers
1990   Preserving the 8th Century B.C. Mudbrick Architecture at Gordion, Turkey: Approaches to Conservation. *Adobe* 90: 289–94.

Körte, A.
1897   Kleinasiatische Studien II: Gordion und der Zug des Manlius gegen die Galater. *Mittheilungen des kaiserlich deutschen archäologischen Instituts, Athenische Abtheilung* 22:1–29.

Körte, A., and G. Körte
1901   Gordion. *Archäologischen Anzeiger* 1:1–11.

Körte, G., and A. Körte
1904   *Gordion. Ergebnisse der Ausgrabung im Jahre 1900. Jahrbuch des deutschen archäologischen Instituts.* Ergänzungsheft 5. Berlin: Georg Reims.

Kuniholm, P. I.
1988   Dendrochronology and Radiocarbon Dates for Gordion and Other Phrygian Sites. *Source* 7,3–4:5–8.

Lawall, M.
1997   Greek Transport Amphoras at Gordion. *Anatolica* 23:21–23.

Le Roy, C.
1967   Les terres cuites architecturales et la diffusion de l'hellénisme en Anatolie. *Revue archéologique*: 127–42.

Leiser, G.
1994   Travellers' Accounts of Mohair Production in Ankara from the Fifteenth through the Nineteenth Century. *The Textile Museum Journal* [1993-1994] 33: 5-23.

Ling, D., and S. Smith
1996   To Desalinate or Not To Desalinate? That Is the Question. In *Le Dessalement des Materiaux Poreux, 7 Journées d'Etudes de la SFIIC*, pp. 65–74. Champs-sur-Marne: SFIIC [International Institute for Conservation of Historic and Artistic Works, Section Française].

Lovell, N. C.
1997   Trauma Analysis in Paleopathology. *Yearbook of Physical Anthropology* 40:139–70.

MacLeod, I. D., and J. A. Davies
1987   Desalination of Glass, Stone, and Ceramics Recovered from Shipwreck Sites. In *ICOM Committee for Conservation: Preprints of the 8th Triennial Meeting, Sydney, Australia*, pp.1005–1007. Los Angeles, CA: Getty Conservation Institute.

Magie, D.
1950   *Roman Rule in Asia Minor to the End of the 3rd Century A.D.* Princeton, NJ:
        Princeton University Press.

Manning, S. W., B. Kromer, P. Kuniholm, and M. Newton
2001   Anatolian Tree Rings and a New Chronology for the East Mediterranean
        Bronze-Iron Ages. *Science* 294,5551:2532–35.

Marsh, B.
1999   Alluvial Burial of Gordion, an Iron Age City in Anatolia. *Journal of Field
        Archaeology* 26,2:163–75.

Marx, K.
1992   [1887] *Capital: A Critique of Political Economy*, trans. Ben Fowkes.
        Harmondsworth: Penguin.

Matson, F. R.
1966   Power and Fuel Resources in the Ancient Near East. *Advancement of
        Science* 23:146–53.

McClellan, J.
1975   The Iron Objects from Gordion, A Typological and Functional Analysis.
        Ph.D. dissertation, University of Pennsylvania.

McClellan, M. C.
1984   Core-Formed Glass from Dated Contexts. Ph.D. dissertation, University
        of Pennsylvania.

Meindl, R. S., and C. O. Lovejoy
1985   Ectocranial Suture Closure: A Revised Method for the Determination
        of Skeletal Age at Death Based on the Lateral-anterior Sutures. *American
        Journal of Physical Anthropology* 68:57–66.
1989   Age Changes in the Pelvis: Implications for Paleodemography. In *Age
        Markers in the Human Skeleton*, ed. M. Y. Işcan, ed. pp. 137–68. Springfield,
        IL: Charles C Thomas.

Mellink, M. J.
1956   *A Hittite Cemetery at Gordion*. Philadelphia, PA: University of Pennsylvania
        Museum of Archaeology and Anthropology.
1980   Archaic Wall Paintings from Gordion. In *From Athens to Gordion. The Papers of a
        Memorial Symposium for Rodney S. Young*, ed. K. DeVries, pp. 91–98. Philadelphia,
        PA: University of Pennsylvania Museum of Archaeology and Anthropology.
1981   Temples and High Places in Phrygia. In *Temples and High Places in Biblical
        Times, Proceedings of the Colloquium in Honor of the Centennial of Hebrew Union
        College–Jewish Institute of Religion*, ed. A. Biran, pp. 96–104. Jerusalem:

          Nelson Glueck School of Biblical Archaeology, Hebrew Union College.
1988   *The Persian Empire: Anatolia. In Cambridge Ancient History 4*, 2nd ed., ed.
          John Boardman, pp. 211–33. London: Cambridge University Press.
1990   Archaeology in Anatolia. *American Journal of Archaeology* 94:125–51.
1991   The Native Kingdoms of Anatolia. In *The Cambridge Ancient History*
          Volume III, Pt. 2:619–665. Cambridge: Cambridge University Press.

Miller, M. C.
1993   Adoption and Adaptation of Achaemenid Metalware Forms in the Attic Black-
          gloss Ware of the Fifth Century. *Archäologischen Mitteilungen aus Iran* 26:109–46.

Miller, N.
1992   Gordion Archaeobotanical Studies: Tracing Human Influence on the
          Vegetation. Paper presented at SAA meeting, Pittsburgh, PA.
1993   Plant Use at Gordion: Archaeobotanical Research from the 1988–1989
          Seasons. *American Journal of Archaeology* 97: 304.
1999   Interpreting Ancient Environment and Patterns of Land Use: Seeds,
          Charcoal and Archaeological Context. *Turkish Academy of Sciences Journal
          of Archaeology (TUBA-AR)* 2:15–29.

Mitchell, S.
1993   *Anatolia: Land, Men, and Gods in Asia Minor. Volume 1: The Celts and the
          Impact of Roman Rule.* Oxford: Clarendon Press.

Neff, H., R. Bishop, and E. Sayre
1989   More Observations on the Problem of Tempering in Compositional
          Studies of Archaeological Ceramics. *Journal of Field Archaeology* 16:57–69.

Olive, J., and C. Pearson
1975   The Conservation of Ceramics from Marine Archaeological Sources.
          In *Conservation in Archaeology and the Applied Arts*. Preprints of the
          Contributions to the Stockholm Congress, 2-6 June 1975, pp.
          63-68. London: International Institute for Conservation.

Özbek, M.
1991   Iznik Roma Açikhava Tıyatrosundakı Kilisede Bulunan Bebek Iskeletleri.
          Belleten Türk Tarih Kurumu 55:315-22.

Parsons, M.
1972   Spindle whorls from the Teotihuacan Valley, Mexico. In *Miscellaneous
          Studies in Mexican Prehistory*, ed. M. Spence, J. Parsons, and M. Hrones
          Parsons, pp.45-79. Anthropological Papers of the University of Michigan,
          Ann Arbor.
1975   The Distribution of Late Postclassic Spindle Whorls in the Valley of
          Mexico. *American Antiquity* 40,2:207–15.

Paterakis, A.
1987   The Deterioration of Ceramics by Soluble Salts and Methods for Monitoring their Removal. In *Recent Advances in the Conservation and Analysis of Artifacts*, ed. James Black, pp. 67–72. London: Summer Schools Press.

Payton, R.
1992   *Retrieval of Objects from Archaeological Sites*. Denbish, Clwyd, Wales: Archetype.

Peacock, D. P. S.
1982   *Pottery in the Roman World: An Ethno-archaeological Approach*. Harlow: Longman.

Phenice, T. W.
1969   A Newly Developed Visual Method of Sexing the Os Pubis. *American Journal of Physical Anthropology* 30:297–301.

Prag, A. J. N. W.
1989   Reconstructing King Midas: A First Report. *Anatolian Studies* 39:159–65.

Ratté, C.
1994   Archaic Architectural Terracottas from Sector ByzFort at Sardis. *Hesperia* 63:361–90.

Rice, P. M.
1987   *Pottery Analysis: A Sourcebook*. Chicago, IL: University of Chicago Press.

Ridgway, D.
1999   The Rehabilitation of Bocchoris: Notes and Queries from Italy. *Journal of Egyptian Archaeology* 85:143–52.

Robinson, H. S.
1984   Roof Tiles of the Early Seventh Century B.C. *Mitteilungen des deutschen archäologischen Instituts: Athenische Abteilung* 99:55–66.

Roebuck, M. C.
1990   Archaic Architectural Terracottas from Corinth. In *Proceedings of the First International Conference on Archaic Greek Architectural Terracottas (Athens, December 2–4, 1988)*, ed. N. A. Winter. *Hesperia* 59: 47–64.

Rogers, M. H.
1989   Site Conservation at Phrygian Gordion. Master's thesis. University of North Carolina at Chapel Hill.

Roller, L.
1987   Hellenistic Epigraphic Texts from Gordion. *Anatolian Studies* 37:103–33.

Romano, I. B.
1995   *Gordion Special Studies II: The Terracotta Figurines and Related Vessels.* Philadelphia, PA: University of Pennsylvania Museum of Archaeology and Anthropology.

Rosen, A.
1997   Environmental Change and Human Adaptational Failure at the End of the Early Bronze Age in the Southern Levant. In *Third Millennium BC Climate Change and Old World Collapse,* ed. H. N. Dalfes, G. Kukla, and H. Weiss, pp. 25–38. NATO ASI Series, Subseries I Global Environmental Change 49. Heidelberg: Springer-Verlag.

Rye, O. S.
1981   *Pottery Technology: Principles and Reconstruction.* Washington, DC: Taraxacum.

Rye, O. S., and C. Evans
1976   *Traditional Pottery Techniques of Pakistan: Field and Laboratory Studies.* Washington, DC: Smithsonian Institution.

Saldern, A. von
1959   Glass Finds at Gordion. *Journal of Glass Studies* 1:23–51.
1970   Other Mesopotamian Glass Vessels (1500–600 B.C.). In *Glass and Glassmaking in Ancient Mesopotamia,* ed. A. Leo Oppenheim, Robert H. Brill, Dan P. Barag, and Axel von Saldern, pp. 203–28. Corning, NY: Corning Museum of Glass.

Sams, G. Kenneth
1974   Phrygian Painted Animals: Anatolian Orientalizing Art. *Anatolian Studies* 24:169–96.
1977   Beer in the City of Midas. *Archaeology* 30:108–15.
1978   Schools of Painting in Early Iron Age Anatolia. *Proceedings of the Xth International Congress of Classical Archaeology,* ed. Ekrem Akurgal, pp. 227–36. Ankara: Turkish Historical Society.
1979a   Imports at Gordion: Lydian and Persian Periods. *Expedition* 21,4:6–17.
1979b   Patterns of Trade in First Millennium Gordion. *Archaeological News* 8,2–3:45–53.
1988   The Early Phrygian Period at Gordion: Toward a Cultural Identity. *Source* 7,3–4:9–15.
1989   Sculpted Orthostates at Gordion. In *Anatolia and the Ancient Near East: Studies in Honor of Tahsin Özgüç,* ed. Kutlu Emre, Barthel Hrouda, Machteld Mellink, Nimet Özgüç, pp. 447–54. Ankara: Turkish Historical Society.
1994a   *The Gordion Excavations, 1950-1973: Final Reports Vol. IV, The Early Phrygian Pottery.* Philadelphia, PA: University of Pennsylvania Museum of

Archaeology and Anthropology.

1994b   Aspects of Early Phrygian Architecture at Gordion. In *Anatolian Iron Ages 3: Proceedings of the Third Anatolian Iron Ages Colloquium held at Van, 6–12 August 1990*, ed. A. Çilingiroğlu and D. H. French, pp. 211–14. Ankara: British Institute of Archaeology.

1995   Midas of Gordion and the Anatolian Kingdom of Phrygia. In *Civilizations of the Ancient Near East II, Part 5, History and Culture*, ed. Jack M. Sasson, pp. 1147–59. New York: Scribners.

Sams, G. K., and I. Temizsöy

2000   *Gordion Museum*. Ankara: Republic of Turkey, Ministry of Culture, General Directorate of Monuments and Museums.

Sams, G. K., and M. M. Voigt

1990   Work at Gordion in 1988. *XI Kazı Sonuçları Toplantısı* 2:77–105.

1991   Work at Gordion in 1989. *XII Kazı Sonuçları Toplantısı* 1:455–70.

1995   Gordion 1993. *X VI Kazı Sonuçları Toplantısı* 1:369–92.

1997   Gordion 1995. *Kazı Sonuçları Toplantısı* 18,1:475–97.

1998   Gordion 1996. *Kazı Sonuçları Toplantısı* 19,1:681–701.

Schaus, G.

1992   West Anatolian Pottery at Gordion. *Anatolian Studies* 42:151–77.

Schumm, S.

1985   Patterns of Alluvial Rivers. *American Review of Earth and Planetary Science* 13:5–27.

Sease, C.

1988   *A Conservation Manual for the Field Archaeologist*. Los Angeles, CA: UCLA.

Seeher, J.

2000   Die Eisenzeit in Zentralanatolien im Lichte der keramischen Funde vom Büyükkaya in Boğazköy/Hattuşa. *TÜBA-AR* 3:35–54.

Sevim, A.

1995   Datça/Burgaz Iskeletlerinin Paleoantropolojik Değerlendirilmesi. *Arkeometri Sonuçları Toplantısı* 11:1-18.

Sheftel, P. A.

1974   The Ivory, Bone and Shell Objects from Gordion from the Campaigns of 1950 through 1973. Ph. D. dissertation, University of Pennsylvania.

Shipp, M. E., and D. Lippert

1997   Cleaning of Archaeological Ceramics: A Comparison of Acetic and Nitric Acid Solutions. Poster presented at the 25th Annual Meeting of the American Institute for Conservation, San Diego.

Simpson, E., and K. Spirydowicz
1999   *Gordion: Ahşap Eserler/Wooden Furniture.* Philadelphia, PA: University of
        Pennsylvania Museum of Archaeology and Anthropology.

Sinopoli, C.
1991   *Approaches to Archaeological Ceramics.* New York: Plenum.

Sparkes, B. A., and L. Talcott
1970   *Black and Plain Pottery.* Athenian Agora, 4,1. Princeton, NJ: American
        School of Classical Studies at Athens.

Stein, G. J., and M. J. Blackman
1993   The Organizational Context of Specialized Craft Production in Early
        Mesopotamian States. *Research in Economic Anthropology* 14:29–59.

Stewart, T. D.
1958   The Rate of Development of Vertebral Osteoarthritis in American Whites
        and its Significance in Skeletal Age Identification. *The Leech* 28:144–51.

Stuart-Macadam, P.
1985   Porotic Hyperostosis: Representative of a Childhood Condition. *American
        Journal of Physical Anthropology* 66:391–98.
1992   Porotic Hyperostosis: A New Perspective. *American Journal of Physical
        Anthropology* 87:39–47.

Sumner, W.
1992   *Gordion Regional Survey.* Oriental Institute. Submitted Field Report, on file
        College of William and Mary, Williamsburg, VA.

Tiverios, M.
1976   *O Lydos kai to ergo tou* (in Greek). Publications of the Archaiologikon
        Deltion 23. Athens: General Directorate of Antiquities and Restoration.
1985–86 Archaische Keramik aus Sindos. *Makedonika* 25:70–87.

Triantafyllides, P.
2000a   *Rhodian Glassware I: The Luxury Hot-formed Transparent Vessels of the Classical
        and Early Hellenistic Periods* (in Greek). Athens: Aegean.
2000b   New Evidence of the Glass Manufacture in Classical and Hellenistic
        Rhodes. *Annales du 14ᵉ Congres de l'Association Internationale pour l'Histoire
        du Verre, Italia, Venezia - Milano, 1998*, p. 30–34. Lochem: Association
        internationale pour l'Histoire du Verre.

Tsu, C. M.
1996   Preliminary Technical Examination of Iron Age Ceramics from Kaman-
        Kalehöyük. *Anatolian Archaeological Research* 5:267–74.

1997 Analysis of Salt Residues from Real-time Ageing Experiment of Terracotta Bangle Fragments. In *Desalination Parameters for Harappan Ceramics,* CAL Report # 5493. Suitland, MD: Conservation Analytical Laboratory.

Ubelaker, D. H.
1989 *Human Skeletal Remains.* Washington, DC: Taraxacum.

Unruh, J.
2001 A Revised Endpoint for Ceramics Desalination at the Archaeological Site of Gordion, Turkey. *Studies in Conservation* 46:81–92.

Van der Leeuw, S. E.
1993 Giving the Potter a Choice: Conceptual Aspects of Pottery Techniques. In *Technological Choices: Transformation in Material Cultures since the Neolithic,* ed. P. Lemonnier, pp. 238–88. New York: Routledge.

Vickers, M.
2000 Lapidary Shock: Meditations on an Achaemenid Silver Beaker "from Erzerum" in the Ashmolean Museum, Oxford. *Archäologische Mitteilungen aus Iran und Turan* 32:261–73.

Vitali, V., and U. Franklin
1986 New Approaches to the Characterisation and Classification of Ceramics on the Basis of their Elemental Composition. *Journal of Archaeological Science* 13:161–70.

Voigt, M. M.
1994 Excavations at Gordion 1988–89: The Yassıhöyük Stratigraphic Sequence. In *Anatolian Iron Ages 3: The Proceedings of the Third Anatolian Iron Ages Colloquium,* ed. A. Çilingiroğlu and D. H. French, pp.265–293. Ankara: British Institute of Archaeology at Ankara.
1997 "Gordion" Oxford Encyclopedia of Near Eastern Archaeology 2:426–31. Oxford University Press for the American School of Oriental Research.
2003 Celts at Gordion: The Late Hellenistic Settlement. *Expedition* 45:14–16.

Voigt, M. M., K. DeVries, R. C. Henrickson, M. Lawall, B. Marsh, A. Gürsan-Salzmann, and T. Cuyler Young, Jr.
1997 Fieldwork at Gordion: 1993–1995. *Anatolica* 23:1–59.

Voigt, M. M., and R. C. Henrickson
2000a The Early Iron Age at Gordion: The Evidence from the Yassıhöyük Stratigraphic Sequence. In *The Sea Peoples and their World: A Reassessment,*

ed. Eleazer D. Oren, pp. 327–60. Philadelphia, PA: University of Pennsylvania Museum of Archaeology and Anthropology.

2000b   Formation of the Phrygian State: The Early Iron Age at Gordion. *Anatolian Studies* 50:37–54.

Voigt, M. M., and T. Cuyler Young, Jr.
1999   From Phrygian Capital to Achaemenid Entrepôt: Middle and Late Phrygian Gordion. *Iranica Antiqua* 34:192–240.

Voyatzoglou, M.
1974   The Jar Makers of Thrapsano in Crete. *Expedition* 16:18–24.

Waelkens, M.
1986   The Imperial Sanctuary at Pessinus: Archaeological, Epigraphical and Numismatic Evidence for its Date and Identification. *Epigraphica Anatolica* 7:37–73.

Wait, G. A.
1995   Burial and the Otherworld. In *The Celtic World*, ed. M. J. Green, pp. 489–511. New York: Routledge.

Waldron T.
1994   *Counting the Dead.* Chichester: Wiley.

Weiss, H., M. A. Courty, W. Wellerstrom, F. Guichard, L. Senior, R. Meadow, and A. Currow.
1993   The Genesis and Collapse of Third Millennium North Mesopotamian Civilization. *Science* 291: 995–1088.

White, T.
2000   *Human Osteology.* San Diego, CA: Academic.

Wikander, Ö.
1988   Ancient Roof-tiles—Use and Function. Opuscula Atheniensia. *Acta Instituti Atheniensis Regni Suecia* 17:203–16.
1990   Archaic Roof Tiles: The First Generations. In Proceedings of the First International Conference on Archaic Greek Architectural Terracottas (Athens, December 2-4, 1988), ed. N. A. Winter. *Hesperia* 59:285–90.

Wilkinson, T.
1992   Gordion 1992: Preliminary Observations on the Natural and Human Landscape. On file, College of William and Mary. Williamsburg, VA.

Wilkinson, T., and D. J. Tucker

1997   *Settlement Development in the North Jazira, Iraq: a Study of the Archaeological Landscape*. Baghdad: British School of Archaeology in Iraq, Department of Antiquities and Heritage.

Willey, J.

1995   The Effects of Desalination of Archaeological Ceramics From the Casas Grandes Region in Northern Mexico. In *Materials Issues in Art and Archaeology IV*, ed. P. B. Vandiver, J. Druzik, J. L. Galvan, G. S. Wheeler, and I. C. Freestone, pp. 839–50. Pittsburgh, PA: Materials Research Society.

Winter, F. A.

1984   Late Classical and Hellenistic Pottery from Gordion: The Imported Black Glazed Wares. Ph.D. dissertation, University of Pennsylvania.

1988   Phrygian Gordion in the Hellenistic Period. *Source-Notes in the History of Art* 7:60–71.

Winter, N. A.

1993   *Greek Architectural Terracottas from the Prehistoric to the End of the Archaic Period*. Oxford: Clarendon Press.

Wood J. W., G. R. Milner, H. C. Harpending, and K. M. Weiss

1992   The Osteological Paradox: Problems of Inferring Health from Skeletal Samples. *Current Anthropology* 33:343–70.

Young, R. S.

1951   Gordion—1950. *University Museum Bulletin* 16, 1:3–20.

1953   Progress at Gordion, 1951–1952. *University Museum Bulletin* 17, 4:2–39.

1955   Gordion: Preliminary Report—1953. *American Journal of Archaeology* 59:1–18.

1956   The Campaign of 1955 at Gordion: Preliminary Report. *American Journal of Archaeology* 60:249–66.

1958   The Gordion Campaign of 1957. *American Journal of Archaeology* 62:139–54.

1960   Gordion Campaign of 1959: Preliminary Report. *American Journal of Archaeology* 64:227–44.

1965   Early Mosaics at Gordion. *Expedition* 7:4–13.

1966   The Gordion Campaign of 1965. *American Journal of Archaeology* 74:267–78.

1968   The Gordion Campaign of 1967. *American Journal of Archaeology* 72:231–42.

1981   *The Gordion Excavations Final Reports Volume I. Three Great Early Tumuli*. Philadelphia, PA: University of Pennsylvania Museum of Archaeology and Anthropology.

CONTRIBUTORS

BRENDAN BURKE is Assistant Professor of Greek and Roman Studies at the University of Victoria, British Columbia, Canada. He received his Ph.D. in Archaeology from UCLA in 1998. He has participated in surveys and excavations in Greece, Turkey, and Ireland. His primary research interest is cultural interactions between Greece and Anatolia. He currently studies cult activity and craft production at Gordion from the Late Classical and Hellenistic periods.

KEITH DEVRIES is Associate Professor Emeritus in the Department of Classical Studies of the University of Pennsylvania and Associate Curator Emeritus in the Mediterranean Section of the University of Pennsylvania Museum of Archaeology and Anthropology. He holds a PhD in Classical Archaeology from the University of Pennsylvania. He served as field director of the Gordion Project from 1974 to 1988 and remains an active member of the staff. His Gordion publications, in addition to seasonal reports, include studies of Phrygian culture, as revealed by excavations at Gordion and elsewhere, and of the Greek pottery that reached the site. Other publications of his have dealt with Greek culture and archaeology from the Early Iron Age down to the Hellenistic period.

MATT GLENDINNING is Principal of the Moorestown Friends School, Moorestown, NJ. With a Ph.D. in Classical Archaeology from the University of North Carolina at Chapel Hill (1996), Glendinning has excavated both in the United States (in New Hampshire and Arizona) and abroad (in Spain, Greece and Turkey) and has taught archaeology at both the college and secondary levels. His work on the architectural terracottas at Gordion has led to publications in *Hesperia* and *The Oxford Encyclopedia of Archaeology in the Near East.*

ANDREW L. GOLDMAN received his Ph.D. in Classical Archaeology from the University of North Carolina, Chapel Hill in 2000. His dissertation investigated the physical plan of and cultural and economic patterns within the small Roman town at Gordion (ca. 0 to 500 AD). Dr. Goldman is currently an Assistant Professor of History at Gonzaga University, and is excavating the Roman-period settlement at Gordion.

MARK GOODMAN was a private consultant specializing in the preservation and presentation of archaeological sites. After supervising a number of projects for the Israel Antiquities Authority, 1989–93, he received a B.A. in Anthropology and an M.Sc. in Historic Preservation at the University of Pennsylvania. His projects included the recreation of an historic village at Nazareth, Israel, and site conservation at Gordion, Turkey. Mark died suddenly in 2004.

PETER GRAVE is a Senior Lecturer in Archaeology and Paleoanthropology at the University of New England, NSW, Australia where he has been on the faculty since 1996. He received an M.A. in Archaeology from the University of Sydney in 1989 and a Ph.D. in 1995 from the same institution. He spent 3 years (1986–89) as a member of the Australian team at Pompeii working on quantitative analysis of decorated wall plasters. He has worked on quantitative analysis of archaeological ceramics in a range of collaborative projects in Southeast and East Asia, Iran, the United Arab Emirates, Jordan and Southern Italy. Since 1996, he has directed the program of ceramic analysis for the Gordion Regional Survey.

AYŞE GÜRSAN-SALZMANN received her B.A. from Robert College in Istanbul and her Ph.D. from the University of Pennsylvania. She has taught cultural anthropology and Near Eastern archaeology at the University of the Arts, the University of Pennsylvania, and Bilkent University. She has conducted archaeological and ethnographic field research in Wyoming, Turkey, Romania, and Uzbekistan. Her project at Gordion represents part of a broader interest in the dynamics of socioeconomic change and material culture in ancient and modern agricultural pastoral societies. Currently a Research Associate in the Near Eastern Section at the University Museum, she is working toward the publication of the Bronze Age ceramic chronology at Tepe Hissar, Iran, and a book on early excavations in Iran by Erich Schmidt, from the collections and archival materials in the University Museum.

R. C. HENRICKSON has been responsible for study and publication of Bronze Age through Hellenistic pottery from the renewed excavations at Gordion since 1988. His research concentrates on reconstruction of ancient craft technologies and their interaction with the societies within which they are embedded, particularly pottery production in the ancient Near East 3500–150 BC. Previously he had done fieldwork in Iran, Iraq, Algeria, and Crete. He earned his Ph.D. in West Asian Archaeology from the University of Toronto in 1984, writing on the socioeconomic development of western Iran during the Bronze Age. He received his B.A. from Vanderbilt University and his M.A. from the University of Toronto. Other interests include sailing ships (naval and merchant, ca.1700-1860), building ship models, and working with stained glass.

JESSICA S. JOHNSON was Head of Conservation at Gordion, 1991–2001, and has worked as a conservator on other sites in Turkey, Cyprus, and Syria. She is currently Senior Objects Conservator for the National Museum of the American Indian, the Smithsonian Institution. She was Conservator for the National Park Service Museum Management Program, the national administrative program for all NPS museum collections. She received an M.A. in Anthropology from the University of Arizona in 1986 and a B.Sc. in Archaeological Conservation (Hons.) from the Institute of Archaeology, University College London, in 1990. She is a Fellow of the American Institute for Conservation of Historic and Artistic Works.

JANET DUNCAN JONES is Associate Professor and Chair of the Department of Classics at Bucknell University, Lewisburg, PA. She received her Ph.D. in Classical Archaeology from the University of North Carolina at Chapel Hill. She specializes in the areas of Greek and Roman art and architecture, ancient technology with a focus on ancient glass production and ancient environmental issues. She has excavated in Greece at Athens and Corinth, in Turkey at Gritille Hoyuk and Gordion, and in Tunisia at Carthage. She is currently glass specialist for the Gordion Archaeological Mission, and the Roman Aqaba Project and Humayma Excavation Project (Jordan).

LISA KEALHOFER is Assistant Professor in the Anthropology and Sociology Department and is cross appointed in Environmental Studies at Santa Clara University. She received her Ph.D. in Anthropology from the University of Pennsylvania. She directed the Gordion Regional Survey 1996-2002. Her research, both at Gordion and elsewhere, focuses on the relationship between land use, environmental change, and the development of political economies. She has also done fieldwork in Thailand, Egypt, and the USA (California and the Chesapeake).

RICHARD F. LIEBHART received a B.A. in English in 1971 and a Ph.D. in Classics in 1988 both from the University of North Carolina at Chapel Hill. He has been a Lecturer on archaeology and ancient art in the Classics Department and the Art Department at Chapel Hill since 1990. He spent three years (1980-83) at the American School of Classical Studies at Athens and worked on excavations in the Athenian Agora and at ancient Corinth. In 1990, he began an architectural study of the tomb chamber of Tumulus MM at Gordion, and this project has evolved into the current structural and environmental conservation project.

BEN MARSH is Professor of Geography and Environmental Studies, Bucknell University, Lewisburg, PA, where he has been on the faculty since 1979. He holds a Ph.D. and an M.S. in Geography from the Pennsylvania State University and a B.A. in Anthropology from the University of California at Santa Cruz. He works as a geomorphologist and geoarchaeologist at several Old World sites and projects. He also works in Pennsylvania on Pleistocene landforms and on human environmental adaptation.

G. KENNETH SAMS is Professor of Classical Archaeology at the University of North Carolina at Chapel Hill. He is President of the American Research Institute in Turkey and, since 1988, Director of the Gordion Archaeological Project. Sams received his Ph.D. in Classical Archaeology from the University of Pennsylvania. He is the author of several publications, including a volume in the Gordion series on the early Phrygian pottery. His specialties include Iron Age Anatolia and the Near East, Greek architecture, and the topography of Athens. Sams has been associated with Gordion since 1967, when he first took part, as a graduate student, in the excavations there led by Rodney S. Young. Other fieldwork experience includes excavations at Corinth (Greece) and Stobi (the former Yugoslavia, present Macedonia), and survey at Patara in southeastern Turkey.

PAGE SELINSKY holds an M.A. in Anthropology from the University of Pennsylvania and is currently a doctoral candidate there in Anthropology. Her research interests include molecular anthropology, ancient DNA extraction and analysis, and skeletal biology. Her previous experience includes an internship with the collections management department and volunteer work with a curator in the physical anthropology section at the Smithsonian Institution's National Museum of Natural History. She has conducted field research at several sites in the Middle East, including Gordion.

JULIE UNRUH holds undergraduate degrees in Studio Art and Liberal Arts, and an M.A. in Art History. She received her Master's of Art Conservation from Queens University, Kingston, Canada, in 1994. She has worked in conservation laboratories at the National Gallery of Art, the Smithsonian Institution, the Royal Ontario Museum, the Getty Museum, the Brooklyn Museum of Art, the Agora Excavations in Athens, and in private practice. She has been a member of the conservation staff of the Gordion Project since 1994. She is currently Conservation Specialist at the Arizona State Museum.

MARY M. VOIGT is Chancellor Professor of Anthropology at the College of William and Mary. She received her B.A. in History and English from Marquette University and her Ph.D. in Anthropology from the University of Pennsylvania. She has taught at Vanderbilt University, Bryn Mawr College, and the University of Pennsylvania. She came to William and Mary in 1990 from the University of Pennsylvania Museum of Archaeology and Anthropology, where she had served as editor of *Expedition* magazine. As an archaeologist specializing in the prehistory and early history of the Middle East, she has conducted fieldwork in Iran and Turkey, and she currently directs excavations at Gordion.

INDEX